DISAPPEARING PEOPLES?

DISAPPEARING PEOPLES?

Indigenous Groups and Ethnic Minorities in South and Central Asia

Edited by

Barbara A. Brower
Barbara Rose Johnston

Walnut Creek, CA

Left Coast Press, Inc.
1630 North Main Street, #400
Walnut Creek, California 94596
http://www.LCoastPress.com

Library of Congress Cataloging-in-Publication Data

Disappearing peoples? : indigenous groups and ethnic minorities in South and
Central Asia / Barbara A. Brower, Barbara Rose Johnston, editors.
    p. cm.
  ISBN 978-1-59874-120-9 (hardback : alk. paper)
  ISBN 978-1-59874-121-6 (pbk. : alk. paper)
    1. Indigenous peoples—South Asia. 2. Indigenous peoples—Asia, Central. 3.
South Asia—Ethnic relations. 4. Asia, Central—Ethnic relations. 5. South Asia—
Social conditions. 6. Asia, Central—Social conditions. I. Brower, Barbara Anne.
II. Johnston, Barbara Rose.
  GN635.S57D57 2004   305.80054—dc22   200702176

07 08 09 5 4 3 2 1

Printed in the United States of America

The paper used in this publication meets
the minimum requirements of American
National Standard for Information
Sciences—Permanence of Paper for Printed
Library Materials, ANSI/NISO Z39.48—1992.

Maps by Jason Clark
Cover design by Andrew Brozyna

Dedicated to the memories of
David R. Brower (1912–2000),
Anne H. Brower (1913–2001), and
Robert I. Brower (1946–2004).

Contents

1

Disappearing Peoples?

Barbara A. Brower and Barbara Rose Johnston

Most people in the developed world know very little about life in the mountains, deserts, and remote valleys of Central and South Asia. Media coverage focusing on extreme events generates an international perception of this region as a terrain of terror, a zone of fanaticism and conflict. We are free to imagine the worst: a place and people dominated by dark forces. But though one can find here the warlords, gun-toting revolutionaries, violent conflicts, and environmental catastrophes depicted in the international news media, South and Central Asia is also a region with a long, rich, complicated history whose current inhabitants—farmers, poets, heroes, herders, mothers, merchants, teachers, students—are far more likely to be peaceful than ferocious. And the lives of these people, many belonging to small groups with unique identities developed over generations in unique encounters with the world, are radically changing. Once a part of the Earth that harbored extraordinary human diversity, South and Central Asia is now the setting for aggressive forces of homogenization.

Today, no place is beneath the radar or beyond the reach of the sweeping force of globalization. No part of the planet can escape the impact of the way one set of peoples—typically characterized as being in the "developed" world—use the planet, its resources, and its people to fulfill a cultural mandate of endless growth, using their power and influence to conquer, redeem, and transform the world and its peoples. The formerly isolated regions of the world are now part of the global mainstream, as illustrated by a quick glance at the headlines in our daily newspapers featuring the issues, problems, and conditions in once-distant lands: Azerbaijan, Tajikistan, Afghanistan, Pakistan, India, Nepal, Kashmir, Tibet.

In this volume we explore some of the cultural diversity of this region, outline the history and current conditions that threaten indigenous peoples and other cultural minorities in South and Central Asia, and examine some of the many ways that people are responding to such threats in their struggle to survive and thrive.

Setting the Stage: People, Environments, and History

Beginning some 60 million years ago in the Tertiary period, a dynamic upheaval began to give shape to the part of the planet we know as South and Central Asia. Tectonic processes rammed the Indian subcontinent into the main mass of Asia, forcing the uplift of the Tibetan Plateau and shoving and distorting the high mountain ranges—Himalaya, Hindukush, Karakoram, Pamir—that distinguish this area of Earth's surface. The highlands blocked the winds sucked from warm seas into the interior of Asia by summer heating, and trapped their moisture in glaciers that formed the headwaters of the great rivers of Asia: the Indus, Ganges, Tsangpo-Brahmaputra, Yangtse, Salween, Mekong, and Huang Ho. In seaming together Eurasia and India, the geophysical forces that created the region brought together widely divergent landscapes and living things, creating the highest mountains, wettest hillslopes, and driest deserts of the Earth.

About 57 million years after this phase of planetary engineering began—2.5 million years ago—the ancestral human *Homo habilis* emerged in Africa. Then, 200,000 years ago, our own species, *Homo sapien sapiens,* gathered plants, hunted animals, and lived in small mobile communities in the forests and savannas of Africa. By 10,000 years ago our human ancestors—furless, without the teeth for defense, speed for flight, or musculature to swing through trees of our primate cousins—had found their way, and ways to make a home, in almost every one of the Earth's varied environments.

Unlike those creatures whose response to harsh or varied conditions was biological adaptation, humans retained their African biology and relied upon ingenuity to survive. They fashioned clothing from skins and plant fiber, rather than growing thick coats of protective hair. They created innovative ways to live and to communicate, and passed this knowledge to their children. Using brains, hands, and the ability to make and transmit culture through language and symbols, we humans survived and thrived—producing a multitude of peoples whose cultures, traditions, ways of life, and languages were finely tuned to our surroundings.

Nowhere else on the planet did our wandering ancestors encounter higher mountains, deeper gorges, or drier cold deserts than in South and Central Asia. Settlers in this region adapted to specific niches within a complex mosaic, becoming forager-hunters, herders, farmers, traders, and conquerors. They ranged in bands across wide territories, or settled in small communities in

favored valleys, or developed cities with complex infrastructures and hier-
archical societies, mostly in well-watered lowlands—and they learned to deal
with one another in constantly changing interactions of power, persuasion,
and commerce. Over long stretches of time people lived in relative isolation,
adjusting and adapting to new people, new ideas, new technologies, and the
varied crises presented by disease, drought, and famine, at a relatively slow,
measured pace. Often, adaptation and change took place over many generations, allowing the old ways to coexist with or modulate new ways. The
wholesale replacement of one culture for another did happen occasionally.
But in the nooks and crannies of a diverse, daunting environment—high in
the mountains and deep in the jungles of Asia, for instance—some groups
were spared, or only lightly touched, by the large-scale forces of change that
swept more accessible places (the Bhil, Tharu, and Tibetans discussed in later
chapters illustrate this). And geographic isolation was not the only way to
evade cultural assimilation: Society provides niches for unique groups by
defining boundaries between peoples through cultural segregation (many
peripatetic groups, as well as the Dom and the Hazara, illustrate cultural differentiation achieved within segregated societies). One way or another, out
of the reach or beneath the notice of most conquerors, traders, missionaries,
and the more powerful, the people in these corners of South and Central Asia
might pick and choose among the cultural transformations imposed on more
vulnerable, accessible, conspicuous groups; their identities would reflect these
interactions without being wholly taken over. Yet these encounters with new
ideas, new ways, whether carried by priests or conquering armies, left patterns
in religions, languages, and lifeways that are apparent across the region and
illustrated in the chapters to follow.

Though modern Americans, until very recently, may have been able to see
South and Central Asia as remote and inconsequential, much of the action
over most of human history happened here—and left many marks.

The ebb and flow of religion accounts for one kind of patterning in the
mosaic of peoples across South and Central Asia. Among significant religions
of this region, the complex collection of beliefs, texts, and practices that we
know as Hinduism is oldest, and retains its importance in the lives of almost
one billion people, most living in India and Nepal. A society ordered in *varnas*—
hereditary occupational castes—is one element of Hinduism that figures in
the lives of several of the peoples profiled in this book (including the Raika,
Tharu, and many peripatetic groups). The tension between Hindu and
Muslim, inflamed during the British occupation of India, and especially by
the terms of the Partition of British India as the Raj collapsed, is reflected in
our account of Kashmir. Buddhism shares deities and some beliefs with
Hinduism, including the central idea of *samsara*, the cycle of life and rebirth—

though the Buddha, born in Lumbini, Nepal, perhaps 600 years B.C., saw escape from samsara to nirvana as the goal for most beings. Buddhism spread widely: Its patron Emperor Ashoka sent missionaries from Afghanistan to Sri Lanka and Southeast Asia; later, the Silk Route became a conduit for Buddhism, and by the 3rd century it was firmly established in Han China, from whence it spread to Korea and then Japan. Only much later, in the 7th century, did Buddhism appear in Mongolia and Tibet (where it remains part of the identity of the Minhe Mangghuer and Tibetans, taken up in the last chapters of this book). Islam, born in Arabia, was carried around much of Asia (indeed to most of the Old World), sometimes on the point of a sword, but also with traders, and among those attracted to its teachings and premise of equality. Islam followed many of the dissemination routes pioneered by Buddhism, eclipsing the older traditions as it spread. As Islam's empires waxed and waned, so did the range and power of its agents, their competing visions of the true faith, and their effect on the region. Today's pattern, as encountered in the profiles in this book, reflects this history: The people of Afghanistan, Pakistan, Tajikistan, Azerbaijan, Dagestan, some parts of northern India, and far western China's Xinjiang are mostly Muslim; typically (though not everywhere) the lowlands are dominated by Sunni and the highlands are home to various Shia groups.

While Hindu and Buddhist pilgrims and Muslim armies further influenced the culture-shaping mechanisms already at work in South and Central Asia, only with the rise of mercantile culture some six centuries ago did the countries of Europe begin to develop an interest in what the rest of the world might provide in the way of resources and markets. Once launched, the rise of European economic and political power had a profound effect across much of the Earth, and certainly in Asia. Particularly significant in South and Central Asia was Britain's role in India, which fell under British control in the mid-18th century and became independent only in 1947. India provided Britain cheap resources and labor and a market for manufactured goods in a classic colonial relationship. The Crown imposed its own laws and values (among the consequences: the expulsion of the Bhil from their forest homelands and the criminalization of some of the nomadic groups described in the chapter on Peripatetics). The strategy of divide and rule helps to explain the relatively recent escalation in hostilities between Hindu and Muslim; its consequence was a former British India divided according to religion. Given its crucial stake in South Asia, Britain sought to repel advancing Russian interests in Central Asia in an elaborate and costly Great Game. Russia—later the USSR—for its part, set itself for the control of Central Asia, and left its own imprint across the region, as shown in our chapters on the Wakhi and Kirghiz, Badakshani, Lezghi, and Hazara. The region's other significant imperial power,

China, retains its influence and exerts its homogenizing power over the peoples directly within its sphere—here, the Mangghuer, Tibetans, and Wakhi and Kirghiz whose territory is now considered part of the People's Republic of China (PRC). And China's influence is only likely to increase as it grows in population and economic strength.

A different sort of imperialism operates today with profound effect on South and Central Asia. This is the economic and political influence exercised by global capital, manifest in multinational trade agreements and their consequent impacts on diverse systems of survival and production. Economic links among countries become conduits for ideas and values, as the Silk Road once was; the pervasiveness and force of contemporary processes of world trade, however, leave no room for the gradual accommodation of historic episodes of culturally transforming invasions.

If cultural diversity was key to the growth and survival of humanity in times past, what does an increasingly homogeneous culture suggest for times to come? Is there a chance to slow the accelerating rate of culture loss? Part of the answer to that question lies in understanding the processes by which cultural diversity is threatened. The imperial impulse that began in the 15th century inaugurated the global integration that probably looms as one of the biggest threats to autonomy and identity for the "disappearing peoples" of South and Central Asia, but that is just the beginning of the story.

Drivers and Dynamics in the Disappearance of Cultural Diversity

Five hundred years ago, as humans entered the age of colonial expansion, there were tens of thousands of cultural groups with distinct languages, values, and ways of life. Today, our world is experiencing a rapid decline in cultural diversity. One in five people in today's world speak the same language: the Mandarin Chinese spoken by the largest single ethnic group in the world, the Han, whose 1.3 billion population represents 92 percent of the mainland China population and 19 percent of the world's population. And, although there are 415 living languages in India, the world's second most populous country, the majority of India's peoples speak Bengali or Hindi. Linguists recognize some 6,000 to 7,000 spoken languages, of which 5,000 are spoken by indigenous peoples and ethnic minorities who represent an estimated 6 percent of the world's population. Over half of these languages are spoken by groups of fewer than 10,000 people. Many of these people, and their languages, face a questionable future. The relatively rapid decline in language diversity parallels declines in cultural diversity. These changes are due in part to the fact that historically isolated peoples have minimal immunity to introduced diseases. Colonizers brought more than their ideas, religion, and economic demands; they brought a host of viruses and bacteria—measles, chicken pox, small pox, the common cold—that swept through "new" worlds at epidemic levels, wiping out entire nations. Imperialist expansion, colonialism, and war have further decimated original, or "indigenous," populations. Today, many of the remaining languages and the cultural groups that speak them are in danger of dying out. Some linguists estimate that over half the world's languages—and thus, the embedded cultural meanings—will not be passed along to the next generation.

These conditions are a product of both historical relationships—imperialism, colonialism, Cold War economic development and militarism—and cultural beliefs that rationalize or justify actions that serve the powerful at the cost of lands and livelihoods of indigenous and ethnic minorities. So, for instance, cultural nations have been fragmented by the imposition—often by imperial powers—of geopolitical borders that disrupt the movements that were essential to the groups' long-term ability to sustain families, kin, ways of life. In this volume, the histories of Hazara, Kashmiris, Wakhi, Kirghiz, and Lezghi illustrate the impacts of closed and militarized borders that deny access to customary lands, resources, and kinfolk. Elsewhere, cultural traditions have been criminalized with the imposition of colonial authority and law: Peripatetic communities viewed as "backward" by the British Raj were classified as criminals; Tibetan Buddhist worship was outlawed by the PRC. The consequences of these histories and actions are profound. The local sustainability of people and their environment has been devastated in the name of national or transnational interests, and this trade-off is not necessarily in the best interests of local peoples, nations, or indeed the world.

Consider, for example, the consequences of water diversion and hydroelectric energy projects planned or already in place to constrain the major rivers flowing from the mountains of South and Central Asia. Reservoirs created by several of these water development projects flood some of the most productive agricultural lands in the world. Across the world, dams and diversions are the primary cause of endangerment or extinction for one-half of the world's freshwater fish, contribute substantially to the decimation of marine fisheries, and have displaced tens of millions of people in the name of projects built to benefit distant cities and agricultural producers. In India alone, an estimated 20 million people have been forcefully evicted from their homes to make way for water development projects. Most of these dam-affected peoples are cultural minorities, and as many as 75 percent were forced to move without adequate compensation or assistance in rebuilding their lives (the case of the Bhil, outlined in Chapter 4, demonstrates the consequences).

And consider the human and environmental devastation accompanying militarization. Cold War militarism and its related quest for nuclear power prompted the Soviets, Chinese, and other powers to mine uranium and other strategic minerals in the distant and previously isolated regions of their respective empires. Cold War mining and processing of uranium in India, Pakistan, Northern Afghanistan, Kazakhstan, Kyrgyzstan, Tajikistan, and China (Tibet) typically relied upon local (cultural minority) labor, and left massive mine tailings that emit radioactive radon gases and other radioactive materials that continue to endanger the health of adjacent and downwind/downstream communities. Nuclear and biochemical weapons development and testing in Kazakhstan severely affected the health of area residents. Similar impacts are likely to have occurred, though there is less documentation in the western literature, around and downwind from the Lop Nur Nuclear Weapons Test facility on the edge of the Tibetan Plateau, home to the Uighur minority in China's Xinjiang Uygur Autonomous Region (known by the Uighurs as East Turkistan).

Global as well as national or regional events have also had serious impacts on this region's cultural minorities and their environment. Anthropogenic climate change, though a consequence of the fossil fuel consumption of the industrialized nations, will have some of its most powerful, potentially catastrophic effects here in South and Central Asia. As the atmosphere continues to warm through the ongoing emissions of greenhouse gases (as well as lag effects), some consequences are already being seen, and others are easy to predict. Rapidly melting glaciers—the largest accumulation of ice outside of polar regions is in this region—first supercharge their rivers with accelerating meltwater, then, as they diminish, will cease to serve as a storehouse of water for the third of the world's population who now depend on these rivers. For the mountain farmers of Central Asia, whose livelihoods are tightly bound to these glacial streams—the Wakhi, Badakshani, Lezghi, Hazara portrayed in this volume, for example—the prospects are not good. Sea level rise brings its own catastrophic consequences for coastal communities (and almost all of Bangladesh): The incremental rise in the sea itself must ultimately compel a massive exodus from coasts; in the meantime, increases in climate instability and the frequency of extreme events will be among the challenges to meet. But it is in effects harder to predict that the true disaster of climate change may be manifest, as for example, in the future patterning of the monsoon. This seasonal shift in the winds controls the climate for much of the region, and in turn schedules the lives and determines the livelihood options for most of Asia's population. Monsoon develops as a result of the differential heating of land (in Central Asia) and the warm sea to the south; its intensity and timing are responses to the rate and degree of warming in interior Asia. Some climate modeling predicts an intensification of monsoon, while other models suggest it could fail entirely. Either effect would make life very different and very much more difficult across the region.

One of the major ways in which governments are responding to threats posed by global environmental change is to propose or authorize massive efforts to capture, hold, and reroute rainfall in the form of a series of dams and river linking projects on both sides of "the world's rooftop." Thus, the Chinese, Indian, and Pakistani governments are all pursuing hydroelectric dam, river diversion, and river linking projects that, if completed, will see the containment of all of the freshwater flowing from both sides of the Himalaya. Such projects are controversial, especially given the limited life of dams, the relatively poor record of such projects in achieving stated goals, and the well-documented environmental and social costs.

For resident peoples living in the small hillside and mountainous communities of the Himalaya, protest is difficult. These people are geographically and socially distant from the central corridors of power. Nevertheless, this region has seen local resistance to development plans and public protests over forced evictions, resettlement with inadequate compensation or assistance, and the burdens of hosting displaced communities. The ulcerating problems from past development, and fears over future development generate conditions and conflict that not only threaten the security of the state but at more fundamental levels, threaten the security of individual and group rights to culture, self-determination, livelihood, and life. As the development controversies play out, new conflict is inevitable.

And finally, global change in the form of the "war or terror," the rise of resource nationalism, and the resurgence of the security state has profoundly impacted this region of the world, where cultural minorities are caught up in the chaotic escalation of militarization and conflict. Throughout the mountainous regions, especially the formerly isolated mountain valleys and passes—the borderlands—identities, homes, and environs are being transformed by militarized construction and destruction. China, Russia, the European Union, and the United States are all in a competitive race to secure bilateral, trilateral, and regional agreements to host military forces and to exploit and ensure continued access to critical energy and mineral resources. Massive infrastructure projects—pipelines, roads, and trains—are being planned and built to ensure the flow of resources and goods in one direction or another. And significant funds and energy are being devoted to secure these routes and resource rights, oftentimes pitting resident communities with customary rights to water, land, and other resources against their nation or the interests of distant nations.

This Book

It is our belief that cross-cultural communication and understanding are the antidote to conflict. Now, more than ever, it is important to know and value the diverse cultural traditions and ways of life in this tense region of the world. In this book we present a sampling of South and Central Asia's cultural diversity, introducing the reader to an array of peoples and their beliefs, histories, and current conditions. While the number of distinct cultural groups in this region is immense and no single volume can hope to represent them in their entirety, we offer here a sampling of cultural traditions and ways of life that span an east-to-west stretch of this largely mountainous region. Taken as a whole, our sampling covers many of the issues and situations that currently threaten the livelihood and lives of indigenous peoples and other cultural minorities throughout South and Central Asia. Recognizing the strength and vibrancy of culture, the authors give significant attention to the varied ways that people are struggling, and at times succeeding, in their effort to survive and thrive. These peoples are briefly introduced below.

Raika

The Raika, whose arid homeland is on the margin of India's Thar desert, know the secret of survival in so inhospitable a place: "Exploit the pockets of high productivity, save for scarcity, and travel to where resources and water are available." Raika farmers grow a quick crop of millet or wheat when the rains come, and herders orchestrate the annual movements of large herds of camels and sheep among widespread pastures, relying on a network of social relations as well as on their knowledge of a changeable and challenging environment. But a lifeway like the Raika's depends on large-scale movement of livestock and access to widely distributed pastureland. Encroaching farms, government restrictions, weakening markets, and a drying climate all spell trouble for the camel-breeding Raika, so Paul Robbins, in Chapter 2, asks: "Can Raika culture, identity, and economy, which is increasingly based on mobility and grazing resources, continue to persist in the face of successive waves of social and environmental change that force settlement and the enclosure of pasture?"

Peripatetics

The Raika's adaptations and obstacles to survival are shared by a large class of peoples who use mobility as a strategy to reach the resources that support their communities, including other pastoralists (such as the Kirghiz, Wakhi, and Tibetans described in this volume). And lifeways premised on mobility also undergird the existence of the highly diverse *peripatetic* peoples found throughout South Asia and described by Aparna Rao in Chapter 3. Peripatetics ("gypsies" in old texts and popular discourse) include many itinerant communities in South Asia whose members move from village to village, town to town, peddling goods or offering specialized skills and services in return for cash or payment in kind. These groups, too, exploit pockets of productivity and travel to find resources, though "productivity" and "resources" are measured in clients and patrons for these commercial nomads.

Usually relegated to the lowest ranks of the caste hierarchy, and labeled "backward" and "criminal" by British colonial administrations, peripatetic groups have never had an easy time of it. And as development replaces the itinerant merchants' clay pots with plastic, Tibetan salt gathered by nomadic herder-traders with a commercial product, and the music and dances of peripatetic performers with movies and television, the niche for these mobile entrepreneurs becomes smaller and smaller. Those whose livelihoods involve the natural world—the bird traders, snake charmers, and bear trainers described here by Rao—must contend not only with shrinking habitat and overexploited species but also with regulations established in ignorance of the connections of endangered peoples to endangered species. Perhaps the best hope for some of these endangered groups is in the resilience provided them by many generations of survival—in spite of the best efforts of the State.

Bhil

The Bhil can be found on Aparna Rao's table of peripatetic peoples; their life, rooted for generations in the relatively small, mountainous river valleys of their homelands, involved a much smaller circuit among available resources. The Bhil—another collective term applied to "tribal" (*adivasi*) peoples who know themselves as Tadvi, Vassawa, and by other names—farmed shifting, burned-and-plowed fields, herded livestock, foraged the forest, and fished the rivers of the Narmada River system beginning about A.D. 1200, perhaps much earlier.

As Judith Whitehead describes, their "multi-resourced" way of life sustained the Tadvi and Vassawa over many generations, in a mountainous region out of the way of the dynamic power shifts of adjacent lowlands. But then the British brought their forest laws to India, and the Bhil's forest home and sanctuary became the Crown's—later the Indian government's—timber store. Though these laws are now being reevaluated, any revision comes too late for Bhil already evicted by forest laws, or those among the 250,000 people displaced by the Sardar Sarovar Dam who live now far from their homeland, and lose their identities in resettlement camps.

Tharu

Rising waters displaced the Bhil; a rising tide of migrants threatens the Tharu. A similarly jungly, river-washed homeland defended the Chitwan Valley Tharu in Nepal's lowland Terai from incursions by others for many generations. The Terai's indigenous people, the Tharu, had some measure of genetic protection from the virulent malaria also indigenous to moist forested hills and valleys of this edge of the Gangetic Plain. There they farmed, fished, foraged the forests, kept livestock, formed communities, worshipped local and remote deities—becoming a people uniquely shaped by relative isolation from the more powerful and much more numerous Hindu Pahari people of Nepal's higher hills. An international malaria eradication program, begun in the 1950s, reduced the threat of disease and opened the Tharu's territory to resettlement from Nepal's crowded hills. Arjun Guneratne, in Chapter 5, explores the consequences: Once the majority, the Tharu are now vastly outnumbered by newcomers whose demands for land and resources push Tharu to the sidelines, and whose values, delivered through religion and education, swamp old ways of knowing the world, and of being Tharu. Nepal's decade-long Maoist insurgency provided a voice for Tharu grievances, but may have exerted its own identity-eclipsing mechanisms. What next?

Dom

The Dom, in contrast to the Chitwan Tharu, are relative newcomers to Hunza, in the Northern Areas of Pakistan. Arriving from different directions, claiming descent from different ancestors, the Dom are united by language and by the way they see themselves—and others see them. Blacksmiths or musicians, the Dom—like many of the peripatetic groups of Chapter 3—made a way of life based on an exchange of their services for support from higher-status clients. The economic and social transformations that are reshaping the rest of the globe reach even here, in "Shangri La." Manufactured tools replace the blacksmith's, and the rulers who patronized Dom musicians and validated their work and Dom identity are now distant history. Always on the margins, the Dom have been squeezed even tighter by these changes. But as Anna Schmid explains, in Chapter 6, by organizing their disparate subgroups, and invigorated by the Aga Khan's endorsement of their traditional work, the Dom are fighting back.

Kashmiris

Kashmir today is contested ground whose people pay a very steep price for a geopolitical struggle not of their own making. The Vale of Kashmir—Ground

Zero in this volatile war zone—is predominantly Muslim, with pockets of Hindus and some Sikhs. So Kashmiris belong to a diverse society of Muslims and Hindus, cultivators and stockkeepers, shopkeepers, office workers, and traders, distinguished historically by amiable relations among disparate groups. Aparna Rao and Michael Casimir tell us "both rural and urban society have been extremely peaceful, with no overt violence between any groups or sections." It is that society, rather than any particular group within it, that has all but disappeared from the world, in the 60-year fight between India and Pakistan over a sublimely beautiful, strategically significant territory in the Himalaya-Hindukush. Chapter 7 lays out history and politics, and illustrates the human cost of war in a place no one would call peaceful today.

Hazara

Decades of war have also harmed Afghanistan's Hazara, though—counterintuitively—war may also have worked to strengthen a sense of identity in this Shia minority. Everywhere in the world, mountains have provided a refuge for displaced and powerless people. Groups who develop the skills to live in mountains (where challenges include steep terrain, short growing seasons, low biological productivity, and instability of weather and landscape alike) can prosper, if they are careful in exploiting the physical advantages of mountains (environmental diversity, availability of water) and can enjoy some autonomy from lowland-based, self-interested governments. The Hazara, descendants of Mongol soldiers from the ranks of Ghenghis Khan's son Chagatai, are mountaineers in this mold (as are other peoples of High Asia discussed in this book, including the Badakshani, Kirghiz, Wakhi, Tibetan, and Lezghi). Distinguished by appearance and religion from their neighbors, the Hazara are living on the margin of the dominant society. Grant Farr, in Chapter 8, explains that "the major threat to the survival of the Hazara is their long and continuing treatment in Afghanistan as a pariah group, where they have been despised, persecuted, murdered, and displaced." Though the Hazara found somewhat safe haven in mountainous Hazarajat, a succession of invaders since the late 19th century has driven many of them from the highlands, across the border into neighboring (Shia) Iran, and into internal refugee settlements. But having chosen the winning side in joining the Northern Alliance against the Taliban, Hazara are, for the first time, in a position to claim the rights of citizenship that their blood has bought them.

Wakhi/Kirghiz

The Wakhi, like the Hazara—and like the Badakshani and Lezghi taken up in this volume—are mountain farmers who combine irrigated agriculture with animal husbandry. Theirs are the green ribbon fields lost in an expanse of desert mountains that we know from photographs. Hermann Kreutzmann, in Chapter 9, describes how the Wakhi, like other practitioners of combined mountain agriculture, grow a hardy crop and plant fruit trees on irrigated valley bottoms, and take or send their herds of sheep, goats, cattle—and in highest Asia, yaks—to graze on mountain pastures. Those mountain rangelands give the place its name: *pamir,* pasture, a landform so characteristic of the knot of mountains at the heart of High Asia that we know this Roof of the World as the Pamirs. And those Pamirian pastures support the Kirghiz, nomadic pastoralists like the Raika already mentioned, and Tibetans of Chapter 12, who use their "fields on the hoof" to tap the widely dispersed, seasonally changing resources of a marginal environment. The peoples of the Pamir, tuned to environmental constraints and experienced at adapting their land use to the capacities of the environment, have experienced different challenges in the last several decades. Once owing some allegiance and tribute only to local amirs and other petty rulers, Wakhi and Kirghiz came under the control of the USSR or PRC. Centrally planned reorganization of herds and farms interrupted the mobility of Wakhi and Kirghiz; local decision making and production based on local needs and values was supplanted, first through collectivization, more recently through decollectivization (in the Chinese Pamirs) and independence (in Tajikistan, now free of the control, but also of the subsidies and opportunities, provided by the Soviet Union).

Badakshani

In the case of the Badakshani, or Mountain Tajiks, Stephen Cunha, in Chapter 10, offers a closer look and explores some implications of the shift from Soviet control. A marginal group within impoverished, war-afflicted Tajikistan, the Badakshani were denied their traditional livelihoods and forced to depend on various subsidies in the Soviet era. Now, in post-Independence Tajikistan, theirs is the last cup to be filled, their needs last to be served. And their mountain homeland—and indeed all of High Asia—is likely the most vulnerable to the perturbations of climate change, so their future, absent the supports of an affluent government, seems particularly precarious.

Lezghi

Mountains again—the southern Caucasus, that long extension of mountains marking the interface between Europe and Asia—are home to some of the Lezghi, though this mostly Sunni Muslim people, divided by the border between Azerbaijan and Russian Dagestan, are also divided by livelihood: they are both mountain agro-pastoralists and lowland farmers (and, increasingly, urban merchants and workers). As Julian Birch, in Chapter 11, explains, one of a number of ethnic minorities concentrated in Russian Dagestan (next door to the better-known Chechnya), the Russian Lezghi, like the Badakshani, cloaked their religious identity during the Soviet period, and contend with the transformed economic and social environment of the new Russia. In-migration of ethnic Russians dilutes the power and strains the resources available for the Lezghi. In Azerbaijan, Lezghi complain that their numbers are undercounted, and that a government already strained to provide for Azeri citizens puts Lezghi last. The Lezghi formed a more cohesive community, inter-acting freely and trading among themselves, before Azerbaijan's separation from Russia in 1991. Now both an intermittently militarized border and national policies of assimilation further threaten Lezghi identity.

Tibetans

Tibetans are better known in the West than most of the peoples discussed in this volume, though once Tibet's objective was to guard its secrets. Their highland homeland (mean elevation: 14,000 feet) and reclusive government kept outsiders at bay, until in recent times first Britain, then the Peoples Republic of China forced open the passes to the hidden kingdom. Cold, very high, and mostly dry, the Tibetan Plateau allows only limited survival options for its human residents, and Tibetans continue ways of life that began millennia ago. Barley (for the staple food, *tsampa*) and other hardy crops grow in the river valleys that draw monsoon moisture around the Himalayan barrier; yak and sheep are herded by *drogpa* in the truly forbidding Changtang and other high, cold rangelands. An almost feudal theocracy directed and diverted some of the production of peasant farmers and herders to the monasteries, where at one time as much as one-third of the male population lived and practiced one of several forms of Tibetan Buddhism. A long history of interaction and shifting suzerainty linked Tibet to Han China, and in 1951 the PRC asserted its authority over the Tibetan territories of what is now the Tibetan Autonomous Region (TAR—Xizang). With the Cultural Revolution came the destruction of traditional institutions, most especially the monastic traditions of Tibetan Buddhism. Today the TAR is home to growing numbers of Han immigrants and institutions; the identity of Tibetans within Tibet reflects this influence, and the classic "Tibetan" is perhaps easier to find in resettled communities far beyond the plateau.

Mangghuer

The Mangghuer of Minhe County (in eastern Qinhai Province, on the eastern edge of the Tibetan Plateau) share some of the subsistence practices, religion, history, and encounter with China experienced by the Tibetans, although the process of assimilation is much further along for the Mangghuer. The formerly forested hills and valleys where Minhe Mangghuer live are now crowded with small farm fields (irrigated in the valley bottoms, rain-fed on the slopes). Despite the care and expertise of Mangghuer farmers, the crop is often insufficient to both feed the household and pay a required government tax; young people leave for construction and other jobs in the cities and lose their connections to the ancestors' place and practices. As Zhu Yongzhong and Kevin Stuart, in Chapter 13, explain, "distinctive Mangghuer culture is threatened by a variety of factors: the presence of skilled workers from outside the area who move into the Mangghuer regions; poverty; language and culture change; the absence of school texts in the Mangghuer language; environmental degradation."

Some Final Thoughts

While the case-specific chapters of *Disappearing Peoples?* outline the lives and ways of life of just a few of the many cultural groups that inhabit the South and Central Asia region, the issues faced by these groups are issues that affect the lives and well-being of dozens and dozens of similar communities in the mountains, deserts, and river valleys of this increasingly militarized region of our world. The stories presented here are the stories of cultural communities that struggle with fundamental threats to the survival of their identity, traditions, ways of life, and life itself. In some instances (Kashmiris, Kirghiz, Wakhi, Lezghi) these cases illustrate the problems and continuing conundrums of cultural groups whose traditional homes and ways of life straddle two or more national borders—problems that are all the more complicated by the political and economic transitions associated with the breakup of the Soviet Union, formation of new States, declining and resurgent interest of China in the region, and the military involvement of the United States and other nations in this region. For many people, it is the natural resource wealth of their homelands that attract intruders with inevitable results, as in the case of Tibet. Other cases (Raika, peripatetics, Bhil, Dom, Badakshani) illustrate the age-old conflict between the rights to a way of life intrinsic to cultural groups and the broader responsibilities of the nation-state in determining legal norms and ensuring social access to critical resources. For some groups, there is a quiet dissolution of traditional identity (Tharu, Mangghuer), barely recognized even by members themselves who see the changes from their parents' lives to theirs as modernization or development—a great leap forward into a new and desirable future. For far too many, the story is of violent, wracking destruction.

We punctuate this book's title *Disappearing Peoples?* with a question mark because the ultimate fate of the indigenous and other cultural minorities in South and Central Asia is not known. These groups, like formerly isolated groups worldwide, are involved in their own efforts to negotiate survival and reshape a way of life. As we look toward the future, we may see a day where the resilience and place-adapted ways of the groups we chronicle are merely archaic footnotes in human history. It is clear that the health of the people and environment of this world is truly endangered by the human environmental crises resulting from overexploitation of finite resources and the many degenerative effects of global climatic change: rising seas, shifting ocean and air currents, melting glaciers, changes in weather patterns, and increasingly violent storms, floods, heat waves, and other disasters. And it is also clear that these groups, with their geographic proximity to critical resources and relative powerless status in society, are clearly vulnerable.

Then again, perhaps we will learn to value these people and respect their rights and traditions not only for what their knowledge and actions have sustained over time, but for what they promise in the future. The traditional knowledge and ability to sustain life in the harshest of surroundings—the flexibility and resilience of these peoples—is something to be celebrated. Indeed, it may be that such lifestyles and belief systems contain kernels of truth that will help other communities, societies, and nations to build new sustainable ways to interact with the planet and one another. It is with this hope that we offer you, the reader, this collection of essays.

Cautionary Note

The area explored in this book is changing fast. As its geopolitical significance has risen, so has the speed with which the dynamics within the region can switch course. This book goes to press at a time—May 2007—when India and Pakistan vow to continue their peace process and, at the same time, are testing and mobilizing nuclear-capable ballistic missiles; when the Taliban has regained control of Afghan villages and increased attacks in the south and east and NATO has acknowledged that force alone will not end the conflict; when a heightened concern for global warming, spurred by the release of the Fourth Intergovernmental Panel on Climate Change (IPCC) Report on Climate Change, suggests far more powerful and pervasive environmental change in the future. This is today's news for the region, and it has significant implications for the people and places chronicled here. What about tomorrow's news? We can't anticipate that, but we hope that with the background provided by these accounts, and with the resources we offer now, plus those that readers may find for themselves, this book will remain a useful resource for those trying to understand the vulnerable cultures of South and Central Asia.

Acknowledgments

In a project as protracted as this one, the list of people to thank could be a chapter of its own. Seven years ago this month I answered an e-mail appeal from Barbara Rose Johnston, who was seeking an editor for the South and Central Asia volume in her series on Endangered Peoples. I'd written a book and edited a journal; could an edited volume be so different? In a word: yes. A variety of complications delayed the completion of the book, and its publisher withdrew the contract, leaving a dozen chapters and maps and a lot of time and effort in limbo—where we remained until Barbara Johnston rode to the rescue with the energy and connections to the wonderful people of LeftCoast Press—to see the volume to a proper finish. She comes high on my thank you list, for envisioning an interesting and important project, trusting me with it, then adding her energy when mine had flagged so that together we could get *Disappearing Peoples?* into the light. My family—parents, brothers, husband, children—either actively encouraged or passively endured my work on this project: Thanks for that! I'm sorry I won't be able to show it off to my parents and elder brother, but I can at least dedicate the book to their memories. My student Jennifer Cesca and extraordinarily gifted editor Marianne Keddington-Lang helped refine two chapters. Jason Clark spent many hours making maps for round one of this project, and generously agreed to rework them to the specifications of our new publisher. I'm sure there are others whose efforts have been important to this undertaking; the fog of years obscures their names. Names I will never forget are those of the contributors to this volume. I hope that Paul Robbins, Judith Whitehead, Arjun Guneratne, Anna Schmid, Michael Casimir, Grant Farr, Hermann Kreutzmann, Stephen Cunha, Julian Birch, Christiaan Klieger, Zhu Yongzhong, and Kevin Stuart are glad they stuck with it; I am certainly glad to have had the chance to work with them and to learn about the people they tell about so compellingly. Again the long, drawn-out process of making this book means that I have left it too late to thank the most substantial contributor to the volume, responsible for our chapters on both Peripatetics and Kashmiris: Aparna Rao. I would like to offer special thanks to her husband and collaborator, Michael Casimir, who helped update Aparna's chapters after her untimely death.

—Barbara A. Brower

***

I, too, have numerous people to acknowledge and thank, not the least of which include my fellow editor and chapter authors whose contributions here will surely help inform the global community of scholars who seek to understand and celebrate the linkages between cultural diversity and biodiversity, and hope to halt the dangerous and troublesome trends of ethnocide, ecocide, and genocide. With regards to our ideas on language diversity and biodiversity, I gratefully acknowledge the work of the late ethnoecologist Darrell Posey, who helped create a global network of scholars examining these links, and linguist Luisa Maffi whose insights and work on bio/cultural diversity with Terralingua are increasingly influencing national and international policy. I have also been influenced by the work of my "Endangered Peoples of the World" series editors—Leslie Sponsel, Robert Hitchcock, Susan Stonich, Milton Freeman, Judith Fitzpatrick, Jean Forward, and Tom Greaves and their many contributing authors. Their work in other corners of the world helped carve out and shape the geographic focus of this book. The conceptual focus of this volume has also been greatly influenced by David and Pia Maybury-Lewis, whose organization, Cultural Survival, and publications have served for many, myself included, as both example and crucial source of information concerning the plight of indigenous peoples and ethnic minorities around the world, and their struggles to survive and thrive. I must also acknowledge the people who helped ensure that this book would truly disappear from my long list of writing obligations. It is only with the encouragement and support of my fellow residential scholars Aneesh Aneesh, Erica Bornstein, Eric Haanstad, Noenoe Silva, Graham St. John, Julie Velasquez-Runk, SAR staff, and foundation sponsors at the School for Advanced Research on the Human Experience in Santa Fe, especially the Weatherhead Foundation, that this project has finally reached its concluding point. I thank Jennifer Collier, a truly brilliant editor and a delight to work with, for encouraging revisions and helping to publish this work. And, finally, I thank Ted, Ben, and Chris Edwards for their patience and belief that, despite the many, many years between inception and completion, this book will be published.

—Barbara Rose Johnston

Resources

Published Literature

Armstrong, Karen. 2000. *Islam: A Short History*. New York: Modern Library.
Green, Richard. ed. 2006. *The State of the World's Minorities: Events of 2004–5*. London: Minority Rights Group International.

Johnston, Barbara Rose. ed. 1997. *Life and Death Matters: Human Rights and the Environment at the End of the Millennium.* Walnut Creek, CA: AltaMira Press.

———. 2007. *Half-Lives and Half-Truths: Confronting the Radioactive Legacies of the Cold War.* Santa Fe, NM: School for Advanced Research Press.

Kolbert, Elizabeth. 2006. *Field Notes from a Catastrophe: Man, Nature, and Climate Change.* New York: Bloomsbury.

Scudder, Thayer. 2004. *The Future of Large Dams: Dealing with Social, Environmental, Institutional and Political Costs.* London: Earthscan.

Skutnabb-Kangas, Tove. 2000. *Linguistic Genocide in Education—Or Worldwide Diversity and Human Rights?* Mahwah, NJ: Lawrence Erlbaum.

Internet

Colchester, Marcus. 2000. "Sharing Power: Dams, Indigenous Peoples and Ethnic Minorities" World Commission on Dams Thematic Paper 1.2 (March 2000): http://www.dams.org/kbase/thematic/tr12.htm

Gordon, Raymond G., Jr. ed. 2005. *Ethnologue: Languages of the World*, Fifteenth edition. Dallas, Tex.: SIL International. Online version accessed December 29, 2006. http://www.ethnologue.com/

Intergovernmental Panel on Climate Change. 2001. IPCC Third Assessment Report—Climate Change 2001. Online version accessed January 6–18, 2007 http://www.ipcc.ch/pub/online.htm

International Work Group for Indigenous Affairs (IWGIA) 2005. *IWGIA Annual Report 2005.* Online version accessed December 30, 2006. http://www.iwgia.org/graphics/Synkron-Library/Documents/publications/Folders/AnnualReport2006.pdf

Iyngararasan, Mylvakanam, Li Tianchi and Surendra Shrestha. 2002. "The Challenges of Mountain Environments: Water, Natural Resources, Hazards, Desertification and the Implications of Climate Change." Briefing paper, Bishkek Global Mountain Summit (28 October–1 November 2002, Kyrgyzstan). Accessed online, December 29, 2006. http://www.mtnforum.org/bgms/papere1.htm

Patwardan, Amrita. 1999. "Dams and Tribal People in India." World Commission on Dams Contributing Paper, Thematic Review 1.2: Indigenous Peoples and Ethnic Minorities: http://www.dams.org/docs/kbase/contrib/soc207.pdf

Skutnabb-Kangas, Tove, Luisa Maffi and David Harmon. 2003. "Sharing a World of Difference: The Earth's Linguistic, Cultural and Biological Diversity." Paris: UNESCO, Terralingua and World Wide Fund for Nature. Online version accessed December 29, 2006. http://www.terralingua.org/UNESCO%20publication.pdf

World Information Service on Energy (WISE) Uranium Project. 2006. "Uranium Mine and Mill Residents—Current Issues." Accessed January 29, 2007. http://www.wise-uranium.org/uir.html

World Commission on Dams (WCD) 2001. *Dams and Development: A New Framework for Decision Making.* Final Report of the World Commission on Dams (November 2001): http://www.dams.org/report/

Sherpa girl near Chaunrikarka, Nepal. Photograph by and © Barbara Brower.

Hazara People. Photograph from the collection of and © Grant Farr.

Boy and goats, Pamir Mountains, Tajikistan. Photograph by and © Stephen F. Cunha.

Tibetan Lama (old man) with prayer beads sitting on a bench facing the camera as a young boy looks over a banister and another man stands in the background. Photograph by and © Joel Correida, made available by the Association for Nepal and Himalayan Studies.

Young monk, Paro, Bhutan. Photograph by and © Gary Goldenberg; made available by the Association for Nepal and Himalayan Studies.

Drogpa–yak herders and their tents, Tibet. Photograph by and © Han Jianlin; made available by the Association for Nepal and Himalayan Studies.

Kashmiri family. Photograph by and © Aparna Rao; made available by the Association for Nepal and Himalayan Studies.

Kashmiri girl with basket. Photograph by and © Aparna Rao; made available by the Association for Nepal and Himalayan Studies.

Kirghiz woman in her yurt in Kara Köl pasture of the Little Pamir, Afghanistan.
Photograph by and © Hermann Kreutzmann; made available by the Association
for Nepal and Himalayan Studies.

Children with flowers: Kabön, Paldar, Jammu & Kashmir. Photograph by and © Isabelle Riaboff; made available by the Association for Nepal and Himalayan Studies.

Raika outside Kumbhalgarh Wildlife Sanctuary in Rajasthan, India. Photograph by and © Paul Robbins.

A Royal Nepal Army patrol passes a Gurung grandmother in the village of Chandrakot, following the 2005 coup by king Gyanendra. This once popular beginning point for trekking in the Anapurna region became a ghost village occupied alternately by Maoist rebels in the evening, and government troops during the day. Photograph by and © Zuzana Sadkova.

Thamel businesses are shuttered in the tourist center of Kathmandu. The civil war was marked by regular Bandhas – shop closures and travel bans – called by the Maoists, and enforced through violent reprisals. Nepal's already fragile economy hit bottom during this time. Photograph by and © Zuzana Sadkova.

2

The Raika of Rajasthan, India

Paul Robbins

Pema Ram Divasi, a gray-haired man in his fifties, stands dressed in a distinctively coiled red turban and white *dhoti* (lower garment) and stares in frustration at the encroaching mesquite trees that blanket the land in front of him. Until recently the land had been useful forest pasture, but now because of the invading plant, the useful grasses and trees are all gone. "That is not a true forest," he says. "A forest has *dhav* trees, *kair* trees, and *palas*. This place has no name" (from an interview, November 1999). For Pema Ram, like other members of the Raika community, this transformation of the landscape is devastating, and may make impossible the adaptive life they have lived for centuries in the desert regions of northwest India.

The People

The Raika of Rajasthan, sometimes also known as Rebaris or Dewasis, are a community of animal breeders and livestock raisers, living a semi-nomadic existence in the northwestern part of India, especially in the arid state of Rajasthan. The Raika are not an ethnic or linguistic group unto themselves but represent an extensive endogamous caste community, meaning that they marry within a larger lineage group and tend toward a common set of occupations. The origins of the community, which today likely numbers more than 300,000, are obscure but they likely originated in Persia or Baluchistan (contemporary western Pakistan) more than 500 years ago. They are now well known in the region for their vast herds of animals and for their extensive ecological and veterinary knowledge. Perhaps because of their historical association with the *rajput* rulers of the region, the Raika hold a distinctive middle position in the region's caste hierarchy. The Raika are also distinctive

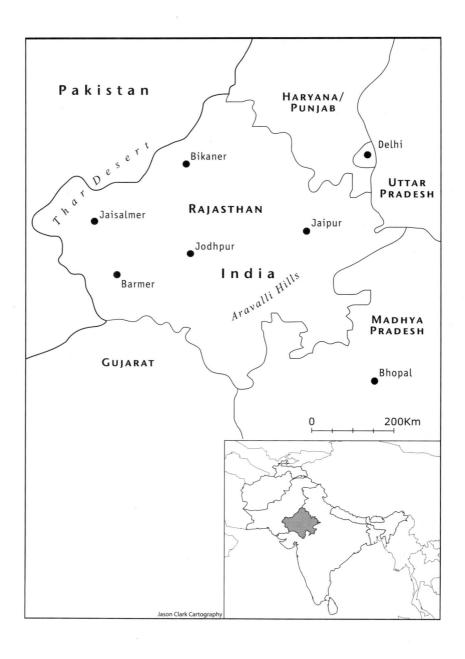

Jason Clark Cartography

in their traditional dress, which includes a unique style of turban and *dhoti* (Kohler-Rollefson 1992, 1994, 1999).

Most important, the Raika have come to be associated with mobility and the annual migrations of their herds. Although the group is not historically nomadic and Raika families keep permanent dwellings in settled villages, many Raika have become increasingly mobile in the last half century. This increasing nomadism is largely a result of changing ecological and economic conditions in the region, to which the group has adapted with success (Agrawal 1993, 1994, 1998). But this raises a fundamental question for the future of the group: Can Raika culture, identity, and economy, which is increasingly based on mobility and grazing resources, continue to persist in the face of successive waves of social and environmental change that force settlement and the enclosure of pasture?

The Setting

Western Rajasthan and the Marwar region, where a majority of Raika make their home, is an arid and semi-arid desert/savanna region on the fringes of the Thar (or Great Indian) Desert. The region receives between 100 and 500 mm of rainfall annually, comparable to the driest desert regions of the southwest United States. Most of this rain, moreover, falls only during the Indian monsoon months of July and August, with some years experiencing totally failed monsoons. Temperatures can climb as high as 110° F during the summer days but can chill and freeze during winter nights. Water is extremely scarce and both drinking and irrigation water comes from deep wells.

Even so, the desert can be extremely productive and the hardy trees and perennial grasses of the area grow like a garden during the rainy season and survive into dry months. Acacia and other tree species are drought tolerant and produce a wealth of fruits, gums, animal fodder, and medicines. The perennial grasses of the region, though invisible during the dry months, grow thickly in the area's pastures with the onset of the rain. Their roots hold soil and sand in place and cover the landscape with productive fodder. As in other desert regions, the secret for survival in such a place is to exploit the pockets of high productivity, save for scarcity, and travel to where resources and water are available. The Raika know these secrets well and are adapted to vagaries of life in an arid region.

Traditional Subsistence Strategies

The Raika has been managing animals since at least the 14th century at which time they bred and supplied camels for the maharajas and rajas (kings) of the vast feudal states of the region, who used camels as pack animals, for racing, and for mounted warfare. The Raika are therefore strongly identified with the camel, but since at least the turn of the century they have also been breeding sheep and goats (Kohler-Rollefson 1999; Singh 1993).

Presently, the community combines agricultural production and pastoralism in a wide variety of strategies, most of which center on earned income from the sale of breeding animals and wool products. Agriculture is generally a single-crop enterprise, using monsoon rains to grow pearl millet (*bajra*), wheat (*gyon*), or a range of arid legumes. These are usually harvested in October. Most Raika families have at least a few sheep and goats, while many households keep herds numbering in excess of 300 (Agrawal 1998, 1999).

The animals are usually herded away from permanent Raika settlements after the harvest and the annual festival of *diwali*. From there, groups of herders combine their animals for safety and efficiency and begin the long and arduous trek, on foot, into the adjacent states of Maharashtra and Haryana, where forests and pasture await them during the hottest months of the year. On the trip they face difficult terrain, sometimes-hostile villages, and even wild animals; the Indian wolf is making a tenuous return, feeding largely on sheep. At the same time, however, they will encounter friendly relatives and economic allies in other castes. In villages where they stay en route, the migration group encamps in fallow fields. These fields, which are not in crop during the dry season and which have a variety of wild grass species mixed in amongst crop stubble (the stalks of harvested crops), provide essential grazing resources. This animal fodder is exchanged with the landowner for the valuable sheep dung that provides fertilizer for the owner's fields. Here, the Raika also have the opportunity to sell both sheep wool and whole animals, the receipts from which are scrupulously saved; herders, often traveling with women and children, live on only the barest necessities (Agrawal 1999; Prasad 1994).

This careful combination of agricultural and pastoral resources can be viewed as a form of risk spreading, practiced by many rural people. By separating their two income streams (crops and herds) in time and space, the Raika lower the chances of failure and disaster. If bad rains cause a poor crop, migration to other areas may offset scarcity. If the migration season is expensive or unproductive, crops will provide for subsistence. This semi-nomadic lifestyle is a carefully calculated investment scheme for scarce resources.

Social and Political Organization

The Raika have historically been politically well positioned. Their alliances to the *rajput* caste, who traditionally governed in Rajasthan as landlords and kings, go far back into remembered past.

The Raika caste is historically divided into a higher-ranked camel-raising group and a lower-ranked sheep-raising group but are linked through many larger social networks. The basis of social organization amongst the Raika is twofold, involving both the larger caste community and the migration group. Though isolated in far-flung small hamlets (or *dhanis*), at the regional scale, households are tied together by their lineage groups and marriage patterns. The Raika are one of the few Indian caste groups that do not practice dowry, and families often have to offer a bride-price to attract a woman to the family. Once joined, these families become economically interdependent to the mutual advantage of each. Extended Raika families call upon one another for mutual support and shared resources, helping one another in times of scarcity and joining together politically to oppose policies that are detrimental to the larger group, such as those involving state enclosure of forest or pasture.

Migration groups are also carefully organized. Individual flocks of 400 to 500 sheep and goats are combined into a *dang*, or huge mobile camp of thousands of animals, and dozens of men, women, and children. The chief decision maker in the *dang* is the *nambardar*, an influential male leader whose talents in dealing with strangers and officials and whose many community connections make him a useful spokesman. His decisions are, however, supplemented and checked by a council of elders and by a second in command. Within this democratic structure, decision-making powers are divided in order to maximize efficiency and make best use of talented individuals (Agrawal 1999).

Religion and Worldview

The Raika trace their roots to a single origin story that binds the widespread community together; they are said to have been created by the Lord Shiva (a creative and destructive god central to the Hindu pantheon) for the specific purpose of caring for the first camel. As such, the Raika are Hindu practitioners with their own distinctive group of heroes and god figures. They are distinctive, however, in the large number of "renunciants" they produce. These ascetics live apart from the rest of the community and renounce worldly matters, while simultaneously filling an important spiritual role for the rest of the community (Srivastava 1997).

Threats to Survival

The Raika have thrived in recent years, owing to their ability to adapt to radically changing conditions. But the limits to these adaptations may be fast approaching and the community is at great risk as it faces the threats of closed forests, intensification of agriculture, disintegrating relationships with other groups, state development projects, a quickly changing economy, and invasive plant species that are transforming the desert.

Efforts to enforce wildlife conservation for the preservation of important endemic species like wolves and panthers have typically taken the form of large-scale enclosures of areas traditionally used for grazing. Whether such enclosures benefit wildlife protection or in fact hinder it (predators in Rajasthan rely heavily on livestock), the loss of dry-season grazing has been an enormous problem for the Raika. As global conservation interest in the region increases, moreover, and local parks achieve International Union for the Conservation of Nature and Natural Resources (IUCN) status and the attention of important international environmental nongovernmental organizations (NGOs), the prospects for maintaining traditional grazing rights begin to look uncertain.

The Closure of Forests

The forests of India have historically been held in reserve by the state. In ancient India, forestlands were held by kings for hunting. In the later colonial era, when Britain ruled the subcontinent, these were placed under the control of a government bureaucracy and expert cadre of foresters. In the post-Independence era, the lands are held by the Ministry of the Environment and managed by state departments of forestry. Over that period, the fundamental conflicts have always been over *who* has the right to use those forests and *what* they have the rights to do. For the Raika, who depend on forestland for dry-season grazing, these large areas of forest are essential. As these forests become increasingly off-limits for animals, a key foundation stone is removed in the Raika's survival strategy.

The closure of forests has increased greatly in recent years. Indian state statistics show that forestland in western Rajasthan has increased three-fold since the 1960s, rising from 40,000 hectares to nearly 120,000 in the four westernmost districts of the state. Rather than representing a real increase in the amount of land under trees, however, these figures represent the tripling of land controlled by forestry officials, which are often restricted against grazing and circled in barbed wire, creating enclosures locals refer to as *tarbandi* (literally: *tar* = wire, *bandi* = closed). In part, the increased zealousness in conservation is a result of international pressure and funding for conservation efforts. As concern around the world grows about the state of forests, Indian officials are increasingly interested in protecting and enclosing forests. Moreover, the proliferation of wildlife conservation areas in India has led to an increased vigilance on the part of officials for keeping livestock out of forestland. A recent Indian Supreme Court decision makes any kind of "resource collection" in wildlife conservation areas illegal. Whether this includes grazing is yet unclear, but livestock prices plummeted as a result of the announcement. Loss of forest grazing represents a fundamental threat for the Raika (Robbins 1998).

Intensification of Agriculture and the Decline of Cooperative Relations

As conservation has removed some dry-season tree pasture for herders, so too has the intensification of agriculture in the area. Agricultural intensification, meaning the increased yield of crop (grain or vegetables) for every hectare of land, is often referred to as the "green revolution," and has led to a fundamental change in the region's agricultural ecology, which has in turn, threatened the way of life of herders. To institute "green revolution" initiatives for increased production in desert crops, which include wheat, chili peppers, and millet, it is necessary to plant crops more frequently than is traditionally possible in an arid monsoon climate. Deep wells must be drilled to provide dry-season water, and the land must be kept in crop during the months of November, December, and January, when it traditionally lays fallow. In the process, the wild grass species that traditionally grow alongside crops in fields are removed through intensive weeding and herbicides.

With dry-season lands in crop, Raika have fewer destinations for grazing on their migration routes. More intensively cropped land, moreover, has fewer grasses and crop waste. At the same time, the fallow land that remains has become more valuable, and is often used by land owners for their own livestock. As a result, the traditional cooperative arrangements established between landowners and migrating herders have begun to disintegrate in recent years. Raika are less welcome in the villages they visit and conflicts sometimes arise that have, on rare occasions, broken into violence between villagers and herders. Many herders do continue to rely on good relations with villagers. Extended family and caste relations are helpful for households on migration, and the nitrogen rich *mingni* (animal dung) that herds provide continues to be a bargaining chip when dealing with local landowners. Even so, the intensification of agriculture has become a serious threat to Raika ecology and economy (Robbins 2004b).

State Development Policy

The Indian government is highly active in development work, with offices and ministries for a bewildering variety of development tasks. In Rajasthan, development programs include the Drought Prone Areas Program, which seeks to ameliorate the effects of poor monsoons, and the Desert Development Program, which seeks to promote modern agricultural and pastoral development under arid conditions. Ironically, however, most of the development activities focused on the pastoral populations of Rajasthan have proven a threat to Raika herders. In one notable example from the early 1980s, the Pasture and Sheep Development Program was initiated in order to settle mobile pastoralists, provide pasture for animals, plant trees, and keep animal numbers in check. The program was a notable disaster and none of the demonstration pasture areas survived. Moreover, the attempts to organize and settle the shepherds also met with failure, actually leading to an overall reduction in the amount of pasture available to herders, rather than an expansion.

The reasons for this failure are several. The system proved extremely inefficient and most of the budgets for the program went to maintaining state salaries and infrastructure rather than helping herders. But perhaps more important, the project failed because it was based on a concept of settled pastoralism, one that fit neither the culture and economy of the Raika nor the ecological and economic conditions of the wool and meat production system. Settled pastoralists cannot respond to changes in the local rainfall pattern, nor can they take advantage of good rainfalls, available forest and fallow, and more reliable markets that exist elsewhere, away from their homes. By enforcing a settled model of pastoral development, the state did more harm than good for the Raika (Agrawal 1999).

Volatile Markets

But neither have "reliable" markets gone unchanged in recent years, and changes in the livestock economy have created new problems and opportunities for the Raika as well. Traditionally, the Raika are large stock herders and have long been associated with the camel, but the camel economy is in a state of transition and herders continue to search for new economic outlets. Camels do remain a part of the rural farm economy; during periods of high fuel costs, the demand for camels tends to rise as producers seek to replace expensive petroleum-powered farm equipment. Even so, the modernization of the agricultural economy and ecology means there is less of a place for large stock as draft power. So too, the traditional purposes for camels, in warfare, racing, and royal procession, have all but disappeared. Some new areas for camels have arisen, including safari tourism, but on the whole the camel component of the Raika economy is much reduced.

Concomitant with those changes, there has been a rise in the demand for small stock. The price of meat has risen far more rapidly than that of milk or grains, and the urban demand for meat and wool increases annually with little sign of stagnation. Meat exports from India, especially to markets in the Middle East, also increase every year. As a result, the Raika have moved from large stock raising to small stock raising, with goats and sheep making up the core of the Raika economy.

But even the meat and wool economies are highly unstable. During bad years, when large numbers of animals die from drought and fodder scarcity, the bottom drops out of the market and prices fall to levels where the price of the animals is far lower than the cost of the maintenance. And even while export markets for meat remain strong, they are subject to wide fluctuations as global trade in meat continues to drive commodity prices downward. As margins become slimmer, the need for larger herds increases. As herds grow, expenses increase and management of the animals becomes more complex. Changes in the market therefore represent a real threat to pastoral household economics (Robbins 2005).

Invasive Plant Species

While human artifacts like "green revolution" technology, forest enclosure, and livestock markets have had a profound effect on the Raika, so too have dynamics in the natural system. Specifically, the invasion of aggressive foreign plant species has created an ecological crisis and threatened what pasturage remains in the region. The two most important invaders, *Prosopis juliflora* and *Lantana camera*, have together rendered large areas of traditional pasture useless for herders.

Prosopis juliflora (or Mexican mesquite) is locally called *Angrezi* (English) *babul*, *Vilayati* (foreign) *babul*, or *Sarkari* (government) *babul*. The tree was probably introduced from North America by the Maharaja of Jodhpur around 1910, in an effort to "green" the desert landscape. It has since that time been a favored plantation species for forestry officials. The reasons for this are several-fold. *Juliflora* is very fast growing, producing a remarkable 15 tons of fuelwood per hectare per year, which far surpasses the productivity of local species. *Juliflora* is also very hardy, surviving on very little rainfall (as little as 150 mm per year), and resilient during failed monsoon seasons. But most remarkable, the tree produces leaves with phytotoxic chemicals, which are released when the leaves fall to the ground. These chemicals are allelopathic, which means they hinder the germination of seeds from competing species.

Thus, the area beneath a *juliflora* tree is usually devoid of grasses or competing shrubs. These features combine to make the tree quick to invade and difficult to remove. Wherever it appears, it quickly outcompetes even the most aggressive local species and soon comes to dominate in vast stands (Robbins 2001).

For herders, the tree is not particularly useful. While the seedpods of the plant can be eaten by livestock, the leaves are useless as fodder. It is also a tree that burns poorly and that makes poor construction material. Combined with the effect of removing fodder grasses in the areas where it grows, *Prosopis juliflora* has become more than just a nuisance for the Raika; it has rendered vast areas of pasture useless, increasing the fodder scarcity problem driven by human actions in the region (Robbins 2004a).

The second species, *Lantana camera*, is not foreign to India but is new to the arid regions of the northwest. It has begun to appear along the migration routes the Raika use in their annual trips into Maharashtra and other adjacent states. The shrub is topped by an attractive yellow, white, and red flower cluster, which is sometimes browsed by sheep during their long migration. The bud is toxic, however, and invariably leads to the death of the animal. As herders attempt to manage hundreds (and sometimes thousands) of animals, therefore, the species represents a dangerous nuisance. Its survival and proliferation is a source of continuous complaint from herders, and along with *juliflora*, the shrub represents a central problem for the Raika.

Response: Struggles to Sustain Livelihoods

The Raika have not faced these transformations passively. Instead the community has organized, adapted, and transformed to meet the challenges they face by involving themselves increasingly in regional and national politics, by modernizing their relationship to the market, and by educating their young.

Politics: Seeking Avenues of Redress

The Raika have never been a "scheduled" caste, meaning that they do not come from the most marginal caste communities and so, unlike some of the poorest groups, receive no special protections or quotas in government planning. Recently, the Raika have organized to more effectively flex their traditional political muscle and secure alliances in regional and national government. Before periodic major elections, Raika elders meet to discuss where their votes will go. Often they vote for candidates preferred by the *rajput* community, which itself meets to choose candidates based on its interests.

These sorts of political alliances are extremely important since local and regional level officials in environmental administration can often be pressured and coerced from above. Raika federations, though representing only a relatively small block of votes, were important to elections in the early 1990s, which brought the Bharatiya Janata Party (BJP) to power in Rajasthan over the traditionally dominant Congress Party. How much influence the shepherds exert at the state level as a result is unclear, but when local forest policy was set recently to enclose large sections of a wildlife preserve in southern Rajasthan, thereby reducing herders' access to pastureland, the Raika were able to appeal to central government officials and have the area reopened. Similarly, by organizing politically, the Raika hope to obtain support through revised state policy on livestock development, including subsidies and infrastructural investment. Overall, the political efforts of the Raika have not been fully successful and government policy is still organized against mobile pastoralism and migrating herds. Even so, the nascent political power of the Raika marks a new adaptation for the community.

More than this, Raika communities have begun to organize through nongovernmental organizations, asserting access to resources (pasture, forest, etc.) but also rights to the genetic heritage stored within the diversity of their many animal breeds, threatened both by decline in herd diversity through modern breeding (promoted by the state) as well as by potential capture by predatory corporate interests (Kohler-Rollefson 2001). This movement has a significant "South-South" component, as local advocacy NGOs seek connections to herders in similar contexts around the world, linking the interests of the developing economies, from those in South Asia to other underdeveloped contexts (Indian Pastoralists and Herders Association 2002).

Marketing: Modernizing Pastoralism

Such political movements have gone hand in hand with changes in economic strategy. Social and economic organizations, including herders' groups, wool cooperatives, and marketing organizations, are increasingly common amongst the Raika. Through these, the shepherds attempt to find new markets, control prices, and achieve economies of scale, meaning that marketing together in large groups reduces the costs for each producer or family. Moreover, political and economic federations like these reduce unnecessary competition between individuals, thereby stabilizing prices for wool and meat. As a result, most animal traders, who depend on the Raika and other groups for animals, report that the regional market is a seller's market, meaning that the herders often have the upper hand in the sale and purchase of livestock (Agrawal 1999). New outlets for nontraditional products have also blossomed, including camel milk, a product not traditionally sold in the region that has found its way onto regional markets (Kohler-Rollefson 1997).

But these new techniques come with a cost. Modernized marketing takes time and effort; meetings must be held and some individuals must take leadership positions in dealing with traders. While much of this work is done along traditional lines, new methods of organization are becoming increasingly necessary. Like political responses to change, volatile markets have forced many changes on traditional Raika culture.

Education: From Traditional Knowledge to Veterinary Science

The Raika are well known throughout the region for their traditional veterinary knowledge. Applying hot brands to camels, for example, has been an effective and well-known technique amongst pastoralists in Rajasthan for treating a range of ailments, though the mechanisms by which these treatments work are poorly understood. Other cures and treatments draw upon easily available plants and materials that Raika find on migration, in forests, and in pastures. Other caste groups sometimes come to Raika healers to treat their livestock (Geerlings 2001a, 2001b).

But as changes in economics and medicine enter Raika villages, these knowledges have proven somewhat insufficient. The Raika have responded by becoming increasingly well educated and seeing to it that at least one member of the family receives at least a rudimentary education. Young Raika are increasingly well schooled and enter professions outside of herding, including engineering and other careers. Some Raika have even become veterinarians, combining traditional and modern knowledges. With the help of regional NGOs, many Raika are being trained in para-veterinary techniques that, while modern by all standards, hold in high regard the traditional knowledge of the community.

But the degree to which the more successful Raika households respond and survive these challenges also represents the degree to which the culture is fundamentally altered. Changing to modern veterinary medicine, for example, has reduced the reputability of extremely valuable traditional ethno-veterinary knowledge. Most younger Raika remain entirely untrained in traditional cures and treatments. Thus, even while the Raika adapt to the changes in the landscape, ecology, and economy around them, their culture is placed at significant risk.

Moreover, these methods and avenues for survival are not equally available to all Raika. Wealthier members of the community have managed to accumulate tremendous amounts of capital while many others remain extremely poor. The degree of stratification among Raika households is not well understood and is difficult to gauge since Raika are traditionally very austere in the way they present themselves to casual observers and all Raika uniformly declare their poverty. It is clear, however, that some Raika are becoming richer while others are becoming poorer and that the concessions made to the changing economy and ecology may foster division within this traditional community.

Food for Thought

Why "Preserve" Culture?

The Raika are a traditional caste of herders who continue to adapt to social, economic, and political turbulence in the world around them. Faced with the closure of traditional pastureland and forest; problematic state development policy; volatile markets for meat, wool, and traction power; and a variety of invasive plant species, the Raika have adapted through innovations in politics, economics, and education. As people, they have proven remarkably resilient. So what is really "at risk" in the socioecological transformation of the Thar desert: a culture or an agro-political economy? This question mark hangs over the case of the Raika, but is similar to that hanging over many pastoral peoples around the world.

First, it seems essential to consider the possible future trajectories of ecological change. To what degree are the changes we see in the desert permanent? With groundwater in serious decline, intensive cropping, especially in the dry season, may end, and with it may come a return of native grasslands. But some ecological transformations cannot be reversed in a simple way, and the new ecosystems that emerge from any disintensification will likely look wholly unlike those of the last two millennia. What does this mean for pastoralism? If we can't "go back," what does it mean to "preserve" a culture?

So, too, it is essential to face the stand-off between local practice and the larger force of conservation imposed in the region. The political economy of biodiversity preservation and the construction of reserve forests for conservation of wildlife have put the state at odds with the economy and ecology of the Raika. Can seeking to protect forestland and charismatic animals that live within be reconciled with pastoral cultural practice? On whose terms?

Finally, some individual Raika will continue to be extremely successful and survive the changes that are occurring around them. Many will not, however, and almost all will be forced to change—through a transition both in material practices and systems of meaning. Does the transformation of their cultural practice make them unrecognizable in any meaningful way? When is a culture "endangered"? And is a desire to "preserve" culture anything more than a colonial or paternalist romance?

It is this last question that perhaps requires the most critical consideration as the idea of "disappearing people" is addressed. After all, is it the *disappearance* of people—many of whom have been effectively "invisible" to development officials since the time of colonialism—that should trouble us, or rather the injustices heaped on people whose way of life fits poorly with the desires and aspirations of those more powerful? Can people be "saved" from disappearance at the will of others, or do people have an opportunity to make themselves understood over the noise of those who, however well intentioned, seek to make them "reappear"? Should we be trying to "preserve" cultures, or instead trying to erect a scaffolding of argument and representation where those long silenced might better be heard?

In sum, the case of the Raika shows the way ecologies, economies, and politics entwine as cultures appear, transform, and vanish. What remains unclear, however, is the normative political path toward a more just and honest way of dealing with "cultures at risk."

Resources

Published Literature

Agrawal, A. 1993. Mobility and Cooperation among Nomadic Shepherds: The Case of the Raikas. *Human Ecology* 21(3): 261–279.

———. 1994. Mobility and Control among Nomadic Shepherds: The Case of the Raikas II. *Human Ecology* 22(2): 131–144.

———. 1998. Profits on the Move: The Economics of Collective Migration among the Raika Shepherds in India. *Human Organization* 57(4): 469–479.

———. 1999. *Greener Pastures: Politics, Markets, and Community among a Migrant Pastoral People*. Durham, NC: Duke University Press.

Geerlings, E. 2001a. Sheep Husbandry and Ethnoveterinary Knowledge of Raika Sheep Pastoralists in Rajasthan, India. MSc thesis, Environmental Sciences, Wageningen University.

———. 2001b. Sheep Husbandry and Healthcare System of the Raikas in South-Central Rajasthan. Sadri (India): Local Livestock for Empowerment of Rural People (LIFE), League for Pastoral People.

Indian Pastoralists and Herders Association. 2002. Alsipura Statement: Issued March 23, 2002, Alsipura, Rajasthan, India.

Kohler-Rollefson, I. 1992. The Raikas of Western Rajasthan, India. London: Overseas Development Institute, 6–7.

———. 1994. Pastoralism in India from a Comparative Perspective: Some Comments. *Overseas Development Institute Pastoral Development Network* 36(a): 3–5.

———. 1997. Camel Milk and Its Marketing: New Hope for the Raikas of Rajasthan. *Livestock International* 1(1): 11–14.

———. 1999. From Royal Camel Tenders to Dairymen: Occupational Changes within the Raikas, in R. Hooja and R. Joshi eds. *Desert, Drought, and Development*. Jaipur: Rawat Publications, 305–315.

———. 2001. Intellectual Property Rights Regime Necessary for Traditional Livestock Raisers. *Indigenous Knowledge and Development Monitor* 9(1): 12–15.

Prasad, R. R. 1994. *Pastoral Nomadism in Arid Zones of India*. New Delhi: Discovery Publishing House.

Robbins, P. 1998. Nomadization in Rajasthan, India: Migration, Institutions, and Economy. *Human Ecology* 26(1): 69–94.

———. 2001. Tracking Invasive Land Covers in India or Why Our Landscapes Have Never Been Modern. *Annals of the Association of American Geographers* 91(4): 637–659.

———. 2004a. Comparing Invasive Networks: The Cultural and Political Biographies of Invasion. *Geographical Review* 94(2): 139–156.

———. 2004b. Pastoralism Inside-Out: The Contradictory Conceptual Geography of Rajasthan's Raika. *Nomadic Peoples* 8(2): 136–149.

———. 2005. Nomadism Now: Cultural Survival in a Changing Desert Environment. *Annals of Arid Zone*.

Singh, M. H. 1993. *The Castes of Marwar: Being Census Report of 1891*. Jodhpur: Books Treasure.

Srivastava, V. K. 1997. *Religious Renunciation of a Pastoral People*. New Delhi: Oxford University Press.

Organizations

The League for Pastoral Peoples, Pragelatostr. 20, 64372 Ober-Ramstadt, Germany. An organization dedicated to the support of livestock raisers throughout the world.

Lokhit Pashu-Palak Sansthan, Bhagwan Mahaveer Colony, Mundara Road, Sadri 306702, Pali District, Rajasthan, India. An organization dedicated to the support and self-improvement of pastoral communities in India.

3

Peripatetic Peoples and Lifestyles in South Asia
Aparna Rao

This chapter introduces and reviews the condition of a variety of nomadic communities in South Asia whose members travel among villages and towns, selling or exchanging goods they make, buying and reselling other goods, or offering specialized skills and services. In return they are compensated in cash or in kind. Such communities—called commercial nomads, service nomads, symbiotic nomads, nonfood-producing nomads, and, increasingly, peripatetics—inhabit most parts of the world. *Nomadism* is understood as regular, usually seasonal movement; the sale of goods and services amounts to a kind of resource exploitation, the resource here being customers with purchasing power (rather than the grazing grounds we associate with pastoral nomads).

The People

Peripatetics have often been dubbed "Gypsies"—a term used in Anglo-American anthropology for endogamous communities who live scattered throughout Europe; North, Central, and South America; and Northern Africa and South Africa, and call themselves Rom, Sinti, Manush, Kale, and the like. Research on "Gypsy" culture in Europe began with the discovery and analysis of the Romani language and its Indo-European roots, and led researchers to look for their origins in the Indian subcontinent. These researchers also turned up itinerant populations in South, West, and Central Asia whose economy, survival strategies, and low social status resembled those of traditional itinerant "Gypsies" in Europe. Travellers, researchers, and later policy makers in Europe and the European colonies lumped these communities together and mislabeled them "Gypsies."

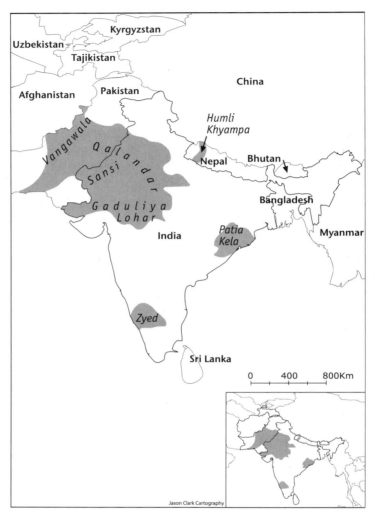

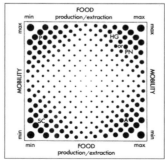

Figure 1

Many nomadic communities of South Asia rely on a variety of subsistence resources: even within a restricted geographical area the categories of pastoralist, forager, and peripatetic can overlap (they are "multiresourced"). Figure 1 models economic categories which are characterized by the degree of mobility and the extent of food production, or extraction. Each of these ideal categories approaches a specific corner of the square. P = peripatetic; SC = sedentary commerce; HG or PN = hunter-gatherer or pastoral nomadic. The model shows that none of these categories is discrete and that an infinite range of "mixed" categories exists; the proportion of this mixture depends on one's present position in the square. Any change in position along either of the two axes implies change in the classificatory category.

Table I sets out examples of nomadic economies in South Asia in which trading, servicing, foraging, animal husbandry, cultivation, and labor overlapped. (While this overlapping still exists, the data in this table omit change through time.)

This fuzziness of economic categories is mirrored in ethnonyms: Ethnic labels such as *Baluch, Banjara, Bhil, Charan, Gujar, Jat,* and *Nandiwalla* are often combined with other terms. *Jat,* for example, designates a cluster of communities dispersed across large parts of South and Southwest Asia; they are mentioned as itinerant camel breeders, camel drivers, buffalo breeders, as guides, spies, "Gypsies," and sedentary farmers. Similarly, the term *Charan* denotes a cluster of nomadic pastoralists, itinerant bards, merchants, farmers, genealogists, guides, transporters, and even priests in western India and Sindh. In official gazetteers and reports and in a variety of ethnographic accounts, many diverse peoples, occupations, and ethnonyms—with only their mobile way of life in common—are often lumped together into a single category. Once recorded, these labels persist, and define prototypic "others" from the perspective of the compilers and authors. Understanding nomadism by examining patterns of multiple resource use, on the other hand, illuminates the realities of economic practice and changing group identity. "Sedentism" and "nomadism" are not necessarily opposites; communities can be composed of nonsedentary and sedentary sections, which may shift over time.

The Setting

South Asia has the world's largest nomadic population and the greatest diversity of peripatetic professions. With some five hundred distinct communities of mobile herders, peripatetics, and foragers, roughly 7 percent of the Indian

Table I Overlapping of Subsistence Strategies among Some Nomadic Communities in South Asia

Group	Gathering	Hunting	Fishing/Hunting	Cultivation	Pastoralism	Trade/Barter	Service	Manual Labor
Aheri	x	x				x	x	x
Andamanese	x	x	x			(x)	x	(x)
Bajanio		x	x				x	
Bakkarwal	(x)			(x)	x			(x)
Bediya	x	x		(x)			x	
Bharwad				x	x	(x)		
Bhil cluster	x	x		(x)	(x)		x	x
Bhotiya				(x)	x	x		
Birhor	x	x				x		
Cholanaickan	x	x	x			x		
Devwalla		x	x	(x)				
Hunzakut	x	x	x	x	x			
Hussaini				(x)			x	
Brahmin								
Jarawa	x	x	x					
Jenu Kuruba	x	x	x	x				
Jogi-Kalbelia	x	x			(x)	x	x	x
Jogi-Nath-Kabelia				(x)			x	(x)

Group	1	2	3	4	5	6	7
Kanjar		x					x
Kashmiri Gujar	(x)	x			x		x
Kathkari	x	x			(x)	x	x
Killekyatha					x	x	(x)
Korava		x	x		x	x	x
Malapantaram	x	x	x		x	x	
Hill Pandaram							
Nandiwalla		x		x	x	x	
Nayaka	x	x		x			x
Onge	x	x	x	(x)			
Palayan	x	x			x		x
Phase Pardhi	x	x			x	x	x
Pohol	(x)		(x)		x		x
Rabari / Raika	(x)	x			x		
Rautye	x	x					(x)
Sentinelese	x	x					
Shompen	x		(x)	x			
Van Vagri	x	x		x	x	x	x
Vedda	x	x	x	x		x	x

Note: x = practiced; (x) = practiced marginally. Pastoralism always includes the sale and/or barter of herd animals and/or pastoral products. Minor horticulture is not taken into account.

population is nomadic, and at least 15 distinct peripatetic communities have been observed in Pakistan. No figures are available for the rest of South Asia, and since the last official community-wide census, in 1931, there are no reliable population estimates for any peripatetic community.[1]

Traditional Subsistence Strategies

Many of today's peripatetic professions are centuries old, and are documented in a variety of sources, including works of art. Miniature paintings, a preserve of the nobility and other high-status groups, often portray performances by peripatetic acrobats, animal trainers, and the like. Several community names are documented in historic accounts. The Banjara were mentioned by Ptolemy, and their own traditions refer to travel as goods porters for Mughal armies. In the 18th century Banjara worked as porters for the Maratha rulers in the Deccan, for the Nizam of Hyderabad, and for the British in their Mysore and Maratha wars. Similarly, the Killekyatha, leather-picture exhibitors and storytellers of Mysore, can be dated back to 1520. Many subcontinental peripatetic communities were probably linked historically to fringe groups of religious vagrants, both Hindu and Muslim. In addition to mobile communities within the subcontinent, groups of itinerant merchants, shepherds, porters, hawkers, moneylenders, and entertainers entered South Asia regularly every year from Afghanistan, western Iran, parts of Central Asia, and Tibet. Every summer peripatetics from the subcontinent crossed into Afghanistan and traveled to what is now Tajikistan to sell goods and services, while others were engaged in trade between Nepal, Tibet, and India. The broad categories of professions practiced by peripatetics including entertainment (as puppeteers, acrobats, animal leaders, musicians, etc.), healing (with indigenous medicines and sometimes possession), and a variety of ritual skills (e.g., display of deities, begging in the name of a deity—in societies where alms giving is considered meritorious—dispensing amulets). Peripatetics have carried with them a variety of little and great traditions and helped in the intermeshing of regional cultures—narrating or singing legends, bringing information about a variety of social, political, and environmental phenomena, and acting as economic links between towns and villages.

Interaction between peripatetics and sedentary peoples varies from region to region and generally diminishes along the rural-urban and the poor-rich continuum. A few decades ago, in the famine-prone tracts of the Deccan where crop failures are frequent, farmers depended on the Tirumal Nandiwalla to take their dry animals to more distant pastures in famine times and breed and keep them until they were once again of use in the village. Settled farmers were provided with game meat by the Pardhi and with medicinal plants by the Vaidu. Yet other Pardhi groups in Maharashtra replaced Pashtun pastoralists—who ceased entering India after the partition of the subcontinent in 1947—as moneylenders of last resort to farmers, to help them tide over hard times.

Peripatetics must take into account the population density and the requirements of their clients and customers, who are their resources, and hence must migrate through regions with enough people to buy their goods and services. A fertile agricultural region with high surpluses is likely to have a higher carrying capacity in terms of the number and variety of circulating peripatetic communities than an arid region. Most peripatetic households have their traditional migration routes between villages and towns within a specific home range and are integrated into local "patron-client" systems. While some communities migrate frequently, others travel only for short periods every year. Migration and agricultural cycles usually follow each other, sometimes because the goods and services offered are required for agricultural purposes, and always because after the harvest there is cash and/or surplus to pay for them.

Social and Political Organization

Peripatetic communities in South Asia can be either castes or tribes. While a caste must be explicitly part of an elaborate ranking system based on criteria of purity and pollution, a tribe does not necessarily have to be part of such a system, though it often is. Most tribes in South Asia, and especially in India, function as part of the vast canvas of hierarchy and repression that is represented by the caste system, and, proactive policies notwithstanding, most of these communities are subject to extreme social discrimination and disentitlement. The tribe/caste/and, increasingly, class equation is extremely complex and, in India, rendered even more so by administrative classifications (see *Source Note 1*). Within South Asia, peripatetic specialists are "attached" to "tribes" just as much as to "castes," to Hindus just as much as to Muslims. In the early 1970s, 23 different peripatetic groups visiting a single village in the Telengana region of Andhra Pradesh could be classified in two groups: those who offered their goods and services to all the villagers regardless of caste, and those who serviced only specific castes.

A caste system necessitates specialization and hence, symbiosis, and in some areas of South Asia, such specialization created specific niches for particular nomadic groups. But many nomadic groups are multiresource communities. This then implies two inherently conflicting "ideal types"—flexible, often multi-occupational nomadic communities operating within a rigid network of essentially uni-occupational community units (castes). How do these two inherently conflicting "ideal types" ("flexible groups" within a "rigid system") pair? Whereas the peripatetic Nandiwalla rank as middle castes, the equally peripatetic Sansi are ranked extremely low. Nomadism per se is, hence, not a criterion for low caste status. It seems that the overall lifestyle of a community— occupations practiced, diet, gender roles, and the like—determines the caste status of a nomadic community within the local hierarchy, and not simply nomadism or the absence of landed property. Furthermore, it appears that the degree of prescriptive specialization influences *varna-jati* status. Peripatetic Vaidu healers and tinkers, for example, faced a problem because their upper-caste Hindu clients could not understand how these two occupations could be practiced by members of one caste. Generally speaking, even today, the impure-pure caste gradient follows an occupational spectrum in which, both synchronically and diachronically, the number of occupations professed is smaller the higher one goes. Conversely, in the "ideal" scheme, the "purer" one is, the less multiresourced one also is – or can afford to be; the greater one's "impurity," the larger the number of things one does (can/has to do) occupationally. In this apparently paradoxical scheme, a sedentary caste whose members have numerous traditional occupations is lower in the caste hierarchy than a sedentary caste with a single occupation. The introduction of the element of nomadism in this structure does not, per se, appear to affect caste status. It is only the multiresourced nomad, and hence numerous peripatetics, who will be somewhere at the bottom of the unending ladder, increasingly subject to harassment and persecution (see below, *Current Events and Conditions*).

Sociopolitical organization varies among peripatetics. Generally, several related households form a unit whose members usually remain together through their lives. Many of them migrate together, depending on the amount of work available in a given area. Though elder members are often more respected, these units lack a single leader, and consensus and group pressure generally drive decision making, even at the level of larger community councils. Most communities have little strict division of labor, and children learn autonomy early.

Kinship systems and terminology follow patterns in a community's home or base area. All communities are patrilineal, some are polygynous, and most inheritance is along the male line. Newlyweds live first with the groom's family, but soon form independent nuclear households. Some communities live in houses in their home regions that are no different from those of sedentary neighbors, but many spend the whole year in temporary shelters (tents, reed huts, etc.) or live in the open.

Religion and Worldview

Many peripatetics, invoking a common rationale to explain low status and poverty, refer to an ancestor who violated some moral code or rule and incurred God's wrath and was cursed. This nuance notwithstanding, they usually share the same broader belief systems as the communities of their home region or the area of travel. Hence some communities are Hindu, others Muslim or Sikh; a few adhere to religions that are often categorized vaguely in South Asia as "tribal." Their ritual practices may differ from the mainstream; some peripatetic communities have a reputation for being more lax. This reputation pairs with that of moral laxity, notably concerning gender roles, especially in areas where women are ideally expected to be inactive and even invisible in public. In recent years Hindu fundamentalist organizations in India have been attacking non-Hindus and all those who refuse to accept their fascist decrees; some peripatetic communities have also been targeted, and violent attempts have been made to convert them (see below, *Current Events and Conditions*). Though despised at the everyday material level, peripatetics in South Asia, as elsewhere, are often ascribed a certain measure of power in the realm of the supernatural. Their "magical" and healing skills and their frequent practice of shamanistic rites or other possession rituals enhance fear and mystery. This apparent contradiction stems at least partially from the inherent contradiction in most societies between social and economic necessity and structures of established power and order.

Threats to Survival

The current situation of South Asian peripaptetics is intimately connected with state policies and practices applied in the region over the last century. The establishment of British colonial rule affected South Asian nomadism, and hence peripatetics, drastically in one or more of the following ways:

- Specific types of infrastructure rendered the occupations of several peripatetic communities—and hence the nomadic strategy involved in their practice—redundant or extremely difficult;
- Decisions based on fiscal policies led to an increase in the distance traveled and/or duration of migration by peripatetics looking for new client pools;
- Migration was simply prohibited in many places.

More modern systems replaced older communications and transport networks in one well-documented instance, with far-reaching effects. Throughout the colonized world ancient trading systems collapsed, and in large parts of South Asia, traditional porters such as the peripatetic Banjara were pushed out of their niche by the railways. Communities dealing in pack animals, and in the animal trade in general, such as the Sansi of Punjab, Sindh, and Rajputana, slowly went out of business as well. Even some of the goods transported were no longer produced as they had been. Salt, once produced from saline soils by peripatetics in many areas, was now brought under excise regulation in a spectrum of restrictions imposed as part of the new fiscal system. Ultimately, such changes in the wider infrastructure led to long-term economic, ecological, and social transformations.

Peripatetic communities had to seek new avenues, yet many professions came to be declared illegal, as new images of "backwardness" and "crime" were imposed on South Asian society at large. The British regarded mobility as "backward" and nomads as uncontrollable and hence potentially criminal. In Europe nomadism had come to be equated with vagrancy and associated conceptually with poverty. The criminalization of the poor led in turn to the idea of "the dangerous classes," and nomadism, or rather "wandering," came to be explained by "wanderlust," which itself was increasingly being considered genetically based and hence incorrigible. Transferred to South Asia, these concepts paired increasingly well with those concerning the newly discovered caste system, within which each entity was conceived of as fixed, with clearly definable features for now and forever. Peripatetic communities came to be seen as "wanderers" without positive goal or definite destination. Peripatetics like the Banjara who had worked as army suppliers (even for the British in their early campaigns) were declared "criminal tribes" after British victory over various local armies left them without work. With changing economic and sociopolitical conditions closing all other avenues of subsistence, highway robbery did sometimes become the ultimate recourse. The close of the 19th century saw colonial legislation define and name "criminal tribes" and fix their places of residence and their "traditional occupations." Numerous peripatetic communities were thus branded at one time or another— and ironically, as with Gypsies in Europe, information about South Asia's nomadic communities in this period comes primarily from colonial records, most of which consider them in "criminal" contexts.

The independent states of South Asia largely followed British concepts and continued considering mobility as a "law and order problem" and the nomad by definition as "backward"; even anthropologists toed this official line. While abolishing the Criminal Tribes Act in 1952, the Indian government promulgated another law, the Habitual Offenders Act, purportedly applicable to any individual but actually applied especially to members of one of the 127 communities (about 60 million individuals) listed in The Criminal Tribes Act Enquiry Committee (1949–1950). In practice, this Act gives the police arbitrary powers even to kill members of these communities. Crime was considered a disease and the criminal a patient. Administrative measures were aimed at sedentarization, through either coercion, persuasion, or both. Contact with "civilization" through the pittance of wage labor, rather than traditional independent resource management, was considered a palliative and the declared goal was absorption into "advanced society," which is by definition sedentary. Numerous attempts to sedentarize peripatetics have since failed miserably and been abandoned. Even when peripatetics obtain land that is not entirely unsuitable for agriculture, existing power relations within villages do not encourage their settlement.

Current Events and Conditions

The last few years have witnessed drastic transformations in the contexts of the three basic elements of peripateticism—labor, customers, and services and goods. These contexts have been affected by crises in two major spheres—socioeconomic and environmental—which are largely interrelated. Of equally great importance are political changes that have hurt peripatetics not only via the socioeconomic and environmental spheres but also directly. Thus, for example, the delineation of new, impermeable international frontiers in South Asia in 1947 cut off, or at least curtailed, numerous migration routes and split entire communities, such as the Kanjar, the Qalandar, the Sansi, and the Jogi. The rare cases of transborder migration were damned as "infiltration," and entire families arrested as "smugglers"—the last resort for some unable to pursue their traditional peripatetic professions. In the 1960s the flourishing transborder trade between Tibet, China, and India diminished, drastically affecting several communities on either side of the borders. An example are the Humli-Khyampa, whose economy had been premised on the absence of salt in Nepal and rice in Tibet—essential commodities that needed to be transported between these regions. The Siwalik range in the foothills of the Greater Himalayas used to be the "salt border" between Tibetan and Indian salt, the former being of major importance for centuries for the whole of Kashmir, Himachal, and Uttaranchal. Changes initiated by national and international policies have led to the gradual disintegration of this economic frontier and opened up new markets, which have adversely affected the traditional barter system of this peripatetic community.

Living in an environment with a rapidly changing infrastructure, most peripatetics are increasingly getting pushed into weaker sociopolitical positions *vis-à-vis* sedentary society. With resources generally being perceived as scarce, peripatetics are increasingly bearing the brunt of stress. Added to this are conflicts rooted in the structures of gender exploitation throughout South Asia and, in India, in the caste system, which has pushed the women of some peripatetic communities throughout India to practice prostitution for a living. Recently, the Bedni and Banchhara of Central India were thus officially branded as susceptible to contracting and transmitting AIDS, and hence condemned to yet more social discrimination. But even peripatetic women of other communities are often considered easy game, especially by men of the rural elites; women are increasingly subjected to great harassment, even rape. Resistance is increasingly met in Pakistan by applying Islamic laws and imprisoning the women on charges of prostitution or adultery. In India it is interpreted as caste-based political resistance against established hierarchies and punished with mutilation and even death of both men and women (see below, *Responses*).

Socioeconomic Crisis

With the spread of cinema, television, and other electronic media, the occupations of many traditional peripatetic entertainers and performers are inevitably declining. The industrialization of South Asia and infrastructural developments have also largely affected demand for a variety of goods and services. An example are the Gaduliya Lohar, smiths and dealers in plough oxen in Rajasthan and Madhya Pradesh. In prosperous areas, tractors replace plough oxen so the need has declined for their services and those of the peripatetic Sattia, who came every year to castrate and trade in bulls. With increasing use of tube wells, traditional open wells need no cleaning, and with increased mechanization, many other peripatetic services are becoming redundant. In the last few years, the skills of the Ghatiya Jogi of western Rajasthan—makers of grinding stones for household use—are also becoming redundant, since already village housewives are, understandably, getting grain milled at the nearest electric mill. Handmade jewelry, toys, or even clay objects are also less in demand, plastic goods being considerably cheaper and more durable. Former low economic overheads have also increased, with trucks and buses replacing pack animals and camping sites near settled areas in short supply. All these processes are rendering a variety of peripatetic professions economically marginal, if not outright redundant. With the opening up of the Indian economy in the 1990s and accelerated globalization, this trend is accelerating.

Environmental Crisis

The current environmental crisis in South Asia has affected a variety of peripatetic peoples intensely. The impact has been twofold, often affecting different parts of one community from various aspects.

First, certain crucial raw materials—such as different species of grasses, reeds, rushes, leaves, bamboo, wood, and specific kinds of clay—used by many peripatetics to manufacture baskets, winnows, screens, cradles, toys, figurines for ritual use, and the like—are becoming very scarce or disappearing altogether, due to massive deforestation and extensive curtailing of a variety of open lands for habitation, agriculture, industry, military use, and development of infrastructure such as roads, power plants, and the like. Unable to obtain access to these traditional resources, many peripatetic communities are being driven to urban slums where they barely survive as daily wage laborers.

The second impact is among those communities who are involved professionally in some manner with birds and/or animals. They trap, snare, and sell birds, while others perform with and/or catch snakes, monkeys, and bears. In India, of the roughly 90,000 species,[2] 60 are highly endangered and 250 are traded regularly, either within India or internationally, as part of the world's trade of many millions of birds a year. Internationally, only about 3.5 million birds survive this trade, and in South Asia many thousands perish in the process. Birds here are trapped and sold not only to zoos but also to individuals, in tiny cages as pets, for sport, to other peripatetics as performing birds[3] for the tables of the rich, and for ritual purposes—such as fortune telling, "purifying" amulets, and above all, earning merit. Throughout the subcontinent almost 50 percent of birds are bought by millions of rural and urban families of all religions in order to let them fly again and thereby earn merit. The precise species as well as the day of the week, time of day, and other details vary regionally and between religious groups. While this practice is not new, its popularity had increased with greater purchasing power, families in some areas spending up to $10 (U.S.) per week. Consequently, the demand for birds grew rapidly, as did the distances they had to be transported and hence the time they were kept caged. This resulted in severe mortality, and this again spiraled the demand, leading to a steady depletion of birds of numerous species. Consequently, the government of India first banned all bird exports in 1990 and in the following year amended the Indian Wildlife (Protection) Act 1972 to ban the trapping of all birds except the crow. These bans are gradually affecting the lifestyles of many peripatetic communities such as the Baheliya, the Chirimar, the Paydami, the Phase, and the Pardhi across large parts of India. Working within a bird market flourishing right across South Asia, some of the 10,000 trappers in northern India alone earned a meager living by selling birds to middlemen, who resold them for 5 to 20 times as much to their customers.

In India the livelihoods and hence also lifestyles of peripatetics who perform with animals are more acutely affected. In 1960 it was made incumbent on all animal trainers and performers to have all wild animals in their possession registered and certificates with details about them issued. However, till the early 1990s the government encouraged animal performers in the tourist industry, employing snake charmers to perform for foreign tourists in government-run hotels and even sending a bear leader with his bear to the government-sponsored and -organized India Festival held in Paris. Animal performances figured in many Indian feature films, and in Pakistan bears were often rented to motion picture companies, since about half of all feature films include rural scenes with dancing bears. By 1990 glamor had entered the lives of many peripatetic animal leaders, but with the intensifying environmental crisis and a growing, if belated, awareness of conservation and animal rights in India, the situation slowly changed. The first sign was the seizure in 1991 of Munna Bhalu, the bear that had been taken to Paris, from his owner. Over the next few years the situation worsened for animal performers in India, and in 1998 the Government of India prohibited the training and exhibition of bears, monkeys, tigers, panthers, and lions. While the latter three effect circus groups, the first two concern peripatetics who work as monkey and bear trainers and performers. There has since been stricter enforcement of laws and voluntary organizations, such as People for Animals, are active in their implementation.

Bear and Monkey Performers

Kalandar or *Qalandar* is the generic term used for communities who perform mainly with bears and monkeys. The *mast Kalandar,* or *bhaluwala,* are the bear performers and are richer than the *bandarwala* or monkey trainers. Yet poorer Kalandar weave and sell baskets, buy and sell astrological rings and charms or do wage labor. Since bear claws and hair are supposed to protect against the evil eye and disease, many mast Kalandar also sell the claw clippings and hair of their bears. Bears bring in higher returns, but are also more expensive and harder to find than monkeys. In Pakistan one brown bear fetches as much as 20 fully trained, healthy monkeys, and one black bear equals 12 to 15 monkeys. A four- or five-year-old monkey can pay for itself in roughly eight months. Every performer has two bears, and in Pakistan performers work 15 days a month on average, earning from $10 to $25 per month.

Peripatetic Kalandar in India and Pakistan trap black bears and brown bears (but not sloth bears). In Pakistan Kohistanis do the trapping, selling them to semi-sedentary Kalandar, who keep them caged in the Peshawar Valley and train them to be led and stand on command. At five to ten months their canine teeth are pulled out and silver rings inserted into their noses. In India, bears are trapped by various communities and transported by a network of friendly truck drivers to the Kalandar buyers who train the cubs. There is a high mortality on the way—mother bears are killed and often the cubs are injured and die. The Kalandar gets one in every ten surviving cubs; the others are killed and their gall bladders smuggled to China, Taiwan, Korea, and Japan. More recently a few Kalandar in India have entered the market as middlemen and commercial traders and have become rich. The process of procuring and training monkeys is similar to that for bears. While Indian Kalandar deny cruelty and claim to love their bears and monkeys like their own offspring, Pakistani Kalandar are fully aware of the cruelty, and hence no Kalandar who performs the initial mutilations keeps his own adult performing bears, for fear of revenge. The subsequent owner does, however, "train" the bears further, through severe beatings and withholding food.

In 1972 bear hunting and capturing were declared illegal in India and hence, no new certificates could be issued after that. With a mortality rate thrice as high as in the wild, it is unlikely that bears issued certificates prior to 1972 are still alive. And yet there are still Kalandar performing with bears, which must have been captured illegally. However, through more recent vigorous efforts, around 1,000 bears have been rescued from their Kalandar owners and kept in a bear sanctuary near Agra. In Pakistan, where less than 300 bears are estimated to survive in the wild, bear baiting has been illegal for several decades, and yet bear and dog baiting continue to be a favorite pastime among feudal landlords, with some 2,400 such fights held every season[4] and hundreds of men and children paying to watch. These bears are trapped, sold, trained and resold in a network of hunters, wildlife dealers, peripatetic Kalandar, and landlords. With its teeth and claws removed, each bear is rendered defenseless before it is left to the mercy of as many as eight trained pit bull terriers in such fights. The dogs are owned and trained by powerful landlords, while the bears are owned by the Kalandar, who are paid by the landlords. Although illegal, many of these events have the full backing of the authorities, including the police. As a result of research by the World Society for the Protection of Animals (WSPA) and publication of its report, the government decreed a stricter enforcement of the law. In 1997 posters and a schoolbook highlighting the cruelty involved were produced and publicly displayed and after this some events appear to have been canceled. Nevertheless, in 2000 some major events hosted by important landlords took place, with hundreds of spectators and police representatives in attendance. In an effort to help ensure that wildlife laws would be enforced, the WSPA developed a fund raising campaign, eventually collecting some £100,000 from residents in the UK, and used the funds to establish a bear sanctuary in Kund Park, Pakistan. The first bear arrived in the park in 2001, after being rescued from a bear-dog fight. By 2004, some seven confiscated bears were residing in the sanctuary. In 2005–2006, some 13 bear fights were held in Pakistan without intervention from local wildlife authorities, with another 40 events stopped by local wildlife authorities.

Performers working with monkeys have been less affected than bear leaders, partly because of the ubiquitous presence of monkeys. Increasing deforestation near cities has led to thousands of monkeys pouring into urban areas in India and making a nuisance of themselves. But Hindus do not by and large kill monkeys—they revere and often even feed them, and Delhi alone has an estimated monkey population of some 12,000. Up until 1972 (when wildlife protection legislation was passed in India) monkey trapping was common, and some 10,000 mainly rhesus macaques were exported annually for medical research purposes. Today, the civic authorities have them trapped, though illegally, by Kalandar, and sell the monkeys to local laboratories. The Delhi Government is now planning a sanctuary for monkeys away from the urban center.

Snake Charmers

Environmental crises have also adversely affected the peripatetic snake charmer. Men from several peripatetic communities of various religions and regions across South Asia—Jogi Nath Kalbelia, Patia Kela, Zyed, Vangawala, and so forth—have long performed with snakes (mainly cobras, pythons, rat snakes, and sand boas), scorpions, mongooses (mostly the common variety), and hedgehogs. Their women often work as harvesters, their children beg, sometimes with snakes around their necks. Formerly, say the Patia Kela of Orissa, they were also itinerant magicians, cured people, and performed as puppeteers. Some Kalbelia men in northern India also play music in wedding bands. The Zyed of Mysore travel from village to village, showing snake shows and snake and mongoose fights, and earning up to $25 a week. Snake charmers across India are also employed by villagers and townsmen to entice away threatening snakes, which are feared but very rarely killed, especially by Hindus and Jains, who regard them as sacred. Pakistan Vangawala perform magic shows and cast spells with snakes and scorpions.

Caught by the men themselves from riverbanks and forests, the snakes are kept in small baskets and hardly allowed to move, and die within 3 months if not released earlier. While catching them, the Kalbelia take a vow to release the snakes on a specific date, and they honor this vow, but by then the snakes are nearly dead. In any case, the breaking off of the two poisonous fangs and/ or the removal of the poison bag immediately after they are caught makes them unfit for survival in the wild after release. The venom extracted is said to have medicinal powers and is sold as a kind of eye ointment cum makeup.

The Indian Wildlife Act of 1972 made the captivity of snakes and mongooses illegal and hence snake charming peripatetics came under threat. Some, such as the Zyed, found a way out by practicing their profession in more distant villages and supplementing their income by selling frogs and lizards to laboratories and schools for dissection and helping civic authorities chase away snakes. But the decision of May 19, 1997, by the Delhi High Court making dissection in all schools, colleges, and research institutions optional will have a further impact.

In Pakistan, snakes are falling prey to deforestation, snake charmers, and virulent pesticides which, though banned, are used extensively and have entered the food chain and thus ultimately part of the snake diet, through insects and small vertebrates. Especially endangered is the python, which peripatetic communities kill in order to sell its skin, to be made into bags, belts, and the like. Though the government banned the capture and trade in snakes in 1998 and the Convention of International Trade in Endangered Species prohibits their killing, every year some 3,000 snakes are killed at the National Institute of Health in Islamabad, after poison has been extracted from them to make antivenom vaccine.

Responses: Struggles to Sustain Cultural Survival

Nomadic societies everywhere are known for their resilience, resourcefulness, versatility, flexibility, and adaptability, and while these qualities have also been true of South Asian peripatetics, the last few years indicate a different trend. Indeed the magnitude of rapid economic, social, political, and ecological change that is taking place in the subcontinent is reflected in exemplary fashion in the situation of peripatetic communities. These changes are being met with an array of responses that range from traditional adaptive skills, with or without outside help, to legally challenging government laws.

Traditional adaptability is widely observable among peripatetic peddlers, who are simply abandoning older products for new ones more in demand and cheaper—plastic instead of glass trinkets, metal ware instead of clay pots—making and selling papier mâché idols instead of stone ones, repairing bicycles instead of tinkering old pots and pans—these are only some examples of such market-oriented adaptability. In some instances, especially among peripatetics in the entertainment sphere, such adaptability is being encouraged by government or private agencies, notably in the tourist trade. So-called heritage hotels and ethnic resorts in India employ peripatetic families for at least part of the year to entertain their guests with puppet and magic shows and dance and acrobatic performances, which have become exotic even for most upper-class urban Indians. In a few largely tourist areas, municipal authorities have even allocated residential zones restricted to peripatetics and their families. A unique case is that of the peripatetic Bhopa minstrels and storytellers of Rajasthan, where in some areas a few families are now being employed to propagate knowledge about AIDS. Indeed, peripatetics, with their access especially to children and women in various rural communities, could be integrated into a variety of informal teaching programs where they could use their specific traditional skills. Another new avenue slowly opening up in India is that of conservation and breeding in which the intimate knowledge many peripatetics have of birds and animals is being put to use. However, it is obvious that not all peripatetic families can find viable alternatives and survive culturally. Sensing this, many Kalandar in India are trying to fight for their right to livelihood, even taking their case before the Supreme Court of India.

Yet, on the whole, peripatetics are fighting a losing battle and many are abandoning nomadism and settling down in urban slums. The trend toward semi-sedentarization began in the 1970s and is now accelerating. As long as there is a demand for their goods and services peripatetic communities will survive, legally or illegally, and no number of laws and raids are going to do more than make their life increasingly difficult. Demand is of course closely linked to a variety of economic, sociocultural, political, and environmental factors, but even if the returns are meager, as long as peripatetic peoples perceive no fruitful alternatives, they will try to cling to the only livelihoods they have learned.

Food for Thought

Students of the social sciences have largely been impervious to a major cultural adaptation—namely the peripatetic lifestyle—although this adaptation has been an integral part of a larger socioeconomic and cultural network in South Asia that they might have long been studying.

Socioeconomic changes in the wider society are severely affecting these peoples. Notably, global market economies and environmental degradation have taken their toll, and the complexity of the problem is all the greater because relatively little research has been carried out among them. Studies among those whose lifestyles survive and who are battling to sustain them are urgently called for.

The inevitable conflict between socioeconomic change and traditional economies, on the one hand, and between the latter and environmental issues, notably conservation, on the other, can be solved in the long run only by adapting to new avenues of livelihood. But these, again, have the increasing prerequisite of modern educational skills. Unfortunately, assumptions of sedentarization have everywhere largely determined education and health care for migrating families. However, at least primary education should not automatically imply sedentarization. Primary schooling must become a fundamental right and it must be made compulsory, and educational norms and values must change to become more creative and practice oriented.

Until recently, many of these societies were resilient and flexible enough to respond successfully to the above threats. However, with inevitable, increasingly rapid change, the question is how long these strategies can be successful, and what the future holds for such peoples. To survive as communities, they must be encouraged to enter the new niches provided by burgeoning market economies, or to create niches for themselves in the spheres of tourism, the media, and environmental programs.

To Think About

1. How does socioeconomic change impact peripatetic lifestyles?
2. How can one address the conflict between economic modernization and people's right to livelihood?
3. Do the laws of demand and supply affect traditional economies such as those of peripatetics?
4. Can globalization, multiresource exploitation, and economic specialization go hand in hand?
5. What relationship, if any, exists between peripatetics and the natural environment?
6. Is there a conflict between animal rights and human rights?
7. What viable alternatives do peripatetics have to their present endangered lifestyles, and to what extent can formal education help in the process of adopting them?

Source Notes

1. An estimated 4,000 Qalandar families live as animal performers in Pakistan alone, and the snake charming Zyed of southern India are estimated at 9,000. The only official demographic data available in India follow the large-scale official categories of "Scheduled caste," "Scheduled tribe," or "Backward caste." All of these are

administrative-cum-political classifications, often cut across families, and include hundreds of nonperipatetic communities.
2. This constitutes 15 percent of the world's avian species.
3. Notably owls, mynahs, and parakeets.
4. November to April.

Resources

Published Literature

Berland, Joseph C. 1982. *No Five Fingers Are Alike: Cognitive Amplifiers in Social Context*. Cambridge, MA: Harvard University Press.

———. 1992. Territorial Activities among Peripatetic Peoples in Pakistan, in M. J. Casimir and A. Rao eds. *Mobility and Territoriality: Social and Spatial Boundaries among Foragers, Pastoralists and Peripatetics*. Oxford, UK: Berg, 375–395.

———. 2000. Nature, Nurture and Kinship: Body Fluids and Experience in the Social Organisation and Identity of a Peripatetic People, in M. Böck and A. Rao eds. *Culture, Creation, and Procreation: Concepts of Kinship in South Asian Practice*. Oxford/New York: Berghahn Books, 157–173.

Berland, Joseph C. and Matt T. Salo. eds. 1986. Peripatetic Peoples. *Nomadic Peoples* (Special Issue) 21/22.

Berland, Joseph C. and Aparna Rao. 2001. *Familiar Strangers and Persistent Others: Peripatetics and their Contexts in Africa, Asia, and Europe*. Westport, CT: Greenwood Publishing Group.

Hayden, R.M. 1999. *Disputes and Agreements amongst Nomads: A Caste Council in India*. Delhi: Oxford University Press.

Malhotra, K.C. and M. Gadgil. 1988. Coping with Uncertainty in Food Supply: Case Studies among the Pastoral and Non-Pastoral Nomads of Western India, in I. de Garine and G.A. Harrison eds. *Coping with Uncertainty in Food Supply*. Oxford: Clarendon Press, 379–404.

Misra, Pramode K. 1975. The Gadulia Lohars. In L.S. Leshnik and G.D. Sontheimer eds. *Pastoralists and Nomads in South Asia*. Wiesbaden: O. Harrassowitz, 235–246.

Rao, Aparna. ed. 1987. *The Other Nomads: Peripatetic Minorities in Cross-Cultural Perspective*. Cologne: Boehlau Verlag (Koelner Ethnologische Mitteilungen Vol. 8).

———. 1995. Marginality and Language Use: the Example of Peripatetics in Afghanistan. *Journal of the Gypsy Lore Society* 5(2): 69–95.

Rao, Aparna and Michael J. Casimir. eds. 2003. *Nomadism in South Asia*. Oxford in India, Readings in Sociology and Social and Cultural Anthropology. Delhi: Oxford University Press.

Ruhela, Satya Pal. 1967. *The Gaduliya Lohars of Rajasthan: A Study in the Sociology of Nomadism*. Delhi: Impex.

4

The Bhils

Judith Whitehead

The People

Bhil is the ethnic name for a group of horticulturalists and pastoralists who inhabit the Satpuda and Vindhya mountains in central western India. Its meaning—bow and arrow in Dravidian languages—indicates that they were hunter-gatherers who migrated from south India. Archaeological evidence documents some of the earliest Palaeolithic settlements in India in this area, and the first written evidence of Bhil settlements is from early medieval times, about A.D. 1200. Their own origin myths identify the Bhil as the original settlers, or *adivasis*, of this region.

The term *Bhil* was given to the subsistence-based hill tribes of the Narmada region by British colonial authorities. However, the "Bhils" include a number of named ethnic groups, including the Bhils and Bhilalas of Madhya Pradesh and the Tadvi and Vassawa of Gujarat. Most hill tribes in Gujarat today identify with their ethnic name and the broader term "adivasi." The Vassawas and Tadvis of Gujarat, who constitute a large percentage of the people whose land is being submerged by a major dam, the Sardar Sarovar Dam, are the subject of this chapter.

The Tadvis and Vassawas in Gujarat were the dominant inhabitants of the region's mountain forests throughout the medieval, colonial, and postcolonial periods. Their mountain fastnesses acted as buffer zones between medieval kingdoms, sometimes providing refuge to defeated kings. In a few regions close to major trade routes, Bhil leaders arose who could control trade, mount small standing armies of lineage followers and Arabian mercenaries, and claim territories as petty kingdoms. Indeed, prior to the invasions of Rajput armies in the later medieval period, the various Bhil groups were considered the lords of the forested hill areas. Even after these invasions (c. A.D. 1500),

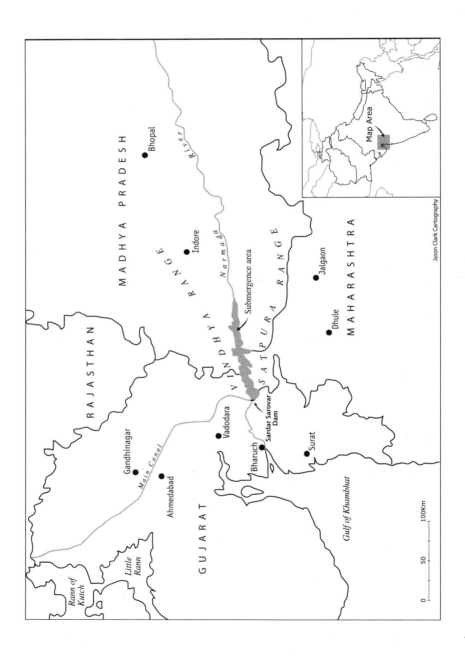

the peoples of the Bhil-controlled forest areas and those of the Rajput plains coexisted in an ethnic symbiosis. Although Rajput rulers were overlords, there was cooperation between the plains and hill communities. Defeated Rajput kings sought refuge in the forest, while successful Tadvi and Vassawa sometimes claimed the Rajput's upper-caste status.

A major challenge to this balance of power arose with the conquest of the region by the British East India Company in 1822. Although a few districts remained princely kingdoms with some internal autonomy, the British colonial government introduced changes in revenue and forest administration that altered the balance between upper-caste Rajput princes and the Bhil population. First, the established princes were vested with permanent and hereditary rights in their landed property and titles, but the hill villages were not. Second, a series of laws was introduced that separated the hill and plains populations. The most important of these was the Indian Forest Act of 1878, which extinguished preexisting rights to land that Tadvis, Vassawas, and other Bhils had held by agreement with Rajput kings. These included the right to plow and cultivate forested areas, and the right to use and trade forest products. Extinguishing these customary rights, the colonial Forest Department declared large percentages of forest area as Reserved or Protected Forests and hence became a major landowner in South Asia. In a Reserved Forest, no habitation or cultivation was allowed, and traditional hill practices such as burning plots of forest to clear vegetation, lopping of trees, fishing, and using minor forest products were prohibited. Protected Forests were those in which some cultivation was allowed; cutting certain timber and burning the jungle were banned. In some cases, Tadvis, Vassawas, and Bhils who lost their land were rehired as workers for the Forest Department.

Introduced for conserving Indian forests and enabling their long-term exploitation, the Indian Forest Act and its later amendments shrank the hill tribes' land base and led to the out-migration of some Bhils from the mountainous regions to other areas for work. This pattern continues to the present day. Despite the fact that the postcolonial Indian government has rescinded the most severe colonial laws that affected the Bhils, such as the Criminal Tribes Act (1871), the Indian Forest Act remains the basic legal tool that shapes Forest Department policies toward forest communities. Indeed, in post-Independence India, the forested area under control of the Forest Department increased from 13 to 27 percent of the total landmass. Because legal rights to land were extinguished by the Act, the possession by Bhils of land inside their former forests, including land left fallow in previous cultivation cycles, is considered illegal encroachment. There are moves underway to change this situation, first by transferring the governance of hill communities from the Forest to the Revenue Department, and second, by introducing a new bill in parliament that will vest tribal communities with written ownership of 2.5 hectares of land. The Scheduled Tribes Act was passed, with revisions, in December 2006. However, this Act has come too late for many Tadvi and Vassawa in Gujarat, since it does not apply to those whose lands have already been appropriated for development purposes, such as large dams.

The Setting

The traditional homeland of the Tadvi and Vassawa is the Vindhya and Satpuda mountains of western India. These rise on either side of the Narmada River about 150 kilometers inland from its mouth on the Arabian Sea and continue eastward for another 200 kilometers. Some Bhils have migrated to the plains north and south of these mountains, and a good percentage have also migrated to cities, especially for work in the construction trades.

Although the Vindhya and Satpuda mountains range from only 300 to 3,000 feet in altitude, they are quite rugged, with steep drops to tributaries that form the watershed of the Narmada River. In southeastern Gujarat, the major tributaries of the Narmada are the Karjan and the Dev Rivers, which form the eastern and western boundaries of this region. The Tadvi live closer to the river valleys, and the Vassawa occupy the hills.

The forests clothing these mountains consist chiefly of deciduous bamboo and teak, but also contain kheir, ebony, mahogany, acacia, and *mahua* trees. Teak (*Tectona grandis*), kheir (*Acacia catechu*), and bamboo, used for house construction by the Tadvi and Vassawa, are also valuable commercial commodities. Various forest plants and fruit trees are used by the Vassawa as food and/or medicine. Fruits include papaya, *sitaphul, sinoti*, and mango. One of the most useful trees is the *mahua* (*Madhuca indica*). Its leaves are edible, liquor is produced from its flowers, and its leaves and roots are used as medicine. The *timaroo* tree provides leaves from which cigarettes are rolled and its wood is used for cart construction. *Neem* is an important medicinal tree whose leaves are dried, ground or crushed, and used as an antiseptic; its twig is an effective toothbrush. At least 42 species of trees, plants, fruits, and vegetables provide important inputs into the region's subsistence economy. Barking deer, wild dog, wild boar, antelope, and panthers are some of the many mammals that are native to these forests, although they are not usually hunted. However, river crabs and various species of fish supplement the Tadvi and Vassawa diet.

Many of the region's streams and rivers have rapids and canyons that make them difficult to navigate. Each shoreline village possesses several flat-bottomed boats that are used for fording the major rivers at advantageous points. The ruggedness of the hills and the river flow kept this area somewhat secluded from trade and commercialization even after the British conquest.

Traditional Subsistence Strategies

The Vassawa and Tadvi practice a type of cultivation known as *jambh*, which can be considered intermediate between shifting (slash-and-burn or swidden) cultivation and intensive agriculture, since it involves features associated with both. As in intensive agriculture, bullocks and ploughs are used in the fields, and cow dung is applied as fertilizer. As in shifting cultivation, however, irrigation is totally rain-fed and fields are left fallow for a number of years in order to regenerate their fertility. Finally, as in shifting cultivation, the forest cover is burned to provide fresh plots for planting.

The cultivation pattern is different from our monocrop fields. In each field, numerous species are typically seeded, a practice referred to as intercropping. This provides resistance to pests and also nourishment to each species. Crops are rotated from year to year. The most common crops are maize, sorghum, rice, Cajan pea (a lentil), castor seeds, chillies, gram, and pulses such as *moong*, *urrad*, and *chana*. Most households possess grinding stones for transforming maize into cornmeal flour, from which delicious *rotis* (unleavened breads) are produced. Coarse cereals such as *khodra* and *bhanti* are also grown by some households. These can be stored for 30 years without spoiling, providing a fallback in bad harvests. As one elder Tadvi woman pointed out, "We can do without outsiders." The Tadvi and Vassawa are proud that their agriculture provides them with "sustainable resources." Since agriculture is mainly monsoon-irrigated, there is generally only one crop per year, except in fields that border the riverbanks, where two crops are typically grown each year. Neither commercial fertilizers nor pesticides are used: Fields are fertilized with either ash or cow dung, while ground leaves from the neem tree are often used as a pesticide.

The Tadvi and Vassawa supplement this subsistence cultivation with vegetables grown on plots located beside their houses and the fishing, hunting, and gathering of forest produce described above. Grazing is a subsidiary occupation for many, and the majority of households have herds that range from 10 to 50 buffalo, cows, and goats. Dairy products, such as buttermilk are produced from their herds. Buffalo milk is sometimes added to tea beverages in a few villages. Herds are a prestige item to the Tadvi and Vassawa. Chickens are also kept by most households, although both chickens and goats are raised for sale or for sacrifice rather than for eating.

Bidis (hand-rolled cigarettes), fowl, fish, and forest produce, gum and honey are the major products made for sale in nearby markets, from the proceeds of which Bhils purchase salt, tea, and clothing. Those communities located on or near the riverbanks can acquire extra cash income from fishing, with a 20-pound fish fetching about 200 rupees in the nearby market. Most households earn an extra income of about 2,000 rupees per month from outside markets and wage work. It should be emphasized, however, that since the economic maintenance of households is not dependent upon market transactions, these communities' economic systems until quite recently were based mainly on economic reciprocity. Indeed, the Tadvi and Vassawa often spoke with pity of those from their community who no longer possessed land and were working as construction laborers. With the average daily wage of a laborer being 18 rupees (48 cents) per day, the advantage of access to both swidden plots and forest resources is obvious.

Sociopolitical Organization

The major social units among the Tadvi and Vassawa are the *faliyas*: patrilineal, and usually patrilocal, descent groups. Each faliya ideally consists of senior males of a grandparental generation, the sons of each grandparent, and their sons and families. However, pragmatism tends to influence post-marital location and even faliya membership. Faliyas are also defined by residence, and the term is often used to refer to a hamlet. For example, in the town near the Sardar Sarovar Dam, one faliya referred to itself as "gas pump" faliya because it was located near a gas station that had been recently built to service the increased traffic to the area. The flexibility of faliya membership is due partly to its association with residence and partly due to the institution of in-marrying sons-in-law. Both Tadvi and Vassawa pay bridewealth, often an indication of their input into the economy. Among the Vassawa, bridewealth consists of grain, cattle, and money, sometimes as much as 30,000 rupees (about $800). A young man who cannot pay the entire bride-price may live with and work for his spouse's father. In one village, there was an entire faliya that consisted of a parental generation, daughters and husbands, and one young son who had not yet married. In Tadvi marriages, since bridewealth is lower, the incidence of in-marrying sons-in-law is not as frequent.

While faliyas are considered patrilocal, it is uncommon for the younger generation to reside in the same household as the older generation. Rather, households are nuclear, consisting of parents and children of a nuclear family, plus the grazing animals owned by the family, kept in a separate room. Yet brothers and their families' houses are typically grouped in the same neighborhood. The creation of nuclear households is facilitated by the ease with which houses can be constructed. The entire village often comes out to put up a house, completing it in less than two days. These dwellings are built from teak beams and woven bamboo walls with thatched roofs, and often consist of a ground floor and an upper story for storing grain and sleeping.

Although parents try to arrange marriages by suggesting suitable spouses, both the young man and the woman will express their preferences, which are considered important for a successful marriage. When a potential partner is identified, the family meets to determine whether he or she is eligible. Faliya and village exogamy are observed. Village males of one generation are considered brothers, women of the same generation their sisters; hence sexual relations within a village are frowned upon and marriageable women were traditionally found from the mother's relatives in other villages. However, female and male chastity before marriage is not highly valued. There are few restrictions on female mobility in the mountain villages, and young, marriageable women are celebrated with a midsummer festival known as *garbadhan*. Opportunities for young men and women to meet occur after the harvest in September and October, when intervillage festivities are arranged. The usual age of marriage today for a young woman is 15 or 16 and for a young man about 18. Divorce and remarriage are not uncommon: As a Tadvi woman said, "It's easy to find another man if we don't like our husbands, but who will replace this land if we lose it?"

The gender division of labor appears fairly flexible, as both men and women take turns caring for children and going to the fields; clearing the forest and plowing is undertaken mainly by men, although I also saw a few adolescent women plowing fields on a few occasions, especially if men were away. Women typically plant the seeds prior to the monsoon rains, and weed, harvest, and thresh the crops from the summer through early fall. They are also usually responsible for care of the mulch animals. Carpentry and playing musical instruments are solely male pursuits.

Political organization among the Tadvi and Vassawa is quite flexible. Each faliya is nominally headed by the elder male brother of a generation. In practice, however, the brother who is considered the best-educated, most articulate, or most astute is the one who becomes the representative of the village to the outside world. Leaders in Tadvi and Vassawa society have to earn and achieve respect, as there is no institutionalized office of political authority per se. Other leaders can be considered spiritual leaders. Known as *bhuva*, such leaders are healers in the community. Although almost everyone in villages has some knowledge of medicinal plants and herbs, the bhuva possesses specialized knowledge of the rituals that accompany healing ceremonies.

Bhuvas are solely male, and were important mediators in village disputes when sickness was blamed on the machinations of a witch, or *dakan*, as occurred formerly in Bhil villages. While women were almost never political representatives in either Bhil society or the outside world, that aspect is changing somewhat due to the outside influences discussed below.

Religion and Worldview

Scholars, government officials, and politicians have debated for the past century whether the Bhils are Hindus. This issue has resurfaced today as nongovernmental Hindu organizations have tried to reincorporate Christianized tribals into the Hindu mainstream, leading to much discussion and debate in national newspapers. In the region inhabited by the Tadvis and Vassawas, however, there has been little missionary activity. The major influence here has been that of Hinduism, the major religion of India, since the Narmada River is considered a sacred river by Hindus and is the locale of major pilgrimages and temple sites on the river's banks.

The diversity of Hinduisms makes it doubly difficult to decide whether the Tadvi and Vassawa are Hindus or animists. Tadvis and Vassawas have a reverence for nature and identify their own local deities and saints. In addition, many eat meat and fish, drink alcohol, and allow divorce. These practices differentiate them from orthodox Hindu practice. On the other hand, the Tadvis and Vassawa worship mainstream Hindu deities, such as Siva and the Mother Goddess, and believe in reincarnation, two fundamental precepts of Hinduism. Given these syncretic elements of Tadvi and Vassawa religion, perhaps the most useful question to ask is not whether the Tadvi and Vassawa are Hindus or animists, but rather what is the relationship between hill and plains religious systems.

A major form of religious syncretism of the hill communities is the *Bhagat* movement. Beginning in the 19th century, Bhagat developed as a movement that involved the worship of a mother goddess. It included trance and possession within its practices, and aimed at introducing social reforms to Bhil communities. These reforms included prohibitions on eating the flesh of cows or other animals, drinking liquor, and giving bride-price. The deity, often a local goddess who possessed the Bhils during trance, commanded that they not cooperate with the British, the forestry officials, or merchants from the plains. The goddess also instructed them to abstain from eating meat and drinking liquor. Yet while the deity urged noncooperation with outsiders and unity within Bhil villages, the social reform aspects of the Bhagat movement also aligned the hill communities more closely with mainstream

Hindu beliefs. The Bhagat movement illuminates hill and plains differences, and can be interpreted as a form of accommodative resistance to dominant outsiders.

The Bhagat movement is currently regaining popularity among Tadvis especially. Deities worshipped include Kalikamata (a local mother goddess), Shrinarainsinghji (a local saint), and Kabir (a 15th century saint who urged unity of Muslims and Hindus). Worship takes the form of hymn singing accompanied by *tablas* (drums) and harmonium. Incense is burned, a coconut is sacrificed to the deity at the end of the event, and *prasad*—or sanctified food—is distributed to all participants. After several hours of singing and clapping, the deity, either Siva or a mother goddess, possesses some of the participants. This ceremony lasts from sunset to sunrise and involves the entire village. Participants start in one household, then move to the households of other faliyas. A successful invocation of the deity may engage participants in a week-long pilgrimage to neighboring villages, although those engaged in wage labor argue that the all-night celebrations should be shortened.

Bhagat ceremonies are most popular in late August, just before the harvest, and in October and November, after the harvest season. These intravillage ceremonies also unite geographically dispersed faliyas into a single unit. Bhagats, or devotees, make up about 50 percent of the population in many villages. Bhagats and non-Bhagats intermarry, dine together, and both are considered integral parts of the wider Tadvi or Vassawa community. Bhagats also participated in specifically adivasi ceremonies such as *garbadhan* and *indool puja*. Individuals may leave the Bhagat movement at their own choice. The dividing line between Bhagat and non-Bhagat, Hindu and animist beliefs is a flexible and ever-changing one. It seems to relate to the assertion of identity in conjunction with the situational stresses that adivasi communities experience in their interaction with dominant outsiders, as are occurring today. It may be a way that this minority community tries to negotiate their entry into and maintain their identity within the larger Indian society.

Threats to Survival

Since the 1970s several large dams constructed on the Karjan and Narmada rivers have been an ongoing threat to Tadvi and Vassawa identity. The Narmada River Project, part of a series of dams that form one of the world's largest water projects, will consist of 30 large, 135 medium, and 3,000 small dams intended to harness the waters of the Narmada and its tributaries to provide electricity and irrigation for development purposes.

Unfortunately, the reservoir areas of the 30 dams will submerge the lands of about 5 million people, and the Bhils are a major ethnic group being displaced. These dams have already displaced hundreds of thousands of villagers as their lands are submerged by the reservoirs impounded behind the two dams. The reservoir of the Karjan River dam drowned 21 Vassawa villages, and the Sardar Sarovar Dam on the Narmada River, located near the boundary between Gujarat, Madhya Pradesh, and Maharashtra, has flooded 19 Tadvi and Vassawa villages. Of the 14 large dams built in Gujarat state since Independence, ten have been located in Bhil homelands, and only the Sardar Sarovar dam has involved some land compensation. In all the others, only cash compensation of varying amounts was given. The numbers of people involved in this displacement in Gujarat have not been calculated. However, the number must be in the millions since the Sardar Sarovar alone has displaced about 250,000 to date. The Sardar Sarovar dam has become the subject of intense national and international controversy over the past 15 years, but it is not the largest in terms of numbers displaced.

In addition to the 19 villages in Gujarat state, 33 villages have been lost in Maharashtra state; in Madhya Pradesh, 193 villages have been submerged. More were projected to be underwater after 2000, when the Gujarat government received a positive judgment from the Supreme Court allowing its height to increase to 90 meters and beyond. More dams are planned upstream, such as the Maheshwar and Narmada Sagar Dams. In addition to those displaced by the Sardar Sarovar Dam itself, hundreds of thousands have been displaced by administrative infrastructure and the irrigation canals. A wildlife sanctuary south of the dam site is being constructed as a conservation adjunct to the dams. It will be divided into core and buffer areas, with no cultivation allowed in the core region of the sanctuary and only limited cultivation allowed in the buffer areas. This wildlife sanctuary will probably displace 38,000 people, unless there is judicial intervention. In addition, teak plantations installed in the buffer areas to provide wildlife corridors for animals have closed off about 50 percent of lands once cultivated. The resource base of the Tadvi and Vassawa, already shrunk by commercial forestry and government fiat in the past century, is being further diminished by contemporary development projects.

A shrinking resource base and a doubling of population in the past 30 years, partly from outsiders moving in, is increasing population pressure. Some ecologists argue that existing land-use practices are unsustainable. The Forest Department, in particular, argues that setting fire to sections of the forest to create garden plots, using them for a decade, and then abandoning them causes forest degradation. The Forest Department also believes that grazing animals in the forest contributes to degradation. Yet Tadvis and Vassawas cultivated forest patches for at least 600 years, suggesting that in the past, with human population low and traditional users managing their own resources, jambh cultivation combined with grazing maintained productive, diverse forests. Further research needs to be undertaken to determine whether shifting cultivation can be sustainable.

The major social and economic effect of these dams has been on the livelihood and subsistence strategies of the Vassawa and Tadvi. Various national and international agreements hold that the level of subsistence of people uprooted in the name of development should be equal to or greater than what they experienced in the preexisting environment. After lengthy deliberations between the three state governments affected, the Narmada Water Disputes Tribunal (1978) awarded compensation for those whose lands were to be submerged by the dam. This compensation included 5 acres of new land—a minimum subsistence holding in India—to every male household head and to those sons who reached the age of majority by 1987, free transport to the resettlement site, money for house construction, 5,000 rupees for leveling new land, and various civic amenities in the resettlement site, including electricity, a school, a threshing ground, a dispensary within 5 kilometers, and wells and irrigation facilities. Those whose lands were appropriated for infrastructure, canal construction, or the wildlife sanctuary, however, received no compensation—in land or cash. Although the described award is generous compared with previous resettlement schemes from other dam projects, its implementation has been plagued by controversy.

The earliest complaints were that people were not properly consulted or even notified about the submergence of their lands: In some villages, those to be displaced came to know of their fate only when government surveyors put up boundary stones. Second, while some village lands were cultivated under written records, a large portion of lands were possessed on the basis of oral deeds, that is, a customary ploughshare system. These lands were not considered subject to compensation. Although an NGO, Arch-Vahini, attempted to record land possession in the early 1980s, the replacement land constitutes a considerable loss of acreage for the Tadvi and Vassawa households, whose plots included fallow as well as cultivated land in the past.

The most serious complaints in the 1990s relate to the quality and quantity of land the displaced have actually received. According to complainants, replacement lands were barren, infertile, or rocky, completely waterlogged during the summer monsoons, or unirrigated; the government had purchased only the most inferior and cheapest lands from nearby farmers. Many adult sons complained that upon resettlement they had received neither the land nor job that was promised in the 1979 Tribunal award.

There has also been controversy about the lack of amenities, nonfunctioning wells and electricity, and the disbursement of tin siding alone for housing, which is cold in winter and hot in the summer. This problem was highlighted in May of 1998, when seven adivasis died in one of the resettlement sites, Rameshwarpurwa, from heat exposure and malnutrition.

A study carried out in the summers of 1997 and 1998 showed many complaints to be well founded. Despite the fact that the resettlement sites were in a well-irrigated area, the majority did not produce any crops because the land was badly waterlogged. It appears that farmers in the region had indeed sold their worst land to the government. In one resettlement site, all households experienced such a severe shortfall between income and expenses during these years that all had at least one person working as a temporary agricultural laborer in order to make ends meet. In some of the resettlement sites southwest of the dam, adivasi oustees from the Karjan project had already been resettled. There, conflict over land and jobs led some of the later resettlers to return to their partially submerged village just behind the dam site itself. Several sites appeared to be nearly deserted.

In addition, social relations have changed through the move from the hills to the resettlement sites. Many of the faliyas from the original village have been dispersed throughout the 180 resettlement sites, which house from 50 to 80 households each. Traditional leaders have thus lost a great deal of their prestige, and those who have taken their places appear to be representatives of the government. Reconfigured settlements lose the traditional bases of support for communal ploughing and house construction. Another major change has been loss of livestock because of the lack of freely available fodder and the impact of new diseases. Not only has this eroded an important source of supplementary income, it has also ended a preexisting form of social prestige. Finally, debt forces many in the resettlement sites to sell both teak furniture and women's silver jewelry during lean harvests.

While output in the plains villages on good land is generally higher, it is also less secure. This reflects the change from a subsistence orientation in the hills to a cash-crop orientation in the plains resettlement areas. In their original villages, Vassawa and Tadvi would sell and purchase some goods and services in the market, but their communities were insulated from the vagaries of the market because they could depend on jambh cultivation with its home-produced inputs. This was an especially secure subsistence since many of these crops could be stored for long periods and there was also a diversity of other resources available, such as fish and forest and dairy products. In the plains sites, in contrast, resettlers must grow mainly cash crops such as wheat, sugarcane, and cotton which are sold in nearby markets. These crops depend on market-purchased inputs such as high-yielding seeds, fertilizers, pesticides, and irrigation. One young man in a waterlogged resettlement site had spent a total of 3,500 rupees on pesticides alone, only to reap no harvest. This shift to a market orientation was summed up by an older Bhil man: "In the resettlement site, everything is bought and sold, but in our original village, women had at least 5 rupees in their pockets."

With so many households experiencing economic difficulties in lean seasons, a great many men have migrated to nearby cities for work. This has altered household structures and also caused many changes in gender relations, as women are left at home to take care of households and fields. Many women are taking up jobs as agricultural workers on nearby farms.

In some resettlement sites, women have to travel longer distances to collect fodder for their animals. In a number of other sites, women have faced some harassment from neighboring farmers, many of whom are upper caste and disdainful of adivasi culture, particularly the relative autonomy that it allows women. In some cases, adivasi women have adopted the upper-caste practice of *purdah*, or female seclusion. A more subtle way in which gender relations are changing is through the adoption of upper-caste attitudes toward bridewealth, free-choice marriages, and right of divorce. A number of women expressed "shame" about some adivasi festivals, such as the garbadhan ceremony, and thought it would be discontinued in the future. In one relatively well-endowed resettlement site, most of the village had abandoned the practice of bridewealth as young men now demanded television sets, household appliances, and money as dowry from their prospective in-laws. Finally, there was a much greater tendency for brothers to live together in the resettlement sites and form joint households with parents. In sum, then, the people of many resettlements appear to be abandoning the greater autonomy that adivasi women experienced in the hills in favor of upper-caste patterns of dowry, female seclusion, and patrilocal, joint-family residence.

Responses to Ecological Threats

The Tadvi and Vassawa Bhils have not been mute in the face of displacement. Helped and spearheaded to some extent by urban intellectuals and farmers, the adivasis of the Narmada Valley have participated in creating one of the best-known environmental movements of recent history in India. This movement has taken the form of a Gandhian-style mass civil disobedience campaign, which can be divided into two major phases.

The first phase, led by the NGO Arch-Vahini, occurred in the early to mid-1980s. Arch-Vahini contended that the resettlement process was unjust because it had failed to register much of the hill land of adivasis. However, the NGO held that resettlement was inevitable, and that just resettlement was possible. The movement involved civil disobedience aimed at registering cultivated lands of adivasis and securing land compensation. In 1986, however, a young social worker from Bombay, Medha Patkar, visited the valley. Upon learning the extent of the planned relocation and the high-handedness of officialdom toward the adivasis, she became convinced that a just resettlement was not possible. Since 1988, she has worked to organize the adivasi communities to stop the dam itself, forming the Narmada Bachao Andolan (NBA), one of India's best-known nongovernmental organizations, in the process.

The Indian government is committed to industrial development via liberalization, and the Narmada Bachao Andolan has both suffered defeats and experienced a few notable successes. In 1990, the movement organized a mass march to the Gujarat border to demand a complete review of the project. This event was well publicized in national and international media; it included a 20-day fast by leading activists and eventually led the World Bank to withdraw from the project in 1993. In fact, it might even be argued that the NBA has fostered an international revision of views on dams, which culminated in the formation of the World Commission on Dams. In 1995, the Supreme Court of India also ordered a stay on construction of the dam until the resettlement process was improved, as the Court believed that families were being broken up and settled in different villages. Recently, the World Commission on Dams, consisting of NGOs, government, and industry representatives, concluded that while large dams bring economic benefits, their social and environmental disruptions are also substantial. Tellingly, it concluded that in no case in the past four decades have dam-displaced people achieved a living standard equal to that in their places of origin.

While the NBA has thus garnered support, the government of Gujarat is determined to press on with what it views as a necessary project. The western parts of Gujarat state, Kutch and Saurashtra, are prone to drought conditions. Environmentalists argue that these drought conditions are exacerbated by capital-intensive tube wells, which have lowered the water tables in the region. Whatever the causes of dessication, it is clear that west Gujarat has suffered droughts in the past decade, and the Narmada irrigation canal promises water to these areas. The NBA argues that the industry-rich corridor between the dam site and west Gujarat will commandeer most of the irrigation. Whatever the truth to these promises and criticisms, the debate about the Sardar Sarovar Dam is a highly emotional one in Gujarat, and there is a strong pro-dam lobby in that state.

A change in the central government of India in 1997 brought a new Supreme Court, and new Court orders in February 1999 and October 2000. These have allowed the dam to be constructed to its full height. This is seemingly a body blow to the NBA, but Medha Patkar has vowed to fight on. However, sentiment in urban Gujarat strongly favors raising the dam's height, and it has been increased several times since the Supreme Court ruling in 2000. A restudy of a submerging village in 2003 indicated that only about 40 percent of those who were seeking a second land resettlement had received it. The 60 percent who did not receive promised compensation are migrating for work as agricultural laborers and construction workers. These and other documented problems with compensation and rehabilitation evidently contributed to the March 15, 2005, ruling by the Indian Supreme Court confirming earlier decisions that dam construction can only continue once every person has been rehabilitated. The political will to enforce this Court ruling is, however, inconsistent, and construction increasing the height of the dam has continued. Political activism by local groups, as well as international advocates, has, however, played a significant role in the financing decisions of international lenders like the World Bank, who have withdrawn from funding commitments for upstream projects such as the Maheshwar Dam. And, in June 2006, following a Ministry of Environment and Forests ruling that Maheshwar contractors had failed to provide a comprehensive resettlement plan, the Indian government announced its decision to halt further construction on this project. This decision followed years of public protest by thousands of farmers, laborers, and fishermen who had set up a protest camp at the construction site.

Despite this apparent "win," displacement from huge portions of the Narmada River Valley is now a *fait accompli*. Even for those who have been equitably compensated, what kinds of changes in their culture and lifestyle will ensue once they are settled in plains communities that practice capital-intensive agriculture? As previously mentioned, research shows that adivasis in the resettlement sites are already adopting a number of upper-caste practices. Whether they will be able to maintain a distinctive culture through a regional tribal identity movement that has emerged in eastern Gujarat remains a highly debatable question.

Food for Thought

The case of the Narmada River dams has generated an important debate on the costs and benefits of large-scale development projects. While we might unconsciously attribute positive values to the notion of "development," as it ideally brings higher living standards, greater literacy, health, and education, the Narmada case shows us that development projects can impoverish many while benefiting a few. It also shows that the legal aspects of displacement, such as recognizing the land rights of indigenous populations, should be addressed before assuming that a "technological fix" is advisable. Otherwise, tribal cultures appear to have very little power in the decisions that are being made about their lives and livelihoods.

This case has spawned a wide-ranging discussion on the meaning of development both in India and internationally. Environmentalists and social activitists have created the term "sustainable development" to identify policies that would provide increased productivity, but without destroying the environment or the livelihoods of people inhabiting areas that are undergoing industrial transformation. While sustainable development means reproducing the environmental conditions to sustain future generations, pro-dam and anti-dam thinkers have very different views of what needs to be sustained. Subsistence producers in South Asia, who depend on fields, forests, and streams for their existence, find that the capital-intensive development projects promoted by global financial institutions have eroded their resource bases to the point of nonexistence. Recent changes, such as the impact of seed patenting on small farmers in India, the effects of global demand for exotic timber on the resource base of indigenous hill dwellers in South Asia, and the marketing and patenting of tropical forest herbs by global pharmaceutical companies have had adverse effects on subsistence producers in the subcontinent. While the urban middle-class workers in the rising industrial or service sectors in India have seen their income rise substantially, about 400 million people in India, especially in its rural areas, remain below the poverty line. Anti-dam activists are therefore on solid ground when they question the benefits of capital-intensive, export-oriented approaches to development, of which dams are a prime example. However, in the context of today's globally oriented, profit-driven world, how labor-intensive, low-technology, decentralized communities practicing sustainable development will be integrated with the wider, globalized economy remains an open question.

Resources

Published Literature

Baviskar, A. 1995. *In the Belly of the River*, Delhi: Oxford University Press.

Dreze, J. ed. 1996. *The Dam and the Nation*, Delhi: Oxford University Press.

Fisher, W. ed. 1995. *Toward Sustainable Development: Struggling over India's Narmada River*, New York: M. E. Sharpe.

Hardiman, D. 1989. *The Coming of the Devi: Adivasi Assertion in Western India*, Delhi: Oxford University Press.

Sanghvi, S. 2000. *The River and the Life: People's Struggles in the Narmada Valley*, Mumbai and Calcutta: Earthcare Books.

World Commission Report on Dams: Dams and Development, A New Framework for Decision-Making. London and Sterling, VA: Earthscan. Available at http://www.dams.org//docs/report/wcdreport.pdf

Films and Videos

Narmada: A Valley Rises, dir. A. Kazimi, 1994.

Drowned Out, dir. Fanny Armstrong, 2001.

Narmada Diary, dir. A. Patwardhan, 1994.

Internet

http://www.narmada.org www.narmada.org, Friends of the River Narmada.

http://www.irn.org www.irn.org, International Rivers' Network

http://www.dams.org//docs/report/wcdreport.pdf

Organizations

Narmada Bachao Andolan
    B-13 Shivam Flats
    Ellora Park
    Vadodra, Gujarat
    390007
    Telephone: 91-0265-282-232
Paryavan Suraksha Samiti
    37/1 Narayan Nagar
    Chandni Chowk
    Near Municipal Office
    Rajpipla
    District Narmada
    Gujarat, India
    Telephone: 91-0264-393-145

5

The Tharu of Chitwan, Nepal

Arjun Guneratne

The People

The ethnic label *Tharu* is shared by more than a million people who live in Tarai, a narrow strip of land running for hundreds of miles along the Himalayan foothills where India and Nepal come together. Most Tharu live in Nepal, but smaller populations also live in adjacent areas of India. Although they share the same name, the people known as the Tharu belong to a number of communities that vary greatly in language and culture as one travels along the Tarai. The various Tharu languages belong to the great North Indian branch of the Indo-European language family, and relate to each other in the same way that the Romance languages do. Culturally, the Tharu vary, from the heavily Hinduized populations of the eastern Tarai living in mixed-caste villages, to the more "tribal" groups in the west who live in villages consisting largely of single ethnic groups, worshipping deities peculiar to their communities. When Tharu from different areas gather, they usually turn to Hindi or Nepali to communicate with one another. These languages are widely spoken by most Tarai people, Tharu and non-Tharu alike. Life for most Tharu has changed dramatically in the last 50 years because the Tarai has become the focus of the largest population shift in Nepal's history, as hill people in the hundreds of thousands have settled in Nepal's fertile lowlands.

No one knows the exact number of ethnically different Tharu communities that live in the Tarai, but five groups predominate. In the far west live the Rana Tharu, whose population straddles the Indo-Nepal border. To their east are the Kathariya Tharu and the Dangaura, whose name is derived from their original home in Nepal's Dang valley. In the center of the Tarai live the Tharu of Chitwan and Nawalparasi districts, whom outsiders sometimes refer to as the Chitwaniya, and to their east are the largest and most far-flung

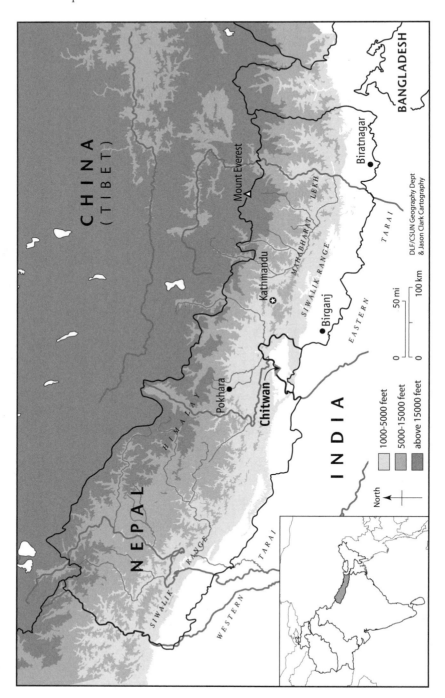

BANGLADESH

CHINA
(TIBET)

Mount Everest △

Biratnagar ●

LEKH

MAHABHARAT

Kathmandu ✪

SIWALIK RANGE

Birganj ●

EASTERN

TARAI

HIMALAY

Pokhara ●

Chitwan

NEPAL

INDIA

SIWALIK RANGE

WESTERN TARAI

TARAI

1000–5000 feet
5000–15000 feet
above 15000 feet

North

0   50 mi
0   100 km

DLF/CSUN Geography Dept
& Jason Clark Cartography

group, the Kochila. While the general points made in this chapter apply in varying degrees to all these groups, it is in particular an account of the social and cultural transformation of the smallest of the five groups mentioned, the Tharu of Chitwan.

There is no firm evidence identifying where the Tharu came from or even if all the different populations known by this name were historically a single people. It is possible that the word came to be applied to people inhabiting what outsiders saw as a malarial and dangerous area. Tharu have probably lived in Chitwan for several hundred years; certainly many places in Chitwan are associated with their sacred geography. During the first half of the 20th century, the Tharu comprised over 90 percent of the population of the Chitwan valley; people from the adjacent hills of Nepal avoided the valley because of the very virulent strain of malaria found there. Since the 1950s, however, immigration has reduced the Chitwan Tharu to a minority of the valley's population.

The Setting

The Tharu consider themselves to be and are thought of by others as being the indigenous people of the Tarai. This region is characteristically marshy and swampy, covered in former times by tall forests of sal trees (*Shorea robusta*) and traversed by wide rivers flowing south from the mountains. In the wet season, these rivers are raging floods; in the dry season the water slows to a trickle, exposing great beds of sand a mile or more in width. This topography has historically made east-west travel difficult, and limited the interaction among the various Tharu populations, which have remained culturally and linguistically distinct into modern times. Today, the forests, especially in the central and eastern Tarai, have been largely felled and the region knit together by a modern highway system that has greatly facilitated travel.

Chitwan is a valley lying between the foothills of the Himalaya and another range of low hills farther south, known as the Siwaliks. Such valleys are referred to as the Inner Tarai and are distinguished from the Tarai proper, the Outer Tarai. The Outer Tarai, especially the part lying east of Chitwan, is economically vital for Nepal, being the site of much of the country's agricultural production and its industries. In contrast, the Inner Tarai has been relatively unimportant until recently. For the first half of the 20th century, Chitwan was sparsely populated and mostly under forest; it was a popular hunting ground for Nepal's aristocracy, but contributed very little to the economy. It is densely populated today and the site of some major industries, including tourism and poultry farming.

Traditional Subsistence Strategies

The Chitwan Tharu have traditionally been rice cultivators, raising a single crop of mainly rain-fed rice in clearings in the forest. In addition to rice, they cultivated oil seed (mustard) both for home consumption and to raise cash. In what used to be a largely unmonetized economy, the cash was used to pay land taxes and to buy certain essentials like kerosene and cloth. Before development programs transformed the valley beginning in the 1950s, the Tharu kept large herds of cattle and goats, which had ample grazing in the forests and pasture lands surrounding the villages. The cattle (including buffaloes) provided milk and traction for plows and manure for fertilizing the fields. Goats were a valued source of meat and were also important in religious rituals: They were sacrificed to the numerous gods and minor deities of the Tharu pantheon. Another culturally important source of protein was (and continues to be) fish; the Tharu are expert fishermen, and fishing is practiced by men, women, and children. Farming was the livelihood for almost all Tharu families; the only other significant source of employment was in the government elephant stables. The Tharu have a well-developed reputation even today as elephant drivers and keepers. While agriculture continues to be the main occupation of most Tharu, since development work began in Chitwan many have entered other fields, including the tourism sector, and a small number have found white-collar employment.

Sociopolitical Organization

Tharu society in premodern times consisted of three social classes. At the top of the social hierarchy were the families of the tax collectors, who were responsible for collecting the taxes levied on cultivation. These tax collectors were known as *jimidars*. The state owned the land and Tharu farmers cultivated it as tenants of the state. These farmers were known as *raiti*. At the bottom of the hierarchy was a servant class—the *bahariya*—who had no land. They worked for the tenant farmers on year-long contracts that would be renewed every February; in exchange for their labor the farmer undertook to feed and clothe them and their families, and make payment in kind (Guneratne 1996).

Kinship ties are important in Tharu culture. A Tharu village in Chitwan consists of a number of lineages (*khandan*), each consisting of one or more households. Members of a lineage trace their relationship to each other through the male line, and precise knowledge of relationships typically goes back no more than three or four generations. Related lineages form amorphous social units known as *kul* (clan). A *kul* is a collection of lineages whose members believe that they share a common male ancestor, although the precise nature of their relationship is typically unknown. The clan, like the lineage, has no precise function; it holds no land in common and has no corporate existence. Its principal purpose appears to be to define the proper boundary for marriage; members of the same *kul* may not marry each other. Members of a *kul* gather together only at funerals, where they ritually reaffirm their kinship.

Tharu live in extended family households, although the economic pressures of contemporary life are forcing such households to break up much earlier than they used to. The head of a household is typically its oldest male member; with him live all of his sons and their families, and his unmarried daughters. His oldest son will take his place upon his death, but as his brothers grow older, they will usually separate from their natal household to set up on their own. Lineages expand in this way. The family land is divided up equally among the brothers, but women may not inherit land (although in rare cases a woman with no brothers may do so). The most important function of such large households (which in their heyday might have numbered more than 50 people) was to organize the labor necessary for farming. Until recently, Chitwan suffered from a labor shortage, and farmers depended on the labor of their households, supplemented by that of their servants, to cultivate. There was thus an economic incentive for landowning households to stay together for as long as possible.

Religion and Worldview

The Tharu of Chitwan are Hindu. However, in addition to the various gods—such as Vishnu, the preserver of the cosmos, Saraswati, the goddess of learning, and Lakshmi, the goddess of wealth—worshipped by Hindus throughout India, the Tharu revere particular gods of their own, in whose worship other Hindus do not join. Every Tharu village, for example, has a particular guardian deity whose worship must be carried out by the chief family of the village (descendants of the tax collectors of former times). Important people are sometimes deified after death and one's parents become guardian deities of the household when they die.

The gods of the Tharu are mostly forest gods. The Tharu believe that their gods draw strength and power from the forests, and are able to provide boons—such as children to the childless—to their devotees. In return, animals—goats, pigeons, and chickens—must be sacrificed to them.

There is widespread belief in ghosts and evil spirits among the Tharu. The Tharu believe that when a person dies, his or her spirit becomes malevolent, and must be hurried into the afterworld with the proper rituals. This is a widespread belief among people in northern India. These rituals take 13 days to complete for a woman and 12 for a man. If these rituals are not performed or are delayed, the evil spirit will linger on Earth and harm the living. A woman who dies before her husband, for example, becomes an evil spirit known as *churaini* who seduces young men and kills them by wasting them away. The performance of the ritual requires the presence of a Brahmin priest, but in former times, Brahmins would come down into Chitwan from the hills only in the winter, out of fear of malaria. In such conditions, with funeral rites postponed until the services of a Brahmin could be obtained, malevolent spirits flourished in the valley and afflicted the living.

Threats to Survival

The threat to the survival of Tharu culture in its "traditional" form comes from the immigration of hill people into the valley and the various programs for economic modernization and state building carried out by the government of Nepal since the 1950s. More recently, the forces of globalization, especially the migration of increasing numbers of young Tharu men to foreign countries in search of work, has been a significant catalyst for change.

Until the early 1950s, the Tharu were the dominant ethnic group that inhabited the Chitwan valley. The people from the surrounding hills avoided the valley in the hot season because of the endemic malaria and the Tharu were able to lead a relatively autonomous existence in which the cultural beliefs sketched out in the preceding section could develop and be reproduced in the context of social life. Beginning in the 1950s, the government of Nepal began to look to the Tarai to relieve the mounting pressure on land in the hills as the population grew. With help from the United States Agency for International Development (USAID), the government launched a malaria eradication project in Chitwan in the 1950s and, following on its success, extended it to the rest of the Tarai as well. With malaria under control through the widespread application of DDT, and with the construction of all-weather roads in the Tarai, hundreds of thousands of hill people began to migrate into that region, including Chitwan. In two decades the Tharu went from being numerically dominant in the valley's population to being a minority of less than 14 percent. The old system of land tenure, under which farmers had been tenants of the state, was abolished, and farmers were given title to their land. The extensive forests that had once covered Chitwan were cleared, until they remained only in the protected area of the Chitwan National Park (established in 1974) and an adjacent forest reserve. Even the pasture land on which Tharu had grazed their large herds of cattle were brought under the plough, while new villages were established and old ones greatly enlarged by immigrants.

Tharu society was radically transformed by these changes. Most fundamentally, Tharu control of land was threatened. Prior to the malaria eradication program, land had been virtually unlimited. Any Tharu who wanted land could have it. Even the servant class followed that occupation more by choice than necessity; their limited wants could be met by working for others and they thereby avoided the onerous responsibilities of tenancy, including the payment of taxes (Guneratne 1996). The immigration of hill people into Chitwan closed off the land frontier and also reduced the land to which Tharu had access. For example, the elimination of pastureland meant that Tharu could no longer maintain the large herds of cattle and goats of former times; the average household today is able to maintain only a few head.

More importantly, the transformation of former tenants to landowners in their own right had a deleterious consequence in the short term. The Tharu, unlike some of the hill people who had moved into Chitwan, were generally illiterate and uneducated, largely ignorant of laws and their rights. Some of the more unscrupulous of the new immigrants quickly took advantage of this illiteracy and lack of awareness. They lent money to Tharu at exorbitant rates of interest, and sometimes forged promissory notes to show that more money was owed than was actually the case. When Tharu found themselves unable to repay their loans, their land was seized in payment of their debt.

The monetization of the economy has also exerted a profound influence on Tharu culture. As the necessities of life expanded—clothing, consumer goods, costs associated with education and travel, the construction of more durable houses and so on—money and time became scarcer. Where once the Tharu grew only one crop in their fields, they raise three today: rice, mustard or wheat, and maize. Intensified cropping has become an economic necessity. Rituals can no longer be as elaborate and costly as they once were. The festival of Holi, for example, one of the most important in the Tharu calendar, which had once lasted for a month, is today celebrated over two days only. Many people now work outside of agriculture and even agriculture has become more demanding of their time and energy. Much of what is used in these celebrations must now be paid for in cash. Goats, for instance, used in animal sacrifice, must now be purchased in the market, whereas formerly every household would have been able to meet its requirements for goats from the stock it raised.

Tharu culture has also been transformed by its intimate relationship to the more prestigious culture of the immigrants into the valley. The culture of

Nepal's hill people (most of whom enjoy higher status than do the Tharu in Nepal's caste system) is more prestigious because it is the culture also of the rulers of Nepal and in recent times has been the basis of the process of national identity formation fostered by the state. This transformation is very visible in religious life. The gods of the Hindu pantheon are today beginning to play a greater role in Tharu religious life as Tharu society becomes increasingly influenced by the immigrant culture that now surrounds it. The popularity of some Hindu deities (for example, Sarasvati) appears to have increased because of the influence of Brahmin-Chhetri immigrants. Sarasvati was once unimportant for Tharu because she is associated with knowledge and learning, and the Tharu were largely illiterate; today, with the introduction of schools and the desire of many Tharu to advance themselves through modern education, Saravati's popularity has spread. Some gods of the Hindu pantheon, such as Hanuman, are worshipped as clan deities.

As Tharu society has become increasingly Hinduized, the role of the Brahmin priest in ritual life has also expanded. Formerly, it was confined to the performance of the Satya Narayan *puja* (worship of one of the forms taken by the god Vishnu) and of death rituals. The adoption of Hindu ritual practices in Tharu marriage ceremonies, however, has greatly expanded the role of the priest, who is also regularly consulted to determine the auspicious time to hold significant activities. Marriage ceremonies has been one of the areas in which Tharu society has been most susceptible to the influence of immigrant culture.

The old gods and minor deities of the Tharu are declining in importance for the younger generation (those who grew up in close interaction with the immigrants who settled in the valley since the early 1960s) for whom the "great tradition" of Hinduism is becoming increasingly important. This is due to a number of factors. Tharu believe that their gods need forests to sustain them. With the disappearance of most of the forest, Tharu believe that the gods abandoned the valley. As older people ceased to worship them, knowledge of these deities—who they are, what favors they can do for human beings, and how they should be worshipped—was increasingly lost to the younger generation. Some gods, such as Bikram Baba, whose shrine has survived because it is in the national park, have survived into modern times, are well known, and continue to be worshipped. But many young Tharu no longer share the knowledge their elders have of the traditional religion and are unlikely ever to acquire that knowledge because the context for that acquisition no longer exists. Cultural knowledge is transmitted from one generation to the next through both discourse and practice, and because the

context in which that transmission takes place has changed dramatically, certain kinds of knowledge are no longer relevant to contemporary
circumstances.

On one occasion, a young Tharu man in his mid-twenties, a student in an
agricultural college, was present at an interview with his neighbor, an old
carpenter. The carpenter spoke at length about the different gods who used
to inhabit the valley and were driven out (or left) because of the extensive
deforestation. The young man said afterwards that, excepting for Bikram
Baba, he had never heard of most of the gods who were mentioned and discussed. In part, this is because many of them are no longer worshipped, or
are worshipped less frequently than before. Knowledge is communicated
not only through formal instruction but also through the everyday practice
of social life, and younger people learn by observing the practice of their
elders and engaging in those practices themselves. Their elders grew up in
a society in which such practices were a central concern of social life. For
young Tharu today, however, a greatly expanded economy and the development of a much more complex society (socially, culturally, and politically)
is a powerful force that draws them away from the core beliefs and practices
of their elders.

"Local knowledge" or "traditional knowledge" as contrasted to knowledge
acquired through a system of modern schooling, is unlikely to be equally
distributed in a society. This is the sort of knowledge that most members of
a society may be expected, in the ordinary course of events, to acquire over a
lifetime, such as knowledge of rituals, or of forest resources on which traditional forms of livelihood depend, and of agricultural practices. Such knowledge is likely to be shaped, and the conditions of acquiring it determined, by
factors such as social status, age, kinship, and gender. For example, boys (and
usually elder sons) assist their fathers in the worship of household deities
and may be expected to acquire their knowledge in that context; girls, typically, do not. The changes that occur are usually not radical enough or dramatic
enough to disrupt this process of acquiring knowledge, but rather make
incremental additions to the total store of knowledge. Some things are gained
while others are lost, but there is no sharp disjuncture with the past, at least
none that we can perceive from our vantage point in time. This was the case
in Chitwan for the first half of the 20th century.

A radical disjuncture in the way knowledge is transmitted has taken place
in the last 40 years in Chitwan, however. New sources and forms of knowledge, invested with greater value for a new generation of Tharu, have developed to challenge the old order. Chief among these is the modern system

of state-sponsored education, which young Tharu and even many of their elders see as a prerequisite for successful participation in a modern economy. The cultural adjuncts of a modern economy, such as the cinema, television, and now, for the better educated and relatively well-to-do, the Internet, also pose a challenge to established practices through which local knowledge was transmitted. For example, the telling of folk tales used to be a principal source of entertainment for Tharu; this has been replaced by the cinema, and knowledge of these stories is dying out. One young man commented that when he was a boy he had been interested in these stories, but now he no longer was. In fact, when I was tape-recording stories or playing them back during my fieldwork,, many young men like himself, drawn there by curiosity, heard these stories for the first time or for the first time since their childhood. Other forms of mass communication, such as radio and television, are making their presence felt in Tharu villages, particularly those that have been electrified. In short, Chitwan Tharu society has been transformed from one focused largely inward to one that must look outward to prosper.

The rituals that will not be abandoned will be principally those associated with the worship of Hindu divinities: Vishnu, Lakshmi, Sarasvati, Durga, and Siva. The contemporary influence of Brahmin society on that of the Tharu virtually guarantees this. The Tharu elite are increasingly adopting Brahmin or Hindu ritual practices which earlier had played little or no role in Tharu life, thereby legitimizing these practices for the rest of their society. The Tharu elite itself is constructing its own linkages with the elites of the wider society in which Tharu society is embedded, and the practices of the dominant elite is a model for local Tharu elites to follow. These practices are further legitimated as a proper model for social action and behavior by their being considered as both (a) Hindu and (b) Nepali, both categories to which Tharu consider they belong.

Beginning in the 1990s, increasing numbers of Tharu have begun to go abroad—to Qatar, Saudi Arabia, Malaysia, and, in far smaller numbers, to Japan, Europe, and the United States—to look for work. While it is still too early to say what kind of cultural impact this migration will have on Tharu society, its economic impact is beginning to be visible: in brick houses (replacing traditional structures of elephant grass and mud), cement latrines, satellite dishes for TV, and other elements of consumption. Before significant labor migration began, the importance of Chitwan as a tourist destination following the establishment of the national park meant that local Tharu had some exposure to ways of being and styles of consumption very different from their everyday experience, reinforced both by the cinema and more recently by television. The increasing presence of television in the villages is another catalyst for change: For instance, the increasing popularity of cricket in Chitwan, as a sport played by boys and young men, which has come about only in the last few years, can be directly attributed to the broadcasting of cricket matches on Indian television (which can be viewed in Nepal). Migrants, tourists, and television are among the conduits through which new ideas, new practices, and new ways of understanding the world flow into Tharu villages, to be taken up, discussed, and perhaps adopted by those best placed to do so.

To sum up, a number of factors have combined to transform Tharu culture and society. The catalyst for these changes was the malaria eradication project, which made possible the processes that are changing Tharu life. The presence of immigrants in overwhelming numbers, speaking a different language and following different practices, has provided a new model for Tharu to follow. It has also generated the social pressures to make them conform to this new model. Along with immigration came new development policies; schools were introduced and the Tharu were taught the national language and culture, which was also that of the immigrants. Various processes of globalization that followed on the heels of these transformations were also catalysts for change. Educated Tharu men and women tend to have less regard for the beliefs and practices of their elders and gravitate instead to the cultural practices of the hill people who now live among them. They see hill people as being successful and powerful, and their culture accordingly gains prestige. Tharu in general have embraced these changes, for they see them as something positive that will enable them to advance themselves in life. Brahmin priests have become more influential even as the power of the traditional Tharu shamans has declined. Whereas once the principal ritual service the priests performed was in the funeral rites, their participation now is essential in marriage and other life cycle rites as well. The monetization of the economy that has occurred has compelled Tharu to grow crops for the market; where once they grew a single crop of rice, they now grow two, with an additional crop of maize to supplement it. This intensive agriculture leaves much less time for other pursuits.

Response: Struggles to Sustain Survival

The Tharu have responded in numerous ways to the challenges posed by the social and economic transformation of the Chitwan valley. They are acutely aware that their culture is being transformed through the influence of both Nepali hill culture and Indian plains culture. Some Tharu welcome these changes, which they view as positive. Others deplore them. Changes seen as positive include the establishment of schools and colleges and clinics and hospitals, the availability of a broader array of jobs and other opportunities for economic advancement, the development of a market economy which has brought for many a higher standard of living than that enjoyed by their forebears, and the opportunity to participate in the wider life of the country to which they belong. On the negative side, these changes have reduced them to a minority, one that is, in their own eyes by comparison with the new immigrants, relatively powerless and impoverished. Many Tharu also feel that they are at a disadvantage in the new economy: They are less educated and sophisticated than their immigrant neighbors and their value system and cultural practices require great expenditure, during life cycle ceremonies, for example, or when hospitality is shown to a guest. Nor have all Tharu benefited from the changes wrought by the market. Poorer people, for example, who must sell their labor power in order to survive, now find themselves competing with immigrant workers from outside the district for work in agriculture.

How have Tharu responded to the situation that has developed since the malaria eradication project of the 1950s? At the national level, Tharu from every part of the country have organized themselves into a national organization called the Tharu Welfare Association (Tharu Kalyankarini Sabha). Although this organization was founded in 1949, it has gathered strength and expanded since large-scale immigration into the Tarai began. Its primary goal is to facilitate the participation of Tharu in the modern economy by establishing hostels and scholarships for Tharu students, and by limiting cultural practices that call for great expenditures. The Tharu Welfare Association has also asked the Nepal government, so far unsuccessfully, to implement a system of quotas for Tharu (in effect, a form of affirmative action) to guarantee them access to both higher education institutions and government service. Tharu from Chitwan are active in this organization.

In Chitwan itself there are numerous organizations whose goal is to improve the Tharu's economic condition and "preserve" Tharu culture. What these activists mean by culture is not the symbolic systems—the beliefs, values, and systems of morality—that shape the way they understand and give meaning to the world, and which are usually taken for granted, but instead, a self-conscious awareness of the salience of certain practices or customs as markers of social identity. It is culture in an objectified sense. For example, most Tharu, like many people, do not reflect on the language they speak; it is taken for granted and used instrumentally. Language, however, is objectified for Tharu ethnic activists, who seek to raise the profile of the Tharu community in Nepal's polity; it is through the language one speaks that a Tharu can be identified in the census of Nepal, which until recently did not use ethnic categories in its enumeration of the population. Thus, it is important to give the language a label (*Tharu bhasa*) and to ensure that it is entered in the census, distinguishing the speakers of that language from the others around them.

An example of an organization seeking to preserve "Tharu culture" was the Tharu Yuva Club (Tharu Youth Club), which existed in southern Chitwan during the early 1990s. The goal of the club was to improve the welfare of Tharu and to develop the Tharu language through literary activities. The club intended to develop the concept of "Tharutva" a neologism coined to describe everything that pertains to being a Tharu, including culture, language, and society. The goal of the Tharu Yuva Club was to halt the decline in the social and economic conditions of the Tharu community that was, according to its founder, "getting weaker as a society day by day" (Guneratne 1998).

Another group with similar aims was the Tharu Kalyankari Yuva Sabha (Tharu Welfare Youth Association). The founder of this organization established it because the youth were dissatisfied with the "slowness" of the Tharu Welfare Association's approach; they wanted "quick results." This organization brought out a magazine *Hamar Sanskrti* (*Our Culture*). It never got beyond the inaugural issue (apparently because of lack of funds to publish it). Publishing such magazines is, however, a significant part of the activities of organizations such as this throughout the Tarai. An important component of these publications are the folksongs that are collected and transcribed in their pages.

A very different kind of organization that has emerged in Chitwan since the democracy movement of 1990 is the Nepal Indigenous Development Society (NIDS), founded in 1993 by a group of young Tharu men who wanted to improve the economic condition of their villages. NIDS has been successful in part because it has received steady funding from international NGOs interested in its goals. Its activities include providing assistance to Tharu farmers to raise pigs, organizing nonformal education programs to raise literacy in the community, improving health and sanitation by building latrines, and setting up credit associations. In addition, NIDS successfully organized villagers, Tharu and non-Tharu, to cooperate in the construction of a 90-meter poured concrete bridge, built with financing from a Belgian NGO.

Such activities are oriented to improving the economic condition of Tharu farmers. NIDS, however, has also involved itself in cultural activities. When the Ministry of Tourism in Nepal, along with the Tharu Welfare Association, decided to sponsor a Tharu cultural program in Chitwan, in the tourist development at the entrance to the national park, NIDS was asked to organize the event. Dance troupes of Tharu were brought from all over the Tarai, and a daylong performance of dances took place before an audience of hundreds of local Tharu. On the one hand, such performances serve to remind

Tharu of cultural practices that may be in decline due to the pressures of contemporary life and the appeal of competing sorts of cultural performances (such as Hindi movies, for example). On the other hand, however, they are no longer embedded in their proper performance context; they have been taken out of context and put on display as a spectacle. That in itself is a form of cultural change; while the outward form of the practice (in this case a dance) is preserved, its meaning has been changed because it is now performed in a different context.

The Tharu as a community were affected to varying degrees by Nepal's Maoist insurgency. Many Tharu throughout the region joined the insurgency, some in local leadership roles, but the Tharu in the far western districts were identified as a community with the insurgency and suffered extreme state repression as a result. Hundreds were murdered or disappeared. Maoists also targeted BASE (Backward Society Education, a Tharu nongovernmental organization based in Dang and active in the far west), harassing and sometimes murdering BASE activists, presumably because they saw BASE as their main rival for Tharu loyalty. Toward the end of the insurgency, Tharu had become disillusioned with the Maoists. But in Chitwan the Tharu as a community were not identified with the movement, although, of course, individual Tharu joined it.

Food for Thought

Cultures are always dynamic configurations of ways of being in the world, ways of understanding it, and practices that engage it. Because the world is changing, culture inevitably changes along with it. The issue is not whether cultures should be preserved in some pristine, objectified form; the question, rather, is who should control the pace, the direction, and the process of change. Where the Tharu are concerned, these matters are largely not under their control, but the same could be said for people throughout much of the world. The direction of cultural change among the Tharu is shaped both by the policies of the state of Nepal—which seeks to create a unified state and a shared Nepali identity among its culturally heterogeneous population—and the globalizing forces that affect Nepal. In the period prior to the malaria eradication project, the Tharu lived lives that were shaped only to a limited extent by forces outside their valley. Although they were obliged to pay revenue to the state, their economy was based on subsistence agriculture and was able to support a cultural life that was distinct from that of their neighbors in both the hills and the plains. This is no longer the case. Nevertheless, the Tharu of Chitwan will survive as a culturally distinct people in Nepal's population, their distinctiveness preserved by their names, their language, their system of kinship, and those cultural practices that have been preserved as a marker of that distinctiveness.

To Think About

1. How is culture transmitted from one generation to the next?
2. A common anthropological understanding of culture is that the concept refers to the systems of ideas, values, and beliefs that people have which help them interpret their world and generate behavior. Is this the notion of culture that Tharu cultural organizations are working with?
3. What are the key factors that have transformed Tharu culture since the malaria eradication project of the 1950s?
4. How are Tharu responding to these changes?
5. How have environmental factors helped to shape Tharu beliefs? How have those beliefs been affected by environmental change?

Resources

Published Literature

Bjork Guneratne, Katharine. 1999. *In the Circle of the Dance: Notes of an Outsider in Nepal.* Ithaca, NY: Cornell University Press.

Guneratne, Arjun. 1996. The Tax-Man Cometh: The Impact of Revenue Collection on Subsistence Strategies in Chitwan Tharu Society. *Studies in Nepali History & Society* 1(1): 5–35.

———. 1998. Modernization, the State, and the Construction of a Tharu Identity in Nepal. *The Journal of Asian Studies* 57(3): 749–773.

———. 2001. Shaping the Tourist's Gaze: Representing Ethnic Difference in a Nepali Village. *Journal of the Royal Anthropological Institute*, 7(3): 527–543.

———. 2002. *Many Tongues, One People: The Making of Tharu Identity in Nepal.* Ithaca, NY: Cornell University Press.

Krauskopff, Gisele and Pamela Deuel Meyer. 2000. *The Kings of Nepal and the Tharu of the Tarai.* Kirtipur, Nepal: Center for Nepal and Asian Studies, and Los Angeles: Rusca Press.

Müller-Böker, Ulrike. 1999. *The Chitwan Tharus in Southern Nepal: An Ethnoecological Approach.* Translated by Philip Pierce. Stuttgart: Franz Steiner Verlag.

Films and Videos

Servants of Ganesh. This film about elephant handlers in Chitwan has footage of the performance of various Tharu rituals and discusses the relationship of the Tharu to elephant handling. Distributed by Documentary Educational Resources: (<http://www.oneworldfilms.com/>http://www.oneworldfilms.com/).

Internet

Resources on the Tharu. This site contains links to various online resources on the Tharu, including an annotated bibliography
   http://www.macalester.edu/~guneratne/Teaching/TharuResources.html
The Tharu of the Tarai. A site that describes the art and architecture of the Tharu.
   http://www.asianart.com/tharu/
Dilli Chaudhary's Anti-Slavery Award acceptance speech. Text of a speech by the leader of the largest NGO in Nepal, honored for his role in ending bonded labor among Tharu in western Nepal.
   http://www.antislavery.org/homepage/antislavery/award/dillispeech.htm

Organizations

Association for Nepal and Himalayan Studies
   Department of Anthropology
   Macalester College
   Saint Paul, MN 55105
Backward Society Education
   Tulsipur,
   Dang. Nepal
   Phone: 977-82-20055
   Fax: 977-82-20312
Nepal Indigenous Development Society
   Ratnanagar, Sauraha Chowk,
   Chitwan, Nepal
   Phone: 0977-56-60069
   Fax: 0977-56-60235

6

The Dom of Hunza (Northern Areas of Pakistan)
Anna Schmid

The Dom are a people in Hunza, a valley and administrative division in the Northern Areas of Pakistan, and until 1974 the state of Hunza governed by a local ruler. The Dom's identity developed out of their work as musicians and blacksmiths. The Dom's status is low and their opportunities have been constrained because these professions, though essential to the smooth functioning of traditional life for Hunza's people, were despised by the wider society. And the Dom's old roles do not fit comfortably in today's changing society and economy, where musicians and blacksmiths are no longer so necessary. They must remake themselves.

The Dom have responded to this challenge by reworking the interactions with members of the wider society that are a central feature of their identity. Because of recent social, cultural, political, and economic changes, the main challenge to their way of life is a desire to be fully integrated into the wider society of Hunza. Dom want to overcome their low social position and engage in the exploration of new economic activities, finding a new path to what they see as a better future. Almost everywhere minority peoples are exposed to this dual challenge: They must deal with the wider society from their disadvantaged position as a minority, and they must organize and structure their own way of life, with all its peculiarities and differences, as wider societal processes compel them to reinvent themselves to suit external demands.

The People

The Dom of Hunza are concentrated today in about 50 households in the village of Mominabad; an additional 50 households are scattered among other villages, for a total population of Dom in Hunza of about 700 (there are Dom in other areas of Pakistan's northern territory as well). They are a group with

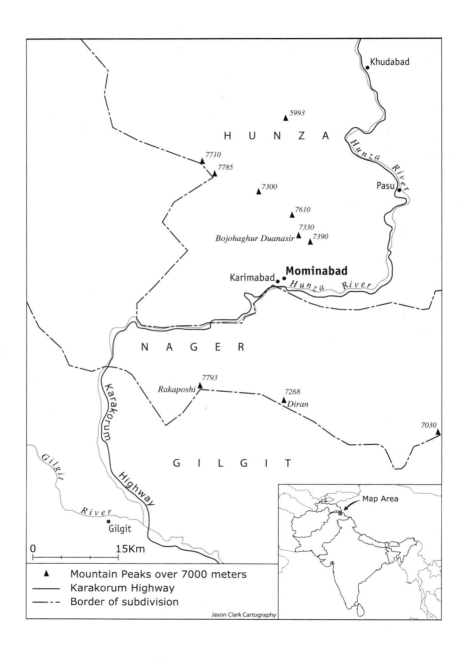

Mountain Peaks over 7000 meters
Karakorum Highway
Border of subdivision

Jason Clark Cartography

heterogeneous origins, developed from a number of different founding families. Each kinship-group has its own narrative to explain the events that led its founders to leave their former homes, and the circumstances of their arrival in Hunza. Most narratives tell of difficulties in the homeland that forced the search for a new one. They tell of the migration itself, and of how newcomers were adopted into the society by the local ruler in Hunza. In one narrative, for example, Noor Shah, a respected personality in Mominabad, the village of the Dom, reported:

> First two brothers reached Hunza and Nager [the principality opposite Hunza, on the left bank of the Hunza River]. Their names were Majun and Dishil. They had left their former homeland. They had lived in Kashmir. In Kashmir they had to endure a heavy crisis: They had not enough to eat and they witnessed a severe oppression. They only wanted to live in peace and without having any quarrels. In the new homeland they hoped for better treatment and a better social position. . . . When they finally reached Hunza and Nager, the brothers decided to split up; Dishil went to Nager, Majun went to Hunza. Before splitting up they agreed upon helping each other in difficult times in the future, therefore they kept their own language [called Domaaki] thus ensuring that they could communicate with each other but nobody else would understand them. . . . Although there was nothing specific to fear, they could not know what they had to expect. . . . They went to the respective local ruler and told him their story. Explaining their background they asked for employment with the ruler. Inquiring about their skills and hearing about their being professional musicians the ruler welcomed them and asked them to stay. First they stayed in the palace, later the ruler gave them some land. In the course of time other migrants joined Majun and Dishil [in Hunza and Nager]: After Majun came Ashur, he was blacksmith, then came Bak, then Gulbeg. The latest to come [to Hunza] was Mishkin, he came during the reign of Shah Silum Khan. That's how the group of the Dom was created." (Schmid 1997: 34; translation)

This reconstruction of the history of the Dom—part fact, part justification for present conditions—illustrates the way that each musician or blacksmith who arrived in Hunza was integrated into the Dom on the basis of his skill. According to Noor Shah's narrative, the last person to be assigned to the Dom arrived in Hunza during the reign of Shah Silum Khan (1790–1824). Such narratives tell that the members of the Dom migrated to Hunza in several waves, arriving from different areas adjacent to the Hunza Valley, often fleeing social or political difficulties in their homelands. The Dom thus do not consider themselves descendants of a common ancestor. Rather, each immigrant initiated his own kin-group, with himself as its founding father. Relations between kin-groups were established through intermarriage, and a sense of belonging to one larger group developed from these unusual beginnings.

The livelihoods of the Dom provided them both a place in the economy and a social identity distinct from the majority population of Hunza, which consists of Shina-speaking people in the lower valley, the Burushos in the central part of Hunza, and the Wakhi (described in Chapter 9) in the upper part. The Dom constitute approximately 2 percent of the population of Hunza.

The Setting

Mominabad is situated in the center of Hunza, an administrative unit of Pakistan's Northern Areas, on the right bank of the Hunza River. The 210-kilometer-long Hunza Valley lies in the Karakoram Range in northeastern Pakistan, where the landscape is characterized by its extreme relief—K2 (8,126 meters) and Rakaposhi (7,793 meters) are two of the highest peaks in the world—and by glaciation, which limits the land available for cultivation. Alluvial fans are the only sites for settlements and cultivation, and all agricultural land requires terracing. Hunza is at the transition from the arid to the subtropical zones, and fields need to be irrigated. Farmers get water to their fields by diverting meltwater from the glaciers through a system of channels that follow contour lines along the steep cliffs. Agricultural land is divided into three categories: (1) arable land on which the principal crops of wheat, barley, millet, buckwheat, legumes, maize, and potatoes are cultivated; (2) orchards, where apricot, apple, and mulberry trees are most frequently grown; and (3) irrigated hay meadows. Farming is complemented by raising livestock, which is constrained by the availability both of high summer pastures and of the winter fodder needed when the cattle are kept in stables.

Traditional Subsistence Strategies

The livelihood of Hunza's majority has long been based on a combination of farming and livestock raising. Each household possesses some land, with only minor differences in size of holdings. In recent years, most households have sent one or more members to work outside the agrarian sector, in government services, development programs, tourism (as drivers, guides, souvenir traders, entrepreneurs in the hotel business, and so forth), or other economic sectors.

For the Dom, however, traditional subsistence strategies were different. Each family of blacksmiths serviced a specific village or a certain area, touring it twice a year in spring and autumn just before and after the main agricultural season, primarily to repair agricultural tools. In return, Dom blacksmiths were entitled to a small amount of grain a year from each household within their sector. In addition, each blacksmith received extra payment in cash or in kind for a major work such as the production of a new agricultural tool (e.g., fork, shovel, or ax).

Dom musicians received their remuneration in cash and kind during and after each musical event. They performed in ensembles of at least three persons (one musician playing a wind instrument—the double-reed clarinet, the fipple flute, or the transverse flute; the second playing a pair of kettle drums beaten with straight sticks; and the third playing the double-headed cylindrical drum beaten with the hands and a curved stick). Each ensemble served a specified village or cluster of villages in the annual cycle of festivals (e.g., at harvest time). Musicians also performed at shamanistic rituals, polo matches, and other events.

Though they have earned their livelihood primarily as musicians or blacksmiths, all Dom also possess some land. The average landholding per household in Mominabad is more or less equivalent to the average in other villages, but the quantity of water allotted is lower and the yearly harvest therefore less. Farmers in Mominabad bring in only one harvest per year even though the village is located in the zone where double crops are possible. Water allocation is strictly regulated; each village has the right to specific quantities. To increase their share a delegation of the Dom applied to the local ruler in the 1960s, then sued a neighboring village, Aliabad. Neither attempt succeeded: Members of the wider society argue that musicians and blacksmiths have a far higher income than the average farmer in Hunza, because they are paid for their professional services in addition to their agricultural resources.

Sociopolitical Organization

The Dom's social organization was initially established by intermarriages between migrants with a specific skill, either as a musician or a blacksmith. Internally, the Dom built up a social organization through obligations and specific rights vis-à-vis other inhabitants of Mominabad. Neighbors had to help in difficult situations—for example, a birth or death, a heavy workload, or compulsory labor obligation. The social structure was also influenced by how land was allocated by the local ruler in Mominabad and by the quality of the performances in their respective profession. A person's recognition as a member of the Dom and status within and outside the group were related to the ruler's assessment of skill and consequent assignment of professional territory. The ruler assessed the quality of a person's work and granted privileges to the most talented musicians and hardest-working blacksmiths. The best workers and performers were allotted the best territories within which to ply their trades, so that large villages close to Mominibad—convenient and sizeable enough to provide a substantial income—were only for the favored. The closer the village to the center of Hunza—Baltit/Karimabad—the higher valued are the skills of the professional and the more profitable. Thus, the musicians and blacksmiths who worked with and for the ruler—who personified the center of the entire society—were the most highly regarded.

Although their skills were highly valued and applied in many important spheres of life, the Dom as a group were despised and relegated to the lowest social status. The Dom had a reputation for being greedy, never satisfied with their payment; they were said not to adhere to common moral values and to indulge in black magic, harming people who hesitated to meet demands. These attributes were translated by the wider society into exclusion from prestigious activities such as dancing—reserved for higher society—and from public offices such as head of one's village.

With the deposition of the last local ruler in 1974, the political changes that had begun with colonization in 1891—to be followed by independence in 1947 and then development of such infrastructure as the Karakoram Highway (KKH) connecting the plains of Pakistan with China—reached a climax. Until he was deposed in 1974, the ruler was the focal point of the cultural, social, and political order. As such, he guaranteed the regular income of the Dom through their professional activities. Although the Dom occupied the lowest social position within Hunza society, the wider society had to observe a standard of behavior vis-à-vis their musicians and blacksmiths. If a customer of a blacksmith or a dancer in a festival misbehaved (e.g., abusing a musician for his inadequate performance or a blacksmith for wasting too much of the scarce charcoal supplied by the customer), the Dom had the possibility of complaining of this unjustified behavior before the ruler. The ruler's response to complaints was often to ridicule the members of the wider society. Many can recall the ruler stating: "If you can't handle these people [musicians and blacksmiths] properly you are not any better." In addition, the Dom's reputation for skill in black magic helped insure reasonable behavior.

In their evaluations of what it was like to live under the local ruler, the Dom have two rather contradictory reactions. Some, especially the older generation, maintain that they had a far better time as long as he was in office. Others, primarily the younger generation, characterize those times as being years of undue hardship, during which they lived at the mercy of the ruler and were deprived of adequate participation in emergent economic and social developments. They were obliged to carry on with their professions as musicians and blacksmiths and to teach their sons, but now "the restrictions of vocation have ended and the Doma are participating in many different fields of employment from driving to engineering to government administration."

Religion and Worldview

The Dom's worldview is in several respects strongly associated with their professions. This is best illustrated by an often-repeated story about how they acquired them:

> The Dom and the ruler belong to the same family: A ruler had four sons. He had heard about a teacher living at a far off place. He discussed with the members of the court council if he should not send three of his sons for education to this teacher. "Only one of them can be my successor." They agreed that the sons should be sent to learn to read and write. . . . On their way they met an old man and it turned out that he was the wanted person. . . . They did not realize that it was *sheitan* (the devil) they had met. He took them home and started teaching them the Holy Quran. But the princes were not interested in these lessons. Instead they discovered curious objects, the musical instruments, hanging at the wall. They asked for instruction in the handling and playing of these instruments. Sheitan complied with their demand. . . . Coming back to Hunza with the musical instruments their father was disappointed. He was surprised by the sweet voices of the instruments and disappointed at the same time. . . . From this time the musicians—as sons of the ruler—walked in front of him wherever he went." (cf. Schmid 1997: 160; translation)

This story tells us that the Dom's fascination for music led to the degradation of the former princes and also to a close relationship with the ruler. They could not assist the ruler in his courtly business, but walking in front of him meant being in his immediate vicinity—in fact, being closer than anyone else. In their capacity as musicians, they announced his departures, his arrivals, and his daily actions; they accompanied him throughout his life. To each of these activities, specific tunes were accorded.

Another part of the story tells us that the profession itself is derived from evil influence: It is the devil who teaches them how to play their instruments. Similar stories are told about the blacksmiths: By being trained as a blacksmith, the son of the ruler loses social status. In a different story, relegating the blacksmith to a low social position is justified through the theft of iron in the forge of their saintly teacher Da'ud. Da'ud, the mythical patron of the blacksmith, was able to forge hot iron with his bare hands. One day while working in his forge he burnt his hands terribly. He immediately understood that something had gone awry. He asked his pupil if he had stolen iron from his forge. The pupil confessed that he had taken a piece of iron. Da'ud was disappointed and declared that from now on the profession of the blacksmith would be very difficult. The pupil, the forefather of the blacksmiths among the Dom, had to develop special tools to work the hot iron. Thus, the act of stealing became the reason for the difficulties in the profession: working in front of the heat, being dirty, and being despised by other people.

These narratives and stories also contain references to religious orientations. Today, the Dom in Hunza belong to the Ismaili sect of Islam, as do 98 percent of the population. The adaptation of the minority group to the religious denomination of the wider society took place across the whole region. For example, in the neighboring principality of Nager, where the main religion is the Twelver-Shi'a sect, the Dom, too, are Twelver. Although the Ismaili faith has prevailed in Hunza since the 19th century, the population started to build Ismaili prayer houses (*jamaat khana*) only in the 1920s. Members of the Dom community claim that they were one of the first to have their own jamaat khana in the village, as early as 1922. This has to be seen as a strategy applied in the local cultural and social discourse in which the Dom try to justify their own interpretation of their position within the wider society. The declaration of their early religious adherence to the prevailing Islamic faith is to be seen as one attempt to counter their low social position. By insisting on their pioneer role in introducing the new religious faith, the Dom claim they are cultural innovators, with the wider society following them— reminiscent of the Dom narrative about their role in introducing music to Hunza. If the wider society were to acknowledge this pioneer role, the Dom would be recognized as leaders instead of low-ranked people.

Threats to Survival

Demographic Trends

The status of members of the Dom community was and still is somewhat ambivalent: On the one hand, they were in the service of the local ruler and had important tasks to perform for the wider society; on the other hand, they occupied a low social position, were despised, and—most important—were excluded from the wider society. Although they were granted land and allotted water rights and a high pasture, agriculture was secondary to the Dom and they were considered to have only basic skills as farmers.

In the early 20th century, the British colonial administration offered the ruler of Hunza the opportunity to cultivate land around Gilgit, the main town in the Northern Areas. This meant first and foremost that the future settlers would construct water channels, a feature for which the people of Hunza were renowned. The ruler selected not only the people who would dig the channels and cultivate the land but also the musicians and blacksmiths. The musicians had to accompany the daily work with their music and the blacksmiths had to repair the tools. Everyone involved in the cultivation of new land was entitled to a share of the land. In addition, the Dom had to act as musicians and blacksmiths for the newly established communities. In this way families from Mominabad settled in other villages within Hunza and around Gilgit.

Through these processes, the Dom had one focal point in the major settlement, the village Mominabad, but they also had households scattered throughout the area. Today, as mentioned earlier, the community consists of about 50 households outside and 50 households inside Mominabad (cf. Schmid 1997: 147), with a total of about 700 people. Figures are not as accessible for the Dom in Nager, but the same processes took place in that community, although on a minor scale. The important difference between the two populations of Dom is that the scattered households are integrated in completely different village formations from those in Mominabad. It is impossible for single families to live on their own in a village setting. They have to collaborate in all aspects of community life, including agricultural activities (such as irrigating the fields and guarding livestock on high pastures) and cultural and social endeavors (such as celebrating life cycle festivals). Over time, the constant interaction with members of other groups changed their worldview and attitudes, whereas people in Mominabad, though to some degree despised and rejected by members of the wider society, are said to have retained their identity. The only permanent connection between people of Mominabad and Dom living outside the village has been marriage, and rarely has a marriage between a Dom and a non-Dom member of other communities occurred. Today, some of the Dom demand intermarriages with people from other communities as a proof of having equal rights and being acknowledged as equals by the wider society. As long as members of the wider society refuse to permit intermarriages with Dom families, the Dom interpret this as exclusion on the ground of their social position.

Current Events and Conditions

Another major factor in the Dom's process of being acknowledged by members of the wider society is their language, Domaaki, one of the Indo-Aryan languages. In the above-mentioned narrative, a separate language was considered to be necessary to communicate within the community. Today, speaking the language signifies low social position. Asked about their language, many of my interlocutors among the Dom denied that they have their own language, claiming that the language of the dominant group is their language as well. It is true that most of the Dom are bilingual. They have a perfect command over the languages of the dominant society—although they speak with an unusual nasal accent—which is Shina in Gilgit town and surrounding areas as well as in the lower Hunza valley, Burushaski in central Hunza, and Wakhi in the upper Hunza valley (see Chapter 6, by Hermann Kreutzmann, in this volume). In Mominabad households, Domaaki is still spoken, although many in the younger generation are no longer fluent in that language. Many scholars have predicted that the Domaaki language is likely to disappear. The process of adapting the language of the dominant group might help the Dom in certain ways, but it is doubtful if abandoning their own language will lead to a recognition of the Dom as equals by the members of the wider society.

Altered circumstances—primarily the abolition of the ruler in 1974, which itself was the result of a process starting with the advent of the British in Hunza in 1891—changed the contexts in which the Dom's professions were situated. After 1974, the ruler no longer dictated the Dom's actions and performances. But, to go further into the past, the political system and the group's cultural orientation started to change considerably after the British conquest: The ruler was no longer obliged to consider the opinions of his council, dramatically changing the power balance within Hunza. This had consequences for the Dom's acting as musicians: Personal tunes were once granted by the ruler to persons who had mastered a difficult task, such as a heroic deed in one of the numerous wars with Nager. Musicians performed these tunes at specific occasions, and only the tune owner and his kin-group were allowed to dance to it. But personal tunes came to be awarded for odd acts, such as bringing an empty whisky bottle to Hunza.

The ruler was abolished by the Government of Pakistan in an effort to integrate Hunza into new worldwide developments, which did not require the professional skills of the Dom. This situation led to a change in the importance of musical activities: Certain festivals were still observed, dancing ceremonies were maintained, private gatherings with music were held, and tourists were entertained, but the focal point of the musical activities had vanished. For the Dom, the new developments meant that their skills as musicians were no longer considered *necessary*, although they continued to perform and they received considerable payment. As a consequence, the younger generation was no longer instructed as musicians. In fact, the worldview of the entire society had changed. The agricultural cycle was no longer the sole determinant for life in Hunza; other factors—such as education, a regular income, and jobs—became just as important.

Musicians were also faced with trying to change their poor reputation, which was derived from the connection of their profession with the devil.

They saw only one possibility: to stop being musicians as long as members of the larger society refrained from making music in public *with* them. This suggestion was rejected by members of the wider society. Although most people from Hunza argue that music is still an integral part of their life, they make a strict division between music making and listening or dancing to music. The implication is that music making is the role of the Dom while listening and dancing is the role of everyone else. As a general rule, members of the Dom community were not allowed to dance in public. For example, when a festival was celebrated, a representative or a group of representatives of each village was allowed to dance. Turn by turn every village was represented in a fixed succession. Only the village of Mominabad was excluded from this turn taking. One of the reasons for the Dom's exclusion was that dancing is considered by the whole society to be a prestigious and graceful activity, not fitting for the Dom. The Dom want to have an equal share in dancing and demand that the members of the wider society share music-making with them.

Whereas music is attached to the culture and worldview, the work of the blacksmith is associated primarily with the economy. Blacksmiths also participated in politics, as producers of weapons; in religion, as those who melted iron to resist evil influences; and in jurisprudence—conducting the fire ordeal to convict thieves and other culprits. In modern times, the only remaining role for blacksmiths is the economic one.

The blacksmiths of Hunza had only simple tools to work with and could not melt iron ore. Therefore, the production of new tools for agricultural purposes or for household use depended on the availability of steel, which was scarce in Hunza. Nonetheless, blacksmiths stress that their profession has been necessary to the cultivation of the land, for a long time the main economic activity in Hunza. With the importation of new technologies and readymade utensils, blacksmithing was reduced to repairing agricultural equipment such as axes, shovels, sickles, and pitchforks. The blacksmiths working in and around Mominabad practice their craft as a part-time job and find other jobs, such as watchman, day laborer, and mason. Some began working in repair shops in Gilgit, while others found employment in technical establishments working on apparatus such as water turbines. These last two sectors are considered to be modern extensions of their original profession.

The problems described above—lack of work, the struggle for recognition by the wider society, and the like—and the necessity of guaranteeing a regular income for an entire family have made it permanently necessary for both blacksmiths and musicians to readapt their identities and perceptions of their trade within the larger society.

Environmental Crisis

One way to deal with the new economic and political realities described above is to make accommodations to new developments. One of the new developments within Hunza is the result of the extension of the infrastructure that will connect all villages with the Karakoram Highway (KKH) to facilitate transport and to give people access to schooling and the medical system. Within the last ten years, the so-called link roads multiplied between villages and between villages and the KKH, diminishing the arable land. In 1999, an older and much smaller link road between Mominabad and Karimabad was abandoned and a new one constructed, linking the village directly with the KKH and with Karimabad. On the new road, trucks can travel to the Bazar in Karimabad, which sometimes causes traffic jams but which also makes it easier to sell the potatoes grown near the road. Various shops and tea stalls are also appearing along the new road. A Dom from another village commented on these developments:

> The new road is bad for Mominabad. It causes disturbances and trouble and the land is lost. For example the carpenter's shop. Four people from Mominabad rented this piece of land and constructed their shop. Shortly afterwards they started a quarrel with the owner; they refused to pay the rent because they had not enough orders. Now they have invested but they don't get back anything in return. They got only problems. They wanted to make big money fast. Instead they should have seen to the education of their children. Another problem is the tea stall with the dish antenna. Many people meet there. It keeps the people away from their daily work. All advantages of the road are going to the people in Karimabad.

Because of the new road, people from other villages wanted to buy land in Mominabad to build a new hotel, but the landowners resisted selling it. "Those are the best fields in all of Mominabad," one owner said. Entrepreneurial desire looms large; but instead of selling the land to people from other villages, the owners might sell it to a denizen of Mominabad who will build a hotel and become a hotelier himself instead of working for hotel owners from the wider society.

This episode should be seen in the context of the place of tourism in Hunza, a valley that is famous for the mythological longevity of its people thought to result from special diets. To give just one example of Hunza hokum:

> Hunza inspired James Hilton to write his modern fable, "Lost Horizon". In winter the people eat flour made from apricot kernels, drink . . . wines from the grapes that grow everywhere, smothering the poplars and roofs. This *unvarying diet* of

fruit and the waters of its rivers—which tastes like a sludge of porridge and gravel—certainly seems to work. *Many centenarians still work their fields in Hunza.* [emphasis added] (http://www.infohub.com/TRAVEL/SIT/sit_pages/ 16075.html; downloaded 22.12.2006)

The area is also known for the natural beauty of the mountainous landscape. One writer described it this way: "Rakaposhi, its snows are like a gleaming kaleidoscope of changing colors throughout the day as the sun shifts across the horizon and filters through the billowing clouds that boil and fret around its crown" (ibid.). Similar descriptions can be found in abundance on the Internet. For Mominabad, it is not the hosting, guiding, and driving that connects them to tourism, but their music. It is common for musicians to be brought to one of the hotels—mainly in Karimabad—to perform for tourists, with sessions lasting between one and two hours depending on the local audience. For the musicians, this has meant a new way to earn money. Many people from Hunza lament the poor quality of music, attributing it to illiterate foreigners, and they lament the newly established market for musical performances that have led to higher prices for musicians who perform in local events.

Sociocultural Crisis

Some people in Mominabad see low school attendance as a major threat. Recent developments in Hunza have occurred so rapidly that it has seemed impossible to catch up on missed education. As a result, people from the Dom have tried to make a living without adequate education. According to one Dom, some parents are still asking for an exemption so their children will not have to attend school. They give as reasons a heavy workload or the illness of family members, but "they are just not aware of the importance of education. They think it is more important to have the boy attending the sheep and goats than the school." This attitude toward schooling is often related to (1) their professions, especially to music, and (2) to the specific history of the Dom. It is said that their profession as musicians consumes all attention and energies. But this reasoning is no longer valid, since literally no Dom now chooses the profession of musician. The second point—the relation to their history and treatment within the wider society of Hunza— might still be applicable to a certain extent: As early as the 1960s some boys from Mominabad wanted to go to school but the ruler and his advisors refused permission because they feared they would lose the services of musicians and blacksmiths: "We don't need clerks, we need musicians and blacksmiths", argued the ruler and his advisors. One of those early pupils, who was initially not allowed to go to school and who is now about 50 years old, devoted a lot of time and money to increasing his generation's awareness of the importance of education. He endowed an award for the best pupils of Mominabad, hoping for improvement of the situation through this stimulus. The results have not been very promising. "I don't know what to do anymore," he said. "There are some students going to college, but most of the pupils are simply not interested in going to school. If they go, their results are pitiful."

Another major crisis—primarily identified by the older Dom—is the diminishing quality of the local music. Although there have been efforts to abandon music altogether, trained middle-aged musicians still perform on a variety of occasions. The atmosphere is no longer stimulating, however; new tunes are rarely composed, musicians have no time to practice, and tunes are forgotten because they were associated with specific occasions no longer observed. Dance ceremonies are still held, but the dancers do not know the basic behavior—that is, to be in control of one's own body and of the musicians playing for them. Members of the wider society lament that the musicians are no longer guaranteed to give their level best in these ceremonies but perform according to the expected award—namely the money paid to them by individual dancers. This is seen as a lamentable loss of tradition by members of the wider society as well as by most of the Dom. Some elders among the Dom emphasize the ability of music—including the dancing as well as playing the instruments—to induce sorrow as well as joy: "We did not have many things then, not like today. But it was a pleasure to see outstanding dancers."

Another problem is the increasing quarrels in Mominabad. Dom have always had the reputation for arguing among themselves. "They quarrel and insult each other without any reason" is a common statement about them. Even the Dom themselves hint that this is a specific feature of their lives. Moreover, they are considered to be envious of better-off neighbors. New developments such as the road, increased business facilities, or competing for tourist work increase the possibilities of inequalities among the Dom: More powerful members of the community often gain better access to new opportunities to earn money. Thus, these already better-off households are further privileged. For example, the village elders are to be informed about a musical performance for tourists. Instead of notifying all the musicians, these elders decide among themselves who takes part in the ensemble. This competitive behavior makes it difficult to work out common goals and to act on them. However, several initiatives have been taken to respond to the challenges of modernity and development by Dom, clearly realizing the necessity to act as a community.

Response: Struggles to Sustain Cultural Survival

Associations and Institutions

Cultural survival for the Dom does *not* mean keeping things as they were for "hundreds of years." Cultural survival means developing strategies and institutions that sustain the Dom's goals in ever-changing circumstances. The Dom have always had to respond to changing circumstances, beginning with their arrival in Hunza, and continuing through their efforts to be integrated in the larger culture and their fights to acquire basic assets for agriculture. While talking about their history, many Dom emphasize a prosperous past, but this is always in relation to certain events, not as a generally accepted perception of the past.

At the same time, common action has always been a difficult task among the Dom, although they have attempted at times to organize themselves. The first attempt at organization was formation of the group called the Associations of Moghuls (*anjuman moghulia*, Moghul referring to the famous Muslim dynasty ruling India from the 16th to the 18th century) in the early 1980s. The initiative for this association came from the blacksmiths among the Dom in Nager, and their primary goal was to safeguard their own interests. With the abolition of the local ruler (1972 in Nager, 1974 in Hunza), the practice of servicing fixed villages by a specific blacksmith could no longer be enforced. Nonetheless, the villagers attempted to get blacksmiths to carry on under the same conditions, repairing their iron tools and being paid once a year in kind. The blacksmiths protested, stressing that they were now in a position to determine the terms of trade. They wanted to be paid in cash and suggested fixed prices for each item they had worked on. It was clear that their claims could only be enforced by group pressure, which meant that each blacksmith associated himself with these ideas. Thus, blacksmiths from Nager approached their colleagues in Hunza to present their ideas and ask them to join the association. After many discussions and an agreement in principle, the Hunza blacksmiths declined the offer, arguing that they would be in a difficult position in Hunza if they did so. Because the people of Nager belong mainly to the Twelver-Shi'a sect and the people in Hunza belong to the Ismaili sect, the blacksmiths from Hunza argued that joining the new association would contradict their participation in the Ismaili institutions that were of prime importance in their lives. The goal of setting new terms finally was achieved, though after a prolonged process, during which many blacksmiths had to struggle on their own. There is still one blacksmith in Hunza who works on the basis of payment per year.

A similar undertaking was the foundation of an association for musicians. In the early 1990s, many discussions took place about the composition of ensembles performing for tourists. After a period when musicians received a meager income and musical performances were obviously being devalued, the growing tourist trade seemed to promise new occasions for musical sessions and acceptable compensation. One ensemble of musicians tried to monopolize the business and to get as many engagements as possible. They did not inform the other musicians of their plan and tried to make deals with hotel owners and others who serviced the tourists. The musicians who had been excluded from the plan held a meeting, discussed the problems, and came to the conclusion that an association should be responsible for all affairs of the musicians, maintaining a rotating system of engagements, ensuring adequate payment, and overseeing the recording of tunes and the selling of cassettes. The association worked for some time, but in the long run the divergent interests of the individual musicians could not be brought together.

The third and most successful association is the Gilgit Hunza Da'ud Social and Educational Welfare Organization, Mominabad, Hunza, founded and registered as a nongovernmental organization (NGO) in 1994. This association has a social and educational program for the villagers in Mominabad as well as for the Dom who live outside the village. One of the members recalls:

> Before the foundation was set up we discussed the purpose of the NGO. We agreed on doing social and educational work. We outlined the bylaws and went for registration with the government office in Gilgit and with the Ismaili council. All the members paid their share and it was a good start. But then a quarrel came up between the founders of the Organization. And nothing was done. Now [in 1999] we have taken over the institution and started to work. The biggest problem is raising funds. But we got some donations. The new school was built from money donated to the Organization.

Asked about the organization's goals, one member said:

> We are trying to offer help to people who are ill but cannot afford to go to the hospital. We hire a vehicle for their transport and support them for their treatment. We support widows and orphans who cannot earn money. There are poor households, they cannot afford to send their children to school, we are trying to help them. We help the poor students who cannot pay the monthly fees. We try to convince the children that they should learn one of our professions when they can't go to school. We encouraged the master musicians to start teaching our children again. Wherever our people are living we have to try to help them whenever necessary. So far only a few people in need got money. We have to raise more funds, but I am confident.

It remains to be seen whether his confidence is justified.

The Impact of a Religious Leader

The members of the Ismaili community belong to a major Shi'a Muslim sect that is scattered worldwide. Their religious leader—the 49th Imam—is His Highness Karim Aga Khan al-Husseini, also known as Aga Khan. His first visit to his followers in Hunza took place in 1960, a day that is still commemorated by festivals. His latest visit to Hunza took place on September 29, 1996, to witness the inauguration of the restored Baltit Fort. The restoration of this roughly 700-year-old fort took four years, cost $2.15 million, and was undertaken by the Aga Khan Trust for Culture. The opening of the restored fort, which is once again a major tourist attraction in Hunza, was eagerly awaited, as was His Highness. To his followers, his speeches as well as his written and other oral advice to his followers are not just reminders but guidelines for the conduct of daily life. His advice on a specific topic is read out in the *jamaat khana*, and every follower is expected to observe it (e.g., when the Aga Khan decreed that drugs should be abandoned, the Ismaili community stopped selling cigarettes). In the speech he gave that day (which is widely available; see http://www.ismaili.net/fair/video/tv_spc.html; downloaded 22.12.2006), he elaborated on the meaning of culture and tradition for human beings in general and for people in Hunza specifically. He stressed the necessity of "community participation in, and in sustenance of, local tradition and cultural identity . . ." while dramatic changes and developments are taking place. "Values and ideals, and the identities to which they relate and give form, have always been important for humankind. They give direction and points of reference in the face of rapid change. Successful development requires community engagement and mobilization, but it also needs to occur in a cultural context which preserves individual local values and ideals." These statements, together with a personal encounter between His Highness and one of the musicians and his remarks on the musical performances during the opening ceremony (cf. http://www.ismaili.net/foto/people1.jpg, downloaded 22.12.2006) dramatically changed the negative attitudes of the Dom toward their music. In his summons, His Highness said, "We must fight the degradation of our traditions in all fields." The musicians recognized this as a task to be reckoned with in the future. The musicians who were involved in the reception of the Aga Khan proudly tell the story of their direct and indirect encounter with him, detailing the order of events and recounting his statements. For instance, he said that he preferred the traditional Hunza music to other imported musical entertainment. Most important, however, was his instruction to one musician that the Dom are the bearers of a long tradition that must be carried on. His Highness also bestowed the most honorable title within the Ismaili community on that musician for the cultural services he rendered to the community. This recognition not only served the image of the Dom, but it also stimulated people among the Dom *and* among the wider society to learn how to play a musical instrument. The elation has lasted, and there are roughly 20 young, new musicians among the Dom. Three ensembles of them were engaged to perform during the visit of His Highness Karim Aga Khan, with Prince Charles and his wife Camilla, in 2006.

How many musical students from the wider society are still active is hard to know. The new musicians are serious about their new task. In one of the villages, a dramatic competition was held between musicians from the Dom and from the other members of the community, an event unheard of before His Highness's visit.

One problem remains to be solved: If a new generation of musicians is to be trained, who will teach them? Several musicians suitable for the job feel too old and have been too long out of the field. The middle generation might be able to teach, but, as one person said, "they have to learn the old tunes themselves. How would they teach a young generation?" The challenge now is to contextualize the music that remains and to see to it that the stigma placed on the Dom is not attached to these new contexts. This means that the wider society will also need to see the Dom in new ways.

New Identities

Another consequence of the restoration of the Baltit Fort was the inclusion of the village Mominabad in the social structure of Karimabad. This means that the group of Dom living in Mominabad is considered the fifth kin-group of the larger village. It is doubtful that this will lead to the longed-for integration in the system of intermarriages, but it has led to the inclusion of the Dom in village planning. The Dom send two members to the Town Management Society of Karimabad, hold jobs at Baltit Fort, are involved in the new environmentally sensitive sanitation projects, to name the most important fields. These arrangements have enabled interactions among people in spheres so far not shared by the Dom with the wider society.

Food for Thought

The identity of the Dom was first established through the professions of music and blacksmithing, a separate language, a common history of migration, kinship, and life in a separate village. This identity was partly ascribed from outside and partly undertaken by the Dom themselves. The features of their identity were at times emphasized and at times downplayed. Whereas the language was first a means of security and communication, it later became the sign for the Dom's low social status. Political changes led to a rupture in their musical activities—not because they no longer took place, but because the value system strongly associated with the ruler was no longer valid, and thus the context of the musical performances had to be reconsidered. New economic developments and close connections to global events also have had consequences for the village of Mominabad. The construction of the new road carries positive as well as negative consequences, and the Dom now participate in the new businesses of tourism as both musicians and as businessmen.

The most immediate problem to solve is to find a balance between subtle adaptation and uncontrolled exploitation of their resources, such as land in the road construction and shop installation. To get close to a solution, common goals must be defined and implemented. The Gilgit Hunza Da'ud Social and Educational Welfare Organization, Mominabad, Hunza might be the institution that can promote a solution. It certainly strengthens an understanding of an overall identity of the Dom, even though they live in many villages. The impact of the Aga Khan's words and actions vis-à-vis the musicians might be an indication of a stronger sense of community. The new organization began its work with a strong social emphasis and a willingness to support members of the community. It may be able to induce a change in attitude as well and involve all community members in the new developments.

To Think About

1. Is the lifestyle of the Dom "threatened" or do the Dom merely need to adapt it to changing conditions? Gather arguments for both positions. What importance does a language have for the identity of a people? Is this importance attached to the language of the Dom as well?
2. What are the positive and negative aspects of the impact of the Aga Khan on the continuation of the musical tradition? Do you think a tradition has to remain unchanged? Is it possible to talk about an unchanged tradition of the Dom with reference to their professions?
3. What impact does tourism have on the culture and life of the musicians?
4. What are the goals of the newly established institution Gilgit Hunza Da'ud Social and Educational Welfare Organization, Mominabad, Hunza? What would be your guess about the success of this institution?

Resources

Published Literature

Backstrom, Peter C. 1992. Domaaki, in Peter C. Backstrom & Carla F. Radloff. *Languages of Northern Areas. Sociolinguistic Survey of Northern Pakistan, Vol. 2*. Islamabad: National Institute of Pakistan Studies & Summer Institute of Linguistics, 77–83.

Dani, Ahmad Hasan. 1989. *History of Northern Areas of Pakistan*. Islamabad: National Institute of Historical and Cultural Research.

Fussman, Gérard. 1989. Languages as a Source for History, in Ahmad Hasan Dani ed. *History of the Northern Areas of Pakistan*. Islamabad: National Institute of Historical and Cultural Research, 43–58.

Kreutzmann, Hermann. 1989. *Hunza. Ländliche Entwicklung im Karakorum*. Berlin: Dietrich Reimer Verlag.

———. 1991. The Karakoram Highway: The Impact of Road Construction on Mountain Societies. *Modern Asian Studies* 25(4): 711–736.

———. 1993. Challenge and Response in the Karakoram: Socioeconomic Transformation in Hunza, Northern Areas, Pakistan. *Mountain Research and Development* 13(1): 19–39.

———. 2000. Water management in mountain oases of the Karakorum, in Hermann Kreutzmann ed. *Sharing Water: Irrigation and Water Management in the Hindukush–Karakorum–Himalaya*. Karachi: Oxford University Press, 90–115.

Lorimer, David L.R. 1939. *The Dumaki Language. Outlines of the Speech of the Doma, or Bericho, of Hunza*. Nijmegen, Netherlands: Dekker and van de Vegt N.V.

Müller-Stellrecht, Irmtraud. 1979. *Materialien zur Ethnographie von Dardistan (Pakistan). Aus den nachgelassenen Aufzeichnungen von D.L.R. Lorimer. Teil I: Hunza*. Graz, Austria: Akademische Druck-u. Verlagsanstalt.

Schmid, Anna. 1997. *Die Dom zwischen sozialer Ohnmacht und kultureller Macht. Eine Minderheit im Spannungsfeld eines interethnischen Relationengeflechts*. Stuttgart: Franz Steiner Verlag.

———. 2000a. Music of the Northern Areas of Pakistan, in Alison Arnold ed. *Garland Encyclopedia of World Music. Vol. 5: South Asia*. New York: Garland Publishers, 792–801.

———. 2000b. Minority Strategies to Water Access: The Dom in Hunza, Northern Areas of Pakistan, in Hermann Kreutzmann ed. *Sharing Water: Irri-gation and Water Management in the Hindukush–Karakoram–Himalaya*. Karachi: Oxford University Press, 116–131.

Tahir Ali. 1981. Ceremonial and Social Structure among the Burusho of Hunza, in Christoph Fürer-Haimendorf ed. *Asian Highland Societies in Anthropological Perspective*. New Delhi: Sterling Publishers, 231–249.

———. 1983. *The Burushos of Hunza: Social Structure and Household Viability in a Mountain Desert Kingdom*. Ann Arbor: UMI Dissertation Information Service.

Tierney, John. 1990. Three Secrets of Shangri-la. *Health* 4(4): 38–48.

Internet

Domaaki, the language of the Dom:
http://www.ethnologue.com/show_language.asp?code=dmk (downloaded 22.12.2006)
Hunza musicians on the Web:
http://www.ismaili.net/foto/people1.jpg (downloaded 22.12.2006), an ensemble of Dom musicians playing in front of the newly restored Baltit Fort at the opening ceremony, inaugurated by His Highness Aga Khan. The musicians are dressed in garments specific for festive occasions.
http://ismaili.net/foto/hunza5.html (downloaded 22.12.2006)
Baltit Fort: history, restoration, and opening ceremony; also, restoration of village of Karimabad:
http://web.mit.edu/akpia/www/AKPsite/4.239/baltit/baltit.html (downloaded 22.12.2006)
http://www.ismaili.net/speech/s960929.html (speech of His Highness Aga Khan from September 29,1996, downloaded 01.06.2006)
http://www.akdn.org/hcsp/pakistan/PakistanBrief_0505.pdf (downloaded 01.06.2006)
http://www.highbeam.com/library/docfreeprint.asp?docid=1G1:19330788& ctrlInfo=Round20%3AMode20d%3ADocFree%3APrint&print=yes (downloaded 01.06.2006)
Ismaili sect of Islam:
http://www.ismaili.net/histoire/main.html (downloaded 22.12.2006)
http://members.tripod.com/~ismailis/ismailism.html (downloaded 22.12.2006)
Tourism (I suggest that the students search for Websites on this topic)

Organizations

Aga Khan Foundation (NGO) http://www.akdn.org/agency/akf.html (downloaded 02.04.2007)
Aga Khan Trust for Culture (NGO) http://www.akdn.org/agency/aktc.html (downloaded 02.04.2007)
Town Management Society, Karimabad (NGO). Karimabad, Hunza, Pakistan.
Institute of Ismaili Studies, London http://www.iis.ac.uk/home.asp?l=en (downloaded 02.04.2007)

7

Peoples and Cultures of the Kashmir Himalayas

Aparna Rao and Michael J. Casimir

> *O land of blue mountains, verdant valleys and murmuring streams!*
> *Whose envy has eaten into your beauty?*
> *Hamlets on fire, wailing women and children, booming guns,*
> *Who has poisoned the fragrant air?*
> *Who are those ravaging the valley of flowers,*
> *And beguiling the innocent people of Kashmir?*

—a Kashmiri song sung by Gul Akhtar, a professional Kashmiri Muslim woman musician who can no longer sing in Kashmir

This chapter discusses the current situation of a range of communities inhabiting the Valley (or Vale) of Kashmir, referred to as "Kashmir," which forms part of a greater political entity known as Jammu & Kashmir (J&K). The chapter illustrates how political violence not only endangers human lives but also tears apart the sociocultural fabric and ecological integrity of an entire region.

Administered as a self-governing province within India since 1947, J&K consists of Kashmir (ca. 15,948 km²), the area immediately south of the Pir Panjal range, loosely referred to here as Jammu (ca. 28,293 km²), and Ladakh (59,146 km²); it constitutes some 65 percent of the ca. 222,237 km² territory of the former feudal state of Jammu & Kashmir ("Greater Kashmir"), one of the roughly 500 princely states in South Asia under British paramountcy. The remaining 35 percent (ca. 85,791km²) is either directly administered by Pakistan (the Northern Territories), or nominally independent (Azad Kashmir). A small portion is under Chinese control. The legal status of the entire area is controversial, with India and Pakistan battling over it, and major sections of the population demanding independence from both

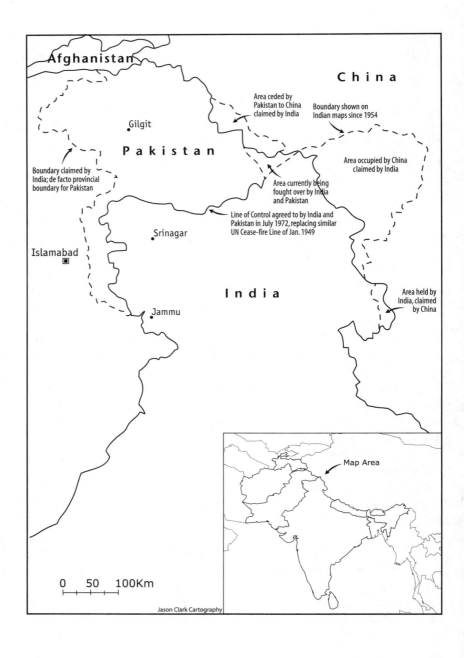

Afghanistan

China

Area ceded by
Pakistan to China
claimed by India

Boundary shown on
Indian maps since 1954

•Gilgit

Pakistan

Area occupied by China
claimed by India

Boundary claimed by
India; de facto provincial
boundary for Pakistan

Area currently being
fought over by India
and Pakistan

Line of Control agreed to by India and
Pakistan in July 1972, replacing similar
UN Cease-fire Line of Jan. 1949

•Srinagar

Islamabad
■

India

Area held by
India, claimed
by China

•Jammu

0   50   100Km

Map Area

Jason Clark Cartography

("self-determination"). Since 1990 Kashmir has become the scene of a major armed conflict.

The People

Several communities inhabit Kashmir. The mother tongue for most is some form of Kashmiri, a Sanskrit-based Indic language, with major vocabulary inputs from Persian (official census figures mention 13,69537 speakers in 1941, rising to 28,06,441 in 1981). There are also large sections of Gujari speakers, smaller numbers of Pahari speakers, and pockets of Punjabi and Dogri speakers. Additionally, nomadic Bakkarwal and Banihara herders speaking Gujari dialects move through the vale between their summer and winter pastures. In the following discussion, the term *Kashmiri* designates exclusively the language and those who speak it as their mother tongue.

The Setting

Kashmir can roughly be divided into three geographical and ecological zones: the basin with Dal and Wular Lakes, the western and southwestern ranges of the Pir Panjal, and the northeastern ranges of the Greater Himalayas (Figure 1). The major river systems of the Jhelum and Sind cut across all these zones, which, in accordance with their climate and soil, are used to grow rice and other crops in the basin, and mainly maize on the subalpine slopes

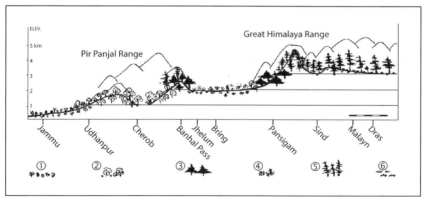

Figure 1   Profile from the Jammu region across the Pir Panjal range over the Banihal Pass and as far as Dras. The individual biotopes encountered are: 1 = subtropical thorn steppe with *Acacia-Carissa-Zizyphus* forest; 2 = forest of *Pinus roxburghii*; 3 = forest of *Cedrus deodar* and *Pinus griffithii*; 4 = Kashmir scrub; 5 = Western Himalayan temperate coniferous forest with *Abies spectabilis* and *Picea smithiana*; 6 = moist alpine scrub and meadows.

up to about 3,500 m. The higher forest areas and alpine meadows (ca. 3,600 m to 4,500 m) are the summer pastures of various communities.

Kashmir has been inhabited since Palaeolithic times. Several Neolithic settlements referred to in early Hindu and Buddhist texts have been identified. In the 3rd century B.C. it was a major center of Mahayana Buddhism, which spread from here to Central Asia, China, and Java. Both Vaishnavite and a mystic Shaivite form of Hinduism slowly replaced Buddhism from the 5th to 12th centuries A.D., to be largely replaced by Islam, especially from the mid-14th century onward. The 13th century experienced a series of Mongol invaders, who carried off slaves and booty and greatly damaged urban and rural life. From the 16th century onward, Kashmir was absorbed into the Mughal (1586–1753), Afghan/Pashtun (1753–1819), Sikh (1819–1846), and Dogra (1846–1947)-cum-British (1899 till 1947) empires and was integrated into the Indian state in 1947.

From the mid-14th century onward, and increasingly from the 17th century, Persian replaced Kashmiri as the official language. Cultural identity was further transformed in the 19th century, when Persian, completely absorbed by the elite, was replaced by Urdu, up to that point an entirely alien language. With the withdrawal of the British and partition of the Indian subcontinent in 1947, the formation of the two independent states of Pakistan and India and the division of J&K polarized political emotions increasingly along religious lines. Sociocultural allegiance wavered between Pakistan and India and the notion of an independent state of Kashmir.

Traditional Subsistence Strategies

Kashmir is mainly rural, and till the early 20th century was often ravaged by famines, floods, and epidemics. Village economy is based on primarily subsistence agriculture (rice at lower altitudes and maize and buckwheat in the upper reaches) and largely mobile animal husbandry (sheep, cows, horses, mules, buffaloes, goats), with significant inputs from horticultural cash crops (saffron, apples, walnuts, almonds) and forestry (timber, mushrooms, etc.). In pre-Islamic times, certain lands were owned by peasants; thereafter, though tenure systems changed, villagers generally enjoyed hereditary occupancy rights. In 1947 most cultivable land was held by Hindu Dogras from Jammu, by local Sayyeds, by once-immigrant Pashtuns, and by a sprinkling of others (Kashmiri Hindus and Muslims and a few Sikhs). Land reforms in 1950 made all holdings the property of the tiller, of whom the vast majority are Kashmiri Muslims. With demographic growth and individual land holdings fixed at 8.8 hectares, many Kashmiris work as tenants—Muslims for other Muslims and Hindus, Hindus for other Hindus, and Sikhs for other Sikhs.

Not every villager was a tiller, and larger settlements have service groups of the Muslim smiths, carpenters, weavers, potters, and the like, required to sustain the agro-pastoral economy. Most village herds are entrusted to shepherds (*pohol*) who drive them to higher pastures in the summer. The Gujar, Bakkarwal, and Banihara take their own herds to pasture in alpine meadows. The land neighboring most nonalpine lakes and waterways, including Dal Lake in the capital Srinagar, is inhabited by one of the eight endogamous Hanz (or Hanji) communities that subsist by growing vegetables, collecting horned waternuts to grind into gruel or turn into cakes, working in summer as menials on tourist houseboats (*doonga*) and in winter as day laborers, hiring out houseboats, fishing, collecting and selling driftwood, or transporting goods along waterways.

Houseboats are important for Srinagar's summer tourist industry, which started in the mid-19th century with mainly British tourists. Europeans were debarred from owning land and hotel development was minimal, but houseboats, which could be owned by Europeans, developed. Europeans also influenced the carpet and shawl industries, and the late 19th to early 20th centuries saw British carpet manufacturers establish their own factories. From the 17th till the late 19th century, shawl weaving depended largely on exports to France, where the Empress Josephine made "cashmere" pashmina shawls a fashion. After 1870, demand declined with the Franco-Prussian war, and many shawl weavers (mostly Sunni, unlike the factory owners, who are mostly Shia), worked in the newly established state silk factory and the new carpet factories opened by Europeans.

Other urban subsistence strategies range from those of administrators, lawyers, doctors, teachers, professional musicians and dancers, to traders, shopkeepers, various craftsmen, bakers, butchers, and manual laborers. Kashmir participated in a trade network criss-crossing the entire Western Himalayas, Tibet, and Central Asia until World War II, when new international frontiers developed and demand for many nonindustrial products decreased.

Until the 1960s, rural production was largely subsistence based, with few extremes of poverty or wealth. Urban poverty, by contrast, was great, with large-scale winter migration of manual labor. The introduction of massive Indian subsidies slowly improved the economy and created a dense structure of family networks between trade, officialdom, artisanship, cash crop agriculture-cum-horticulture, and politics. A broad Kashmiri Muslim middle class emerged, increasingly alienated from Kashmiri Hindus and united with the landed gentry and the urban mercantile class in a system of unparalleled corruption that exploited the vast numbers of Muslim poor. With subsidies in agriculture and horticulture, economic gains gradually percolated to the villages, bringing vastly improved food availability, clothing, and communication. The population grew and rural surplus labor increased. But rising incomes coupled with free schooling made Kashmiri Muslim youth disdain manual labor, migrate to towns, and add to the urban unemployed. Seasonal emigration declined, and long-term job migration was negligible. Instead, seasonal immigrant Indian labor was recruited to supplement local Gujars in a variety of manual jobs, from construction to harvesting. Minimal natural resources and a fragile ecology render heavy industry impossible. No private industrial investment took place and unemployment among the minimally educated grew. In the late 1970s and 1980s Kashmiri Muslim professionals started emigrating to the Gulf and the West, creating a remittance economy that fueled land speculation and rapid urbanization among the middle class, whose opulent lifestyle was disapproved of by conservative urban working- and lower-middle classes, most of whom also had some formal education by now.

Religion and Worldview

Hinduism

Kashmiri Hindus follow a distinctive form of nondualistic Shaivite faith and practice (*trika* philosophy). Numerous mountain peaks, springs, rivers, and lakes have mythological moorings, often bear mythological names (e.g., Ganishbal, Sita Nag, Dodh Sar), and are considered sacred. They are associated with a variety of spirits, "local goddesses," and other essentially benevolent personae. Hindu pilgrimage sites are spread across southern Kashmir.

Ancient temples were built near prominent landmarks, but the vast majority were either destroyed in the 14th–15th centuries or fell into disuse thereafter. Their smaller remnants were often targeted and destroyed in more recent decades, especially in urbanized areas. More recent temples were built near small towns and most homes had a prayer room or niche.

Islam

By the early 14th century, Islam had entered Kashmir and Hindus of various castes, except the *kshatriya*, had converted, influenced by mystics (*sufis*) from various parts of the Islamic world. While unconverted brahmins increasingly isolated themselves and became apolitical, the political-military elite and the common people built a composite Hindu-Muslim culture, with extensive intermarriage and syncretic beliefs and lifestyles. This changed with the advent of Sayyed 'Ali Hamadani in the last decades of the 14th century. Still revered and loved by Kashmiri Muslims as Shah-e Hamadan, this central figure is controversial among scholars. While most consider him responsible for a radical Islamization that resulted in the forced conversion of most Hindus, destruction of most of their temples, flight of most remaining brahmins, heavy taxation of those who remained and resisted, and the mass destruction of Sanskrit texts, some suggest that he only worked to create a culture more oriented toward the *Sharia*.

Kashmir also has a long tradition of indigenous mysticism that was largely syncretistic. The influence of these ascetic mystics, known as *rishis*, on conversion is also controversial. Some suggest it was minimal, since as hermits they had little contact with the people; others suggest they played a major role. The most celebrated *rishi* was Nur-ud-Din (or Nand Rishi, d. 1439, also known as *Alamdar-e Kashmir*: Kashmir's standard bearer), whose shrine in Chrar-e Sharif is a major pilgrimage site for both Muslims and Hindus, as well as a place where traditional Muslims also offer *Eid* prayers. In 1990, leaders of the Jammu Kashmir Liberation Front (JKLF) vowed here to lead Kashmir to independence, but in May 1995 it was largely destroyed when Indian troops battled Islamist militants of the *Harkat-ul Ansar*, who had placed bombs within the shrine. It has since been partially repaired (see *Responses*). Another important mystic was the brahmin woman Lalla (Lal Ded or Lalleshwari), whose poetry in the North Indian *bhakti* tradition influenced Nur-ud-Din, and through him other *rishis*. Over the centuries their sayings have had great impact on popular spirituality and on the development of the ethos of *kashmiriyat*.

From the mid-18th until the 20th century Kashmir was subjected to a series of bigoted rulers. The Afghans persecuted Shias and Hindus; the Sikhs persecuted Muslims, banning the muezzin's call to prayer, closing many mosques, making cow slaughter punishable by death, nearly destroying the Shah-i-Hamadan mosque, and introducing forced labor. The Dogras continued with oppression, but restored the *azan* in 1932, following massive agitations against their repressive anti-Kashmiri and anti-Muslim policies (see *Political Organization*).

Wahabism, introduced in the late 19th century, had little impact on the faith and practices of common Muslims, who continue to believe in fairies, *jinns,* and other personae in mountains, caves, and springs. They revere their *rishis*, visit their shrines on pilgrimage and for rites of passage (see below and *Sociocultural Crisis*), and faithfully follow spiritual guides (*pirs*) who dispense charms and amulets. Discord and suspicion reigns between Sunnis (the majority) and Shias, who rarely inter-dine. The Shia are feared and despised for a variety of alleged practices, from black magic to cannibalism. Since the 1970s, the *Jama'at-e Islami* (*JI*) of Kashmir has preached a conservative Sunni culture in nearly 3,000 mosques and systematically inculcated radical Islam and contempt and hatred for Hindus in *madrasas* attended by thousands of children. Though their women's wing, the *Dukhtaran-e Millat*, counts some 10,000 members, in poorer rural areas gender relations do not adhere rigidly to the dominant and repressive South Asian patriarchal model. Veiling among women is very rare, except among wealthier, traditional families actively aspiring to higher social status, notably in small towns. Polygyny is rarer still. Dowry is transacted among the urban middle and upper classes, while bridewealth is common among the rural and working classes.

Relations between Muslims and Hindus

Since the 14th century relations between Kashmiri Muslims and Kashmiri Hindus have been ambiguous and controversial. Observers have commented equally on the "fanaticism" of Kashmiri Muslims (e.g., Pelsaert in Ahmad 1979:18) and on their liberality and ". . . the friendly relations existing between [them] and Hindus . . . partly to be explained by the fact that many Hindu customs have survived . . . among Muslims" (Ernest Neve in Bamzai 1987). Perhaps both observations are valid and reflect different aspects of the reality, in different contexts. Three factors exacerbating ambiguity are: the extent of the purity and pollution taboos among different Hindu (see *Social Organization*) subgroups (i.e., the degree of social intercourse between Muslim and Hindu families at different periods); the class characteristics of Muslims and Hindus (Hindus adopted Westernized education earlier than most Muslims, while traditional Muslims tended toward Islamization); the role and propaganda of political players in Pakistan and India (there were no "communal riots" between 1933 and 1986, but political discourse in both countries increasingly underlined religious differences between Kashmiri Muslims and Hindus and unrelenting Pakistani propaganda stressed the importance of Islam).

In spite of deepening mistrust, especially in urban areas, and increasing minor differences in food, dress, and speech, similarities and commonalties are strong between Kashmiri Muslims and Hindus, especially in rural areas. Festivals honoring many *rishis* and the three secular spring festivals (following the Kashmir, Persian, and Hindu calendars) are often celebrated together in villages. Other areas of common concern are attempts to sustain the Kashmiri language, traditional music, folk theater, and *unani* medicine. A few decades ago female personal names were common to both communities and even earlier, Kashmiri Muslim and Hindu males often bore Persian personal names. These have all given way to Arabized and Sanskritic names respectively. Both Muslim and Hindu women wore the traditional *pheran* till 1931, when the latter adopted the *sari*, as a sign of "modernity"; both Muslims and Hindus, Kashmiris and non-Kashmiris sported beards till British influences began dominating. The spiritual, artistic, and linguistic commonalities are often considered to inform a specific lifestyle—*kashmiriyat*. Drawing succor from vague notions of sociocultural harmony and a "simple lifestyle," these values represent a "golden age" of what can be termed "cultural security." Many of the politically conscious use the term, though in diverging ways. For Hindus *kashmiriyat* represents intercommunity togetherness. They link this to an allegedly specifically Kashmiri form of Islam which they think harmonizes with the secular ethos informing the idea of the Indian state. For Muslims, feeling betrayed by the political attitudes of most Kashmiri Hindus, *kashmiriyat* developed from a vague longing for political-cum-cultural identity into a form of Kashmiri Muslim identity, both intimately linked to the concept of an independent Kashmir ("self-determination" for J&K or "Greater Kashmir") state. Islamists reject the term outright, as contradicting the ideals of the global Islamic community and negating their aim of union with Pakistan as a Muslim nation.

Social Organization

Kashmir is predominantly Muslim, with pockets of Hindus and some Sikhs. While Muslims practice all professions, Hindus engage in petty trade and agriculture, hold government jobs, work as white-collar professionals, and as domestic and agricultural labor for other Hindus (especially in northern Kashmir). Sikhs are engaged in agriculture, forestry, petty state services, and small-scale trade.

Both rural and urban society have been extremely peaceful, with no overt violence between any groups or sections. Yet society is marked by extreme class differentiation—reflected among Kashmiri Muslims even in personal names—which follows urban-rural faultlines as well as concepts of descent and origin. Though conversion over the centuries broke down earlier patterns of endogamy, new sociopolitical structures created new, preferentially endogamous categories. Kashmiri Muslims consist of Shias, most of whom entered in the 15th century, and of Sunni Muslims, who classify themselves in the following broad descent categories:

- *Sheikh*: local converts, subdivided into numerous subgroups. Most largely retain their family names, or patronyms (*kram*), indicating their original profession, locality or community—such as Khar (carpenter), Pampori (a place), Butt and Pandit (*brahmin*), Dar (*kshatriya*)—but with increasing Islamization, some have dropped these;
- *Sayyad*: traditionally following spiritual professions; some also belong to the landed aristocracy;
- *Mughal*: immigrants from what was broadly known as "Khorassan" and "Turkistan"; descendants of Central Asian traders and of converts from other parts of South Asia who settled mainly in Srinagar's trading localities.

Additionally, in rural areas there are numerous non-Kashmiri-speaking Gujars and some Pathans (Pashtuns who came with Afghan rule), and in urban areas, a few Punjabi Muslims who immigrated during the construction of the Jhelum cart road in 1890–1891. Relations among these various Muslim communities are strained, the Gujars being despised and the Punjabi Muslims suspected as intrinsically pro-Pakistan.

Kashmiri Hindus are all Saraswat brahmins, known by the exonym *Pandit* (the endonym being *Batta*), a term first reserved for emigrant Kashmiri brahmins in Mughal service. Their surnames (*kram*) designate their original professions or their ancestors' nicknames (e.g., Hakim, Kaul, Dhar, Raina, Teng). Tradition holds that they descend from 11 families who survived the reign of King Sikandar (nicknamed *But-Shikast*, the idol breaker, d. 1413) and his neo-convert minister Suha Bhatta without converting, and others who returned to Kashmir when Sikandar's son and successor Zain-ul Abidin (known to Muslims and Hindus alike as *Bud Shah*, the Great King) reversed the policies of persecution. This flight and return led to two divisions: the *malamasi* (who remained and survived and follow the lunar calendar) and the *banamasi* (who returned from exile and follow the solar calendar). The Islamic environment also created a further economic division marked by differences in customs, speech, dress, and dietary practices between the *bhashyabhat* or *guru* (comprising the *gor*, priests studying the scriptures, and the *jyotishi*, astrologers) and the *karkun* (workers), who constituted the majority and were wealthier. Each of these largely endogamous divisions subdivides into several hundred exogamous lineages. Further differences in dress and speech distinguish the urban (mostly middle and lower middle class, with at least 70 percent literacy) from the rural, the former working in government, entering trade, and also becoming absentee landlords. The rural remain poor and less literate. Further hierarchy consists of families with greater genealogical depth in state service being considered superior.

Finally, some non-Kashmiri Hindus originally from Punjab and Jammu inhabit urban ghettos, notably in Srinagar. Traditionally wholesale traders, their ancestors ran the Dogra administration and had little intercourse with Kashmiris, whom they despised and referred to as *hattos* (coolies). British Residency brought more such families, along with a handful of Kashmiri Hindus descended from long-time emigrant families, to help run the administration in Urdu, which then replaced Persian.

Political Organization

The British assumed power because of their fears of Russian designs on Kashmir—hence the dismissal and enthronement of Dogra rulers according to British preferences, and British introduction of trusted non-Kashmiri and Kashmiri administrators. These manipulations intensified the distrust between Dogras and Kashmiris; it also drove the wedge deeper between Kashmiri Hindus and Muslims, who perceived the British as their saviors.

The increasing influx of non-Kashmiris led to the idea of a discrete Kashmir citizenship. The 1920s saw local Kashmiri Hindus, increasingly eased out of their generations-old positions of administrative power by Hindus from Punjab, agitate for a formal definition of local citizenship (*mulki*). In 1927 a law was passed defining "hereditary state subjects"; only they could hold public office and own land. The 1920s and 1930s witnessed political ferment, with movements for greater religious and political freedom. Political and social organizations and parties formed to represent explicitly Muslim identity. In 1931 some Muslim organizations called for a holy war against the Hindu Dogra rule; others represented secular interests and various economic and social concerns. By 1947 a variety of interest groups and organizations existed. With the decolonization of South Asia and the bloody partition of the subcontinent, Kashmir's last Dogra Maharaja opted for independence, rather than join either India or Pakistan. Internal revolts and an invasion organized by Pakistan forced him to call for Indian help and sign J&K's accession to the Indian Union. Its finality was, however, conditional to ascertaining the peoples' wishes through a plebiscite. While India and Pakistan fought their first Kashmir war, the United Nations declared a ceasefire, and J&K was split between India and Pakistan; the Jammu Kashmir Liberation Front formed, aiming to free Kashmir from both Indian and Pakistani rule. Various arguments and opinions debate India's noncompliance with the promised plebiscite; it suffices here to note that it was not held.

Between 1949 and 1953 J&K was an autonomous member of the Indian Union and was ruled by the National Conference, a local party dominated by Kashmiri Muslims but with non-Muslim members, which carried out numerous reforms, ruled with an iron hand, and aspired to complete independence. In 1953, this government was dismissed, its celebrated leader, Sheikh Abdullah was incarcerated, and a new government was established with Indian help and electoral rigging. New interest groups emerged to function along vertical patron-client chains and cut across networks of wealthy and politically ambitious men, jostling for power by projecting themselves in terms of community and religious allegiances. Especially from the late 1960s, religious affiliations were used to convert economic resources into political representation. Ordinary Kashmiri and Punjabi Muslims were expected to "prove" their allegiance and loyalty to India's ruling elite, which was increasingly demanding monolithic identities and affiliations and rewarding these with greater access to resource networks. Such loyalty was assumed for the Gujars, Sikhs, and Kashmiri Hindus who never protested Indian efforts to establish and maintain a series of nominally elected, puppet regimes.

Threats to Survival

Increasingly, all organized political opposition was muffled and local opposition parties were banned or prevented from electoral participation. Mostly working-class Kashmiri Muslim youth were routinely manhandled, humiliated, and arrested for demonstrating, pelting stones, and shouting "anti-Indian" or "pro-Pakistani" slogans; others were picked up as suspected spies and tortured. The continued suppression of basic democratic rights of Kashmiri Muslims who dared protest became the driving force for Kashmir's nationalist resistance. In 1972, one year after the third Indo-Pakistan war and the formation of Bangladesh, India and Pakistan signed an accord, blending out the wishes of the people of Kashmir.

In the 1980s, Islamist organizations, abetted and funded by Pakistan's Inter Services Intelligence (ISI), increasingly tutored and preached an orthodox and intolerant Islam, while their Hindu counterparts, fostered by constituents of the *Sangh Parivar* and encouraged by India's ruling Congress party, inculcated monolithic and intolerant "Hinduism." Culture in Kashmir split along alleged "Hindu" ("Indian") and "Muslim" ("Pakistani") models. The Soviet defeat in Afghanistan, the demise of Soviet rule in Central Asia, the Iranian revolution, and the rising violent power of right-wing obscurantist and fanatic Hindu and Sikh groups in India encouraged Kashmiri Muslims to increasingly conceive of politics, nationalism, and their own empowerment in terms of religion. Increasingly, Kashmiris of all faiths sought solace in fundamentalist forms of their respective religions, and while most Kashmiri Muslims looked in vain for political alternatives, Kashmiri Hindus asserted their loyalty to India.

With the fraudulent elections of 1987, in which the Muslim United Front (MUF), an opposition conglomeration, was declared defeated despite receiving 60 percent of the vote, most Kashmiri Muslims concluded that parliamentary opposition within the Indian Union was futile. The components of the MUF formed armed outfits (*Al Barq, Al Fateh, Al Jehad,* etc.) and by 1989, secession from India was preached in mosques. Waves of strikes, assassinations, bomb blasts, and arson hit the Valley, peaking in 1990. The initial battle for *kashmiriyat* and the establishment of a Muslim state (*Nizam-e Mustafa/Nizam-e Muslimeen*) soon turned into a holy war (*jehad*) against India. Thousands took up arms funded through Pakistan, proclaiming that every God-fearing man's duty was to fight for justice. This justified extortion, kidnappings, torture, property encroachments, and forcible entry even into Muslim homes, since noncombatants should provide funds. Many wealthy Muslims left Kashmir, and much in-fighting ensued within these multiplying, segmenting and criminalizing militia—*Allah Tigers, Al-Umar Mujahidin, Hizbullah, Ikhwan-ul Mujahidin,* and the like—said to number 177 at one stage.

Aspiring to political power, the Muslim middle and lower middle class supported them all in the name of *kashmiriyat* and Islam.

The call for *jihad* hastened the exodus of almost all Hindus and thus the demise of a common Muslim-Hindu culture. From 1947 on, Kashmir's roughly 700,000 Hindus felt increasingly uneasy and discriminated against, and youth emigrated to India and the West, with small peaks of panic-induced emigration in 1965, 1971 (Indo-Pakistan wars), and 1986 (brief anti-Hindu riots when 36 temples were said to have been attacked). In 1989 the remaining Hindus (about 250,000, of whom 2,000 were government employees) were confronted by posters that made their continued presence conditional on converting. Threatening letters, such insults as *Batta Kafirs* (Brahmin heathens), and attacks on houses followed. Considered "informers" per se, several were shot or burnt alive; even pregnant women, elderly men who had sheltered armed youth, and some Muslims who protested these acts were not spared by JKLF militia, while their leaders killed Indians working in Kashmir and spoke of *kashmiriyat*. With local newspapers spreading rumors that those who stayed would be killed, the militia declaring a holy war, and the Indian governor fueling their fears, most Hindus fled with Indian government help. Only a few of the poorest remained in remote villages, trusting their neighbors and convinced of their safety. Between 1989 and 1992, 49 Hindu temples are said to have been attacked and damaged to varying degrees, while roughly 30,000 homes typifying local wooden architecture were burned or damaged in cross-fire or arson; roughly 200 houses were occupied by militiamen and many hundreds occupied and ruined by Indian armed forces. Some Sikhs also fled, but many remained or returned.

To combat the armed struggle (or "insurgency"), India sent 400,000 soldiers and para-military troops. Kashmiri Muslims were suspected, harassed, and persecuted while a guerrilla war was waged by Kashmiri militants with Pakistani inputs in money, arms, and mercenaries. Gradually, in dread of the troops and the militia, about 1,500 Muslim families fled to India and many thousand to Pakistan. Intermittent shelling by Pakistan and India and the Kargil war (in which Pakistani fighters invaded Kashmir and were eventually driven back by the Indian Army) brought further misery to villagers, notably Gujars, living close to the ceasefire line (or "Line of Control"). Today, there is no civil authority worth the name and *de facto* weapons reign supreme.

Current Events and Conditions

Over a decade of war has seen Kashmiri Hindus flee en masse. It has witnessed common Kashmiri Muslims (about 10,000 of them) "disappear," be robbed, arbitrarily arrested, tortured, raped and killed by Indian forces and pardoned ex-militants ("*Ikhwani*" or "renegades") working for the Government as "counterinsurgents"—and held for ransom, raped, and killed (about 7,000) by their own militias and mercenaries from a variety of Muslim countries. Indian soldiers use their sweeping powers to harass and humiliate, blow up houses, and extract forced labor from craftsmen and manual workers. They are hated and despised for their atrocities, indiscipline, corruption (see *Environmental Crisis*), vandalism, and drunken and marauding behavior, and for selling arms, fuel, uniforms, and ammunition to the very militia they are fighting. The latter are also feared for kidnapping, torturing, torching houses, killing, avenging personal enmities, and fighting over women. Dominated first by the mainly urban JKLF, then by the mainly rurally recruited *Hizb-ul Mujahidin* (HM), the JI's armed wing, and then increasingly by foreign Islamist mercenaries, they kill anyone considered an informer (*mukhbir*): their own or friends' opponents in property disputes and family quarrels, men and women who do not acquiesce, members of all political parties and of other militias. However, fear of being killed and/or of being dubbed "pro-India" and the atrocities of the hated Indian forces discourage complaints (but see below, *Responses*). To curb indiscipline and in-fighting, the All Parties Hurriyat Conference (APHC) was formed to press for "self-determination" and the establishment of a society in keeping with Islamic values. But the APHC is mired in corruption, does not represent even all Kashmiri Muslims, and is split over the means, aims, and implications of their struggle and over the relevance and meaning of *kashmiriyat*, self-determination, and justice. The emergence and military successes of Islamist militias from Pakistan and Azad Kashmir, like the *Lashkar-e Toiba* (LT)—who, drawing on the Sufi concept of returning to God by repenting (and hence fighting), view the struggle as "a war between Islam and paganism"—further complicate the issue of a religious vs. political struggle. The current ceasefire of the Indian government is based on no clear policy perspective and has brought little relief to the common people who yearn for peace; it has, however, exacerbated internal discord, since both the APHC and Islamist groups have rejected peace talks.

The ceasefire between HM and Delhi was renewed twice, but expired in March 2001 without a further extension. An attack on the Indian Parliament (Lok Sabha) in December 2001, with the presumed involvement of Pakistani militants, heavily strained the already fragile bilateral relations and the danger of a nuclear war seemed immanent. In its aftermath a general mobilization of troops along the Line of Control took place, followed by the breaking off of diplomatic and economic ties, the closure of the consulates in Mumbai and Karachi, and the cutting of almost all infrastructural connections. However, recent developments indicate a durable detente in the region: In March 2003 the then prime minister Atal Behari Vajpayee offered his Pakistani counterpart Parvez Musharraf his "hand of friendship" in a public speech in Srinagar.

First steps toward an improvement of bilateral relations were taken in the commitment of New Delhi and Islamabad to agree upon the so-called 12 Point-Program, a detailed plan to resume cooperation in specific areas including culture, economy, and politics. Established under the banner of a "composite dialogue" in autumn 2003, this program provides the basis for the ongoing peace process. The outstanding feature of the recent approach is an explicit clause declaring the aim of reaching "a permanent, peaceful and honorable solution to the Kashmir problem." In November 2003 Islamabad unexpectedly proposed a ceasefire along the Line of Control, and, with the extension of its proposed scope to the disputed Siachen glacier, the agreement was implemented. With the South Asian Association of Regional Cooperation (SAARC) Conference in spring 2004, Indo-Pakistani relations were further strengthened by a joint declaration on fighting terrorism. Some months later the Indian government took up a dialogue with the APHC, which is considered another milestone toward peace in the region. Yet the political meaning of the continuous dialogue is heavily contested inside the sociopolitical scene in Kashmir, since the Indian and Pakistani governments, in accordance with the Simla Agreement of 1972, stressed their will to solve the issue bilaterally. The reversal of the Pakistani government in abandoning the demand for a plebiscite is regarded by many Kashmiri leaders as an act of treason. However, in 2005 another symbolic breakthrough was marked with the establishment of a bus route between Srinagar and Muzafarrabad, connecting the divided parts of Kashmir for the first time in almost 60 years. With the resumption of further infrastructural links between the two countries, notably the Thar Express (connecting Sindh in Pakistan with Rajasthan in India) and the Punjab Express (Lahore-Amritsar), the positive trend of increasing bilateral ties is making progress. What kind of developments will result from the intended nuclear cooperation between Washington and Delhi remains to be seen.

Demographic Trends

For centuries frequent famines, floods, epidemics, wars, and religious persecution made people flee and return after the crises. Such great demographic fluctuations have affected communities differentially, causing fluctuations in intercommunity demographic balances. The last decade was marked by 30,000 to 80,000 deaths and a 70 percent increase in the number of graveyards, every fifth or sixth family losing on average one, usually male, member between 15 and 30 years of age; 2–3 percent of all children have lost their fathers. It is also marked by a massive population exodus of Hindus (see *Political Organization*) now living as refugees in Jammu, Delhi, and elsewhere, and of several thousand Muslims who fled or went off to fight and also ended up as refugees in Pakistan. Both groups suffer from great physical and psychological stress.

In the last 20 years, J&K's entire population has greatly increased (it was at least 10,069,917 in 2001), but figures for Kashmir are vague, since the official decennial census was banned by the militants. Impacted by a reportedly high rate of suicide, especially among the youth, and a growing AIDS problem, the demographic trend in Kashmir remains uncertain.

Environmental Crisis

Over the last several decades the natural environment has been increasingly damaged by population pressure and land speculation. Because of growing demands of urban and rural populations for timber, food, and firewood, cultivation and grazing areas have expanded and extensive tracts of woodland have been cleared for unbridled construction. Erosion and landslides have steadily increased with the overexploitation of forests, where much illegal felling is tolerated. Prior to the war, the expanding tourist industry also posed an increasing threat to the fragile mountain ecosystem. Tourist and trekking firms contributed little to local rural economies, but created waste disposal problems.

The war saw illegal felling increase dramatically, with all armed outfits indulging in the commercial exploitation of forests and powerful networks of well-organized and armed timber smugglers. All counterinsurgency leaders, numerous middle ranking military personnel, and countless militia commanders make fortunes by forcing villagers to illegally fell and transport logs, which are then sold to these smugglers. The net result is rapid deforestation, accompanied by erosion and landslides. One immediate effect has been on the Dal Lake, in Srinagar. Its surface is covered by large patches of red algae, which disrupts the entire natural food chain. Elsewhere, the extreme corruption of several forest department personnel has also led to extensive poaching in national parks and eco-reserves.

Recent years have seen drought, with even the Jhelum drying up in parts and the dry rivulets encroached upon for habitation. Horticulture is badly affected, and in some areas maize is replacing the rice crop which requires more water. In January 2001, with an acute shortage of drinking water and hydroelectric power, thousands convinced that the drought is a punishment for evil, un-Islamic deeds assembled in mosques and offered prayers (*nimaz-e istaqa*) for winter rains. This was in response to an official call for prayers by Kashmir's *Mir Waiz*, himself a member of the APHC, to ask for the pardoning of sins such as greed and corruption and to vow to lead a simpler, uncorrupted lifestyle (see *kashmiriyat* above and below).

Indeed, the war has brought tremendous wealth to most militant leaders and many other politicians, government officials, and their friends and relatives. Indian subsidies have increased and huge amounts of cash are channelled via Pakistan from a variety of sources such as Islamist organizations, Islamic countries, Kashmiri Muslim fund raisers in the West, and migrant labor from Azad Kashmir in the Gulf and in the West. Meant primarily to pay for the families of militants, much of these funds are siphoned off by high-ranking leaders of the various militia, the APHC, and other members of the elite, who use them partly to build palatial houses. With workers imported from India, the construction industry is flourishing and vast amounts of open land are encroached upon with impunity. Even the oldest Srinagar graveyard, founded by Shah-e Hamadan's son, has fallen victim to such encroachment.

Sociocultural Crisis

A decade of violent uprising, brutal Indian repression, and massive Pakistani inputs has left a deep mark on every section of the increasingly shredded sociocultural fabric of Kashmir. The Muslim-Hindu-Sikh culture, disrupted in the early 1990s, was further destroyed in March 1997 and January 1998 with the murder of the remaining Hindus in Sangrampora and Wandhama villages and the massacre of 35 Sikh families in Chhattisinghpora in March 2000. The Gujar are more alienated than before from Kashmiri Muslims, who, though seemingly united, are deeply fissured, if one judges by the frequency with which Indian troops are called upon by individuals to threaten and harass neighbors and relatives with whom they have some personal score to settle. The extensive official deployment of ex-militants as counterinsurgents to raid houses and to interrogate and even summarily kill suspects is possible partly because of this social rupture, but it also exacerbates it.

Living daily with death and the mutilated generates an extremely depressing atmosphere; women especially are affected and suicides are not uncommon. Addiction to opium and hashish, locally grown as well as brought in notably by Pakistani *Jaish-e Mohammad* militia, is also increasing. In a decade of war, children have witnessed torture, rape, and murder by troops and the militia, often in their own homes; they have been used by relatives and neighbors as messengers during curfews, to plant weapons in enemy homes, and as couriers, spies, and hostages. The poorer their families, the greater their exposure to the new culture of violence. Even in villages, with few schools functioning (many schoolteachers were either Kashmiri Hindus or Muslims who became militants), the gun is now a favorite toy and armed children threaten adults for fun or money. This "empowerment" of armed youth has also initiated a breakdown of traditional systems and institutions of family and community authority.

Many young people are also economically sustained by the ongoing war. Not only do many work as contractors for the Indian forces—stitching uniforms; selling meat, poultry, walnuts, vegetables, and fruits; weaving blankets; and making ammunition boxes—but they and their relatives also get a great deal of cash from Pakistan to make up for a variety of financial losses incurred during the war. India also regularly pays families and even entire hamlets to work as informers.

While those in positions of power find the war lucrative, many, including 25,000 women, are reduced to destitution; urban and semi-urban areas are witnessing frequent armed robberies. Given Kashmir's inheritance laws, widows and their children have no right to their husband's or father's property. Child labor is increasing, and fatherless girls find it hard to marry. So do girls who have been raped. Women compelled to look for employment are more than ever sexually harassed; many are forced into prostitution, many more beg in order to survive, and yet others are compelled to remarry, thereby losing their rights over their minor children. Caught between all sections of society, the families of deceased counterinsurgents are the worst affected.

The Islamization of the armed movement has transformed many local religious practices among the urbanized. Formerly Muslims vowed by tying a knot at a local shrine; now instead women pray at home and men in the mosques. The common Muslim-Hindu custom of offering thanks to God has also changed. Formerly both distributed *tahar* (rice cooked with turmeric) among neighbors and the needy, as part of *niyaz* for Muslims; now they donate blood instead. Formerly weddings were merry occasions, with special food (*wazwan*), songs, dancing, and good clothes. So were village fairs and post-harvest gatherings, many closely associated with shrines (e.g., Kambar Sahib at Ganderbal or the *dargah* of Khwaja Muain Shah). All these practices are increasingly criticized and partly even banned. Many new mosques have been built following West Asian architectural models, rather than indigenous styles.

Indeed, as the war progresses, various ideological barriers within Islamic groups have broken down. For example, after 1994, JKLF men joined the far more radical LT or the *Harkat-ul Ansar/Harkat-ul Mujahidin* that is linked to the Islamist *Jama'at-ul Ulema-e Islami*. Increasingly, no discrete boundaries divide fundamentalists from nonfundamentalists, Islamists from non-Islamists—simply shades of grey, representing varying ad hoc strategies based on different aspects of faith and on attempts to fulfil personal commitments to principles of specifically Islamic justice.

Violence-engendered heroes and cultural change brought about the glorification of murderers and "rocket launchers." Young men going to Pakistan for military training were anointed by their mothers with henna; they were welcomed back as heroes by young women who often ran off with them against their parents' wishes. Today militants are no longer heroes, but "martyrs'" graveyards dotting the landscape have become new pilgrimage sites and the funerals of militia leaders sites of popular protest. Numerous older sites of pilgrimage were attacked (see *Responses*) by Islamist militia and on one occasion (*urs* at Aishmuqam) all village men were taken hostage and two were killed. As of this writing the Srinagar office of an Indian newspaper was attacked for publishing a brief report that referred to a book by a renowned Kashmiri Muslim historian who opines that the *rishi*-mystic tradition has Indian connections.

The *rishi* shrines are also connected with Kashmir's long tradition of classical music (*Sufiyana musiqi*) and theatre (*Bhand Pather*). Developing from courtly traditions, the latter has one secular aspect of direct sociopolitical relevance and one mystic and spiritual aspect. The performers are Kashmiri Muslims, and most belong to specific communities of musicians and actors. Their status is extremely low and their meager income derives from their rendering Sufi compositions on feast and memorial days and from wedding performances. Such performers were evicted from shrines (e.g., Khwaja Muain Shah, Rahim Sahib at Safapora, Zain Shah Sahib), their costumes and props were burned by HM militia, and Shameema Akhtar, a rare Kashmiri Muslim woman stage performer, was murdered. A few continued performing in private, deleting women's and Hindus' roles from their repertoires.

Kashmir has no ideology of martyrs, no violent historical role models; instead, in the broader South Asian framework dominated by ideals of machismo, Kashmiris have been stereotyped through the centuries as pusillanimous and without a sense of honor. A belligerent form of Islam provides self-respecting role models from a pan-Islamist repertoire stretching from Afghanistan to Algeria. This repertoire also provides the notion of cultural security intrinsic to all homogeneous and monolithic sociocultural systems, and the new empowering ideology soothes the fears of youth, ill-equipped to cope with increasing globalization, whose effects they reject as nefarious (such as women wearing jeans), yet use (foreign media, videos, and the like, to disseminate political perspectives) and dream of enjoying (such as Western aid money and living standards like those in the Gulf countries). The failure to attain their political and sociocultural aspirations in a decade of war, coupled with the enormous suffering and the political manipulations whereby Kashmiris are not recognized as having contributed to this pan-Islamic repertoire, have led to the intensification of these contradictions and to attempts at resuscitating local Islamic traditions. Several discordant cognitive schemas are now emerging.

Responses: Struggles to Sustain Cultural Survival

Shrines are a major symbol of local Islam and of *kashmiriyat*—and are the site of maximum resistance to Islamist forces. This fact surfaced at Tangmarg during the *urs* of Baba Payamuddin Rishi, whose mausoleum was partly burned down, as it did in Batmaloo at the *urs* of Batmoal Rishi. In 2000, hundreds flocked once again to Suache Kral's shrine in Pulwama, planned to build a mausoleum, and sang songs once again. Similarly, in October 2000 Muslims and some Hindus living in exile prayed at the annual *urs* of Nur-ud-Din/Nand Rishi in Chrar-e Sharif; many others sent donations. Children's heads were shaved as in the past and in 2001 *Eid* prayers were also offered here. In spring 2001, in a much reduced one-week period, rather than the traditional two-months, 20,000 peasants celebrated the festival of lights to herald the sowing season at Zain Shah Sahib.

Many musicians, actors, and actresses who still cannot perform in Kashmir seek venues in Jammu and in India and the West, desperately attempting to keep alive their ancient cultural traditions. Women performers are worst affected, just as women are in general. But women's attempts to sustain culture and to resist cultural domination also appear to be strong.

Women participated in large numbers in the early days of the struggle for independence, demonstrating, planting bombs, throwing grenades, and the like. In April 1992, 5,000 Muslim women openly protested the murder of a Hindu family. After the forces of Islamization took over, stifling their overtly political role, they continued for a while to act as couriers, and whenever possible tried to protect their men from the atrocities of the Indian forces and the extortion attempts of militiamen. Their resistance to Islamization was passive and yet largely successful. Attempts to close women's hairdressing salons; prohibit traditional wedding feasts, music, and dances; and, for a while, ban cosmetics and videos succeeded, but they failed to enforce veiling, forbid colorful clothes, and shut down girls' schools and colleges. Though bands of armed youth combed the lanes to enforce proper behavior and cinema houses were closed, many men refused to grow obligatory beards or regularly attend Friday prayers. The ban on smoking could not be enforced and after 1996 the ban on alcohol was often flouted. Gradually, since 1999, feasting is again a part of many weddings and even music is increasingly heard. In 2000 some Kashmiri Hindu and Muslim women in and beyond Kashmir joined to form Women in Security, Conflict Management and Peace (WISCOMP), an organization that helps them meet, present and discuss their various perspectives, listen to one another, and thereby diffuse tension and create avenues for bringing about peace in their wartorn land.

In Kashmir some local NGOs have also organised help for the needy, especially widows and children of deceased militants; some of these help sustain knowledge and skills in traditional crafts. Numerous community-specific organizations have also emerged outside Kashmir among both Muslims and Hindus. Muslim supporters are mostly located in the West, and are represented by Internet newsgroups and Websites. Kashmiri Hindus additionally organized several conventions, started Kashmiri-language newspapers, and, in December 1991, formed the organization *Panun Kashmir* ("Our Own Kashmir") with the aim of creating a specific political identity and returning to form a separate homeland in southern Kashmir. They have also formed cultural associations in numerous Indian cities, to sustain linguistic, musical, and religious traditions.

Food for Thought

This chapter seeks to illuminate how political violence affects societies, invigorating various ephemeral processes of community identity and ethnicity and devastating cultural cohesion and ecological frameworks. It shows how vested interests can prolong warfare through ties of kinship, friendship, and alliance among the elite on all sides of the political spectrum. It also demonstrates that resistance and collaboration are not discrete practices—middle class Kashmiri Muslims collaborate with India, either directly through political patronage or indirectly through finances, simultaneously supporting and encouraging various militia fighting India. Lastly, it indicates that war tends to break down ideological boundaries, which may be relevant in times of peace.

To Think About

1. Compare the relationship between war and culture in preindustrial and more industrialized societies.
2. What is the relevance of culture in the context of human rights abuses, and can such abuses be perpetrated only by the state or also by other groups and institutions?
3. Can the social sciences play a role in peace initiatives? If so, how? If not, why not?
4. Is field work on any aspect of culture feasible in a situation where countless families grieve over some member who has been killed, tortured, or raped; is in prison; or has disappeared?
5. How would you react if you learned that your research informants were persecuted militia men who had themselves murdered, abducted, or raped?

6. What is the role of culture in defining "freedom fighters" and "terrorists"?
7. How do you think Kashmiri Hindu culture will be affected if the community cannot return to Kashmir?
8. Do you think that the institution of shrines in Kashmir could be used as centers of cultural revival?
9. Discuss the effects political violence can have on gender roles and relations.
10. Comment on:

A. Social cohesion and ethnicity are both processes that are intimately linked to economic and political conditions.

B. "What has happened during these years has been a war by our own against ourselves, for a people who destroy their culture destroy their very being"—a *Bhaand* performer, 1998.

Resources

Published Literature

Ahmad, A. 1979. Conversions to Islam in the Valley of Kashmir. *Central Asiatic Journal* XXIII: 3–18.

Ames, F. 1997. *The Kashmir Shawl and its Indo-French Influence*. Delhi: Timeless Books.

Asia Watch. 1991. *Kashmir under Siege. Human Rights in India*. An Asia Watch Report. New York/Washington, D.C.: Human Rights Watch.

Balagopal, K., M.J. Pandey, S. Rajeshwar and V. Shetty. 1996. *Voting at the Point of a Gun: Counter-Insurgency and the Farce of Elections in Kashmir*. Bombay: Lokshahi Hakk Sanghatana.

Bamzai, P.N.K. 1987. *Socio-Economic History of Kashmir*. Delhi: Metropolitan.

Bose, S. 1997. *The Challenge in Kashmir: Democracy, Self-Determination and a Just Peace*. Delhi: Sage Publications.

Casimir, M.J. 1991. *Flocks and Food: A Biocultural Approach to the Study of Pastoral Foodways*. Cologne: Böhlau Verlag.

Casimir, M.J. and A. Rao. 1985. Vertical Control in the Western Himalayas: Some Notes on the Pastoral Ecology of the Nomadic Bakrwal of Jammu and Kashmir. *Mountain Research and Development* 5(2): 221–232.

———. 1998. Sustainable Herd Management and the Tragedy of No Man's Land: An Analysis of West Himalayan Pastures Using Remote Sensing Techniques. *Human Ecology* 26(1): 113–134.

Chadha Behera, N. 2000. *State, Identity and Violence: Jammu, Kashmir and Ladakh*. Delhi: Manohar.

Chattoo, S. 1992. *The Angel of Death in Disguise: A North Indian Case Study*. University of Western Australia: Centre for Asian Studies, Occasional Paper, 4.

Dhar, D.N. 1989. *Socio-Economic History of Kashmir Peasantry from Ancient to Modern Times*. Srinagar: Centre for Kashmir Studies.

Ganguly, S. 1997. *The Crisis in Kashmir. Portents of War, Hopes of Peace*. Washington, D.C.: Woodrow Wilson Center Series.

Hangloo, R.L. 1995. *Agrarian System of Kashmir*. Delhi: Commonwealth Publs.

Incore. 1999. *Incore Guide to Internet Sources on Conflict and Ethnicity in Kashmir*. NETZ-Kashmir.htm

Indian People's Tribunal. 1997. *Wounded Valley . . . Shattered Souls*. Sixth Indian People's Tribunal Report. Bombay.

Ishaq Khan, M. 1978. *History of Srinagar 1846–1947*. Srinagar: Aamir Publs.

———. 1997. *Kashmir's Transition to Islam: The Role of Muslim Rishis*. Delhi: Manohar.

———. 1998. Kashmiri Muslims: Social and Identity Consciousness, in M. Hasan ed. *Islam, Communities and the Nation: Muslim Identities in South Asia and Beyond*, Delhi: Manohar, 201–228.

Joshi, M. 1999. *The Lost Rebellion: Kashmir in the Nineties*. Delhi: Penguin Books.

Kaul-Bhatia, A. 2001. Other Side of Truth: The Kashmiri Woman's Cry for Peace. *Times of India*, February 1, 2001.

Kaw, M.K., S. Bhatt, B.B. Dhar, A.N. Kaul and G. Bamezai eds. 2001. *Kashmiri Pandits: Looking to the Future*. Delhi: A.P.H. Publ. Corp.

Kishwar, M. 1998. Kashmir and Kashmiriyat: The Politics of Language, Religion and Region, in M. Kishwar, *Religion at the Service of Nationalism and Other Essays*. Delhi: Oxford University Press.

Lamb, A. 1992. *Kashmir—A Disputed Legacy 1846–1990*. Karachi: Oxford University Press. (reprint of 1991)

Lawrence, W. R. 1967. *The Valley of Kashmir*. Srinagar: Kesar Publs. (original published 1895).

Madan, T.N. 1973. Religious Ideology in a Plural Society: The Muslims and Hindus of Kashmir. *Contributions to Indian Sociology* (ns) VI: 106–141.

———. 1989. *Family and Kinship: A Study of the Pandits of Rural Kashmir*. (2nd ed.). Delhi: Oxford University Press.

———. 1992. Pandit of Kashmir, in *Encyclopedia of World Cultures*. Vol. III, South Asia. Boston: G.K. Hall & Co.

Madan, T.N. and A. Rao. eds. (forthcoming). *The Valley of Kashmir: The Making and Unmaking of a Composite Culture?*

Malik, Y. 1997–98. The Right to Self-Determination and Human Rights in Kashmir, in *Fifty Years of the State and Human Rights in South Asia. The Second Amiya & B.G. Rao Memorial Lecture*. Delhi: The Champa Foundation.

Misri, U. 1991. *The Child and Society: A Study of Pandit Children in a Kashmiri Village*. University of Delhi: PhD Thesis.

Puri, B. 1987. Fundamentalism in Kashmir, Fragmentation in Jammu, *Economic and Political Weekly* 22(22): 835–837.

Qureshi, H. 1999. *Kashmir: The Unveiling of Truth*. Lahore: Jaddojuhd Publs.

Rafiqi, A.Q. n.d. *Sufism in Kashmir from the Fourteenth to the Sixteenth Centuries*. Delhi: Bharatiya Publ. House.

Rahman, M. 1996. *Divided Kashmir: Old Problems, New Opportunities for India, Pakistan and the Kashmiri People*. Boulder, CO/London: Lynne Rienner Publs.

Rao, A. 1991. 'I am the Judge and I am the Jury'. Report of the Press Council on Kashmir, *Economic and Political Weekly*, December 14, 2856–2857.

———. 1998. *Autonomy: Life Cycle, Gender, and Status among Himalayan Pastoralists*. Oxford/New York: Berghahn Books.

———. 1999a. The Many Sources of Identity: An Example of Changing Affiliations in Rural Jammu and Kashmir, *Ethnic and Racial Studies* 22(1): 56–91.

Rao, A. 1999b. A Tortuous Search for Justice: Notes on the Kashmir Conflict. *Himalaya Research Bulletin* XIX(1): 9–20.

———. 2000. Blood, Milk, and Mountains: Marriage Practice and Concepts of Predictability among the Bakkarwal of Jammu and Kashmir, in M. Böck and A. Rao eds. *Culture, Creation, and Procreation: Concepts of Kinship in South Asian Practice*. Oxford/New York: Berghahn Books, 101–134.

———. 2001a. Wildlife Sanctuaries and Pastoral Nomads in Times of Peace and in Times of War: The Case of Dachigam, Kashmir, in M.J. Casimir and L. Lenhardt eds. *Environment, Property Resources and the State. Nomadic Peoples* 5(2) (Special Issue).

———. 2001b. Access to Pasture: Concepts, Constraints, and Practice in the Kashmir Himalayas, in A. Rao and M.J. Casimir eds. *Nomadism in South Asia. Oxford in India, Readings in Sociology and Social and Cultural Anthropology*. Delhi: Oxford University Press.

———. ed. 2007. The Valley of Kashmir: The Making and Unmaking of a Composite Culture. Delhi: Manohar.

Rao, A. and M.J. Casimir. 1985. Pastoral Niches in the Western Himalayas (Jammu and Kashmir), *Himalayan Research Bulletin* 4(2): 6–23.

Schofield, V. 1997. *Kashmir in the Crossfire*. London: IB Tauris & Co.

Sender, H. 1988. *The Kashmiri Pandits: A Study of Cultural Choice in North India*. Delhi: Oxford University Press.

Sharma, D.C. 1983. *Kashmir under the Sikhs*. Delhi: Seema Publs.

Sikand, Y. 1998. For Islam and Kashmir: The Prison Diaries of Sayyed Ali Shah Gilani of the Jama'at-i-Islami of Jammu and Kashmir, *Journal of Muslim Minority Affairs* 18(2): 241–249.

———. ed. 2000. *Islam and the Kashmiri Struggle: The Writings of Sayyed Ali Shah Gilani*. Bangalore.

———. 2001. Changing Course of Kashmiri Struggle: From National Liberation to Islamic Jihad? *Economic and Political Weekly* 36(3): January 20–26.

Sinha, A. 2000. *Death of Dreams: A Terrorist's Tale*. Delhi: Harper Collins.

South Asia Analysis Group. 2000. *Islam and the World Wide Web*. Chennai, India: Institute for Topical Studies.

Taylor, D. 2000 comp. *Kashmir*. Oxford: Clio Press (World Bibliographical Ser. 225).

Thomas, C. 2000. *Faultline Kashmir*. Middlesex,UK: Brunel Academic Publs.

Internet

http://www.jammukashmirinfo.com/
http://www.markazdawa.org/
kashmir-global-network@yahoogroups.com
http://www.ekashmironline.com/

8

The Hazara of Central Afghanistan

Grant Farr

The last three decades of war and turmoil in Afghanistan have left the country in tatters, and despite five years of relative stability under the Karzai government, many tensions and conflicts still remain just below the surface. Among these tensions are the ethnolinguistic, religious, and sectarian conflicts that have always been a part of Afghanistan but that have been fundamentally altered by the decades of war, revolution, and insurgency. Although the status ranking of the groups appears on the surface to be relatively unchanged, in fact groups at the bottom of the pecking order—many of whom participated in the fighting to drive the Soviet Union out of Afghanistan in the 1980s and then to rid Afghanistan of the Taliban in 2001, and have suffered greatly from the years of war—are now emboldened and beginning to demand a greater role in the Afghan power structure. Among the ethnolinguistic groups demanding a new role in Afghanistan are the Hazara. This group has long suffered social, economic, and political discrimination and disenfranchisement in Afghanistan, but they vow that they will not go back to their subordinate status in a new Afghanistan. Time will tell.

The People

The Hazara are a Persian-speaking people of Mongol ancestry living in the high mountains of central Afghanistan, in an area called the Hazarajat. Unlike other Afghan ethnic groups, the Hazara population resides completely within the borders of Afghanistan, and the Hazara have no related ethnic kin in neighboring countries, except those who have fled Afghanistan recently as refugees. The Hazara population is reported to be approximately two to three million, although a modern census of Afghanistan has never been taken. As a people their way of life is endangered by a number of forces, including

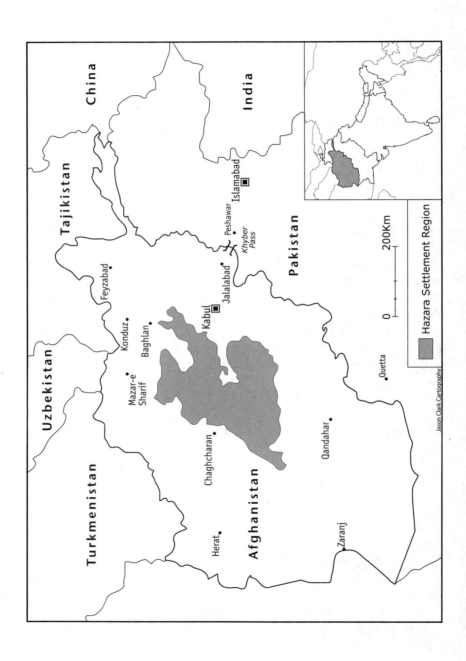

out-migration, political marginalization, environmental degradation of traditional farming and grazing lands, and the killings of civilians during the fighting.

The Hazara, sometimes called the Hazara Mongols, represent the last remnants of the great Mongol dynasties that came through the area that is now Afghanistan in the early part of the 13th century. Although the historical evidence is sketchy, it appears that the Hazara entered central Afghanistan sometime between 1229 and 1447 and are probably descendents of Chagatai soldiers who came originally from the area around the Oxus River. Chagatai, son of Genghis Khan, was installed as leader in this region in the early 13th century. In the later part of the 13th century, Chagatai armies crossed the Hindu Kush, the high mountains of central Afghanistan where the Hazara now live, attempting to conquer the Indian subcontinent. This effort eventually failed; the Chagatai army never reached the Indian subcontinent, but some remnants of the army remained in the Hindu Kush to guard important passes. These soldiers eventually intermarried with local Tajik women, and this intermarriage is thought to be the origin of the modern Hazara people.

This Mongol ancestry is evidenced in a few Mongol words found in the vocabulary of the present-day Hazara. There is also some evidence that remote tribes of the Hazara spoke the Mongol language up to the last century. The Hazaras' Mongol origins can also be seen in their Central Asian facial features, including high cheekbones, sparse beards, and epicanthic eyefolds, which distinguish them from the surrounding ethnic groups. The name Hazara is thought to derive from the Persian word, *hezar*, which means "thousand," referring, perhaps, to a military unit in the Mongol army, but there is no historical evidence of this.

The Hazara now speak a dialect of Persian, called Hazaragi, and are Shi'ah Moslems of the "Twelver" or *Jafari* order, also practiced in Iran. Since most other Afghans are Sunni Moslems, their religion is a source of religious discrimination. Their language and religion indicate that the Hazara were under Iranian influence at one time, although the exact timing is not known.

The total number of Hazara in Afghanistan is estimated to be around two million, although some Hazara leaders argue that the true population is closer to eight million. In fact, no accurate census has ever been taken in this remote region, and the exact population size is difficult to estimate. Population estimates are also complicated by disputes regarding who is Hazara and also because part of the Hazara population has fled the fighting in Afghanistan in the past three decades, either to areas outside the country or to other areas within Afghanistan. It is also clear that the Afghan government in the past purposely undercounted the Hazara population so as to minimize their political role, and drew provincial boundaries so as to divide Hazara populations into several provinces, effectively reducing their collective political power.

Table 1 Hazara Population, 1990

Province	Total Population	Hazara Population	Percent Hazara
Kabul	2,054,781	410,556	20
Parwan	488,748	87,975	18
Ghor	302,497	241,997	80
Bamiyan	301,530	241,224	80
Ghazni	700,794	560,635	80
Uruzgan	460,932	368,746	80
Wardak	372,202	148,881	40
Total	4,681,484	2,060,014	

The Setting

The Hazara live in high mountains of central Afghanistan along the central spine of the Hindu Kush. Hazara areas extend south to the city of Ghazni and west to near the city of Herat. This area is generally called the Hazarajat, but was referred to historically as Babaristan (connoting the Mongol ancestry), as Zabulistan by the Arabs in the medieval period, and has also been known as Bamiyan, for the central province famous for its immense sculpted Buddhas (destroyed by Taliban target practice). Some Hazara prefer to call the area Hazaristan, using the more modern "istan" ending. The Hazarajat is made up mostly of high mountains and narrow valleys at an average altitude of 10,000 feet. Because of the high elevation, the growing season is short, and the winter snows last from October to March or April. In the summer there is little rain and agriculture depends on the water from winter snows. The mean maximum temperature in the summer varies from 29 degrees centigrade in the lower foothills to 13 degrees centigrade in the high mountains. Winter temperatures drop below zero degrees centigrade in most regions of the Hazarajat and as low as minus 15 in the higher areas.

The higher mountains have permanent glaciers—now rapidly melting as a consequence of rising global temperatures—but below the snow line there is a vegetation of thin grasses and stunted trees. There are small areas of forest, mostly deciduous hardwoods, and historical accounts suggest that large areas of the Hazarajat below the tree line were once forested. However, population pressures have led to overgrazing and the harvesting of trees for building timber and for cooking and heating fuel so that very little forest area remains.

There are no major cities or even large towns in the Hazarajat and much of the region is inaccessible by road. In the 1930s, a primitive road was built from Kabul into the Hazarajat, following the Thorband and Surkh Ab river valleys, but it is closed much of the year from snows and spring floods. In the 1960s a major north-south road was built to connect the southern and northern areas of Afghanistan. This road, which passes through the eastern edge of the Hazarajat, was the first route over the Hindu Kush and was engineered by constructing a tunnel through the heart of the Hindu Kush. This tunnel, which is just south of the summit of the 11,100-foot Salang Pass, is the highest mountain tunnel in the world.

Subsistence Strategies

Given the severe conditions created by the elevation of the Hazarajat, the Hazara must use every resource carefully in order to survive. To maximize crop production, the Hazara build elaborate irrigation systems in the narrow valleys and construct irrigated terraces on the hillsides. These irrigation systems are built with rock and tree branches to channel water from melting winter snow into the fields. Wheat and barley are the most common crops, but maize is also grown in some of the lower-lying areas. Several kinds of fruit trees are also cultivated, along with melons and grapes in the lower areas. The higher mountain slopes are used for grazing animals. Goats and sheep are kept for meat, milk, skins, and wool, and horses and donkeys are used for transportation. In good years, sheep herds can grow quite large, but in difficult years their numbers quickly diminish.

This combination of subsistence farming supplemented with animal herding produces a marginally adequate diet in good years, but in years of summer drought or unusually cold winters, food stocks begin to dwindle. Hazara have only limited means to accumulate or store food from year to year, except through their herds; several bad weather years in a row can often lead to hunger and starvation. This occurred in the late 1990s when a devastating and prolonged drought afflicted much of Afghanistan. During this period, many Hazara had to leave the Hazarajat to find food for themselves and their families in other areas of Afghanistan, or face starvation. Even in good years, however, it is common for Hazara men to travel to the major cities (particularly Kabul) after the main crops are planted in the spring to work in menial jobs for income to help feed their families back in the Hazarajat.

Sociopolitical Organization

The Hazara are made of eight subgroups or tribes. Five of these, the Dai Kundi, Dai Zangi, Polada, Jaghuri, and Uruzgani, are called *Sad-i Qabar*, or the "original tribes." Hazara legend has it that the people in these tribes are the direct descendents of the Mongol soldiers. Other, more peripheral tribes include the Dahla, the Dai Khitai, and the Dai Chopan groups, which are called *Sad-i Sueka*, or those of mixed descent. Each of these groups constitutes from 50,000 to 100,000 people. These sub-tribes are identified largely by the area they are from and by lineage, but there is also a considerable amount of intermarriage among these groups so that in actuality it is not always clear who is in one group and who is in another.

While these groups are generally referred to as "tribes," they do not exhibit the strong patrilineal kin-based structure that is usually found in traditional tribal systems. Rather, Hazara generally identify themselves by where they live, rather than to whom they are related. The most salient social organization is on the village level, where people interact on a daily basis and where important social and local political events take place. Each village (a *qaryah* in the Hazara dialect of Persian) or cluster of villages constitutes a hundred or so people, usually interrelated. There are two common types of village physical organization in the Hazarajat: linear villages that occur along a river valley, and clustered villages surrounding a larger village or town. Given the topography, most villages in Hazarajat are linear. Houses are constructed with whatever materials people can find. In the lower elevations, houses are built with sun-dried bricks covered with mud and straw plaster. In the higher elevations, especially in areas with heavy snowfall, houses are often made of stone, with roof beams made of tree trunks. Roofs are constructed of interwoven branches covered with mud and must be shoveled free of snow in the winter and remudded every spring.

Most villages have a guesthouse for visitors and a meeting place for village councils, which often also serves as the local mosque. In some of the colder areas, houses have a type of traditional forced hot-air tunneled heating system, *tawkhanah*, under the floor. A fire is built at one end of the tunnel and the floor stays warm throughout the night. Another, simpler heating system is to put a charcoal brazier, *manghal*, on the floor under a small wooden table with a blanket spread over the table draping to the floor. The family then gathers around the table for the night, putting their arms and feet under the blankets to stay warm in the cold winter nights.

Most villagers are primarily farmers and there are very few fulltime craftsmen or artisans. Therefore, while the Hazara villagers are relatively self-sufficient in basic foods, other items, such as tea, rice, salt, cloth, and the like, must be obtained from other sources through barter or trade. With no real trading towns in the Hazarajat, many of these items are bought from itinerant peddlers who travel through the region, or from occasional trips to the nearest city or trading town outside the Hazarajat, trips that often takes several days. The principal means of local transportation is by foot. For longer distances ancient jeeps or four-wheel drive pickups are used, often piled high with people, sacks of wheat, and sheep. There are few bridges—they tend to wash out in spring runoff, and the Hazara fashion hand-drawn ferries out of inflated goat hides to cross mountain rivers.

The village leader is called the *mir*. The position of *mir*, always an older male, is most often inherited, but in some cases a village may unseat and replace an unpopular *mir*. The *mir* plays a role as a secular leader of the village or sometimes of several villages in the same proximity, ruling over the economic and social life of the village. *Mirs* also represent the local villages in dealing with local or national government representatives. Some *mirs*, especially important ones, use the title of *khan*.

There are also several types of religious leaders in the Hazarajat. A *sayyid* is one who claims to be a direct descendant of the prophet Mohammed through his son-in-law Ali and the Prophet's daughter Fatima. *Sayyids* live as an elite and somewhat separate caste in Hazara society and play an important role in the religious life of the Hazarajat. *Sayyids* often travel on pilgrimages to the important Shi'a religious sites in Iraq and especially Iran, therefore maintaining a connection between the Hazarajat and Iran. The *sayyids* also collect a religious tax, called *khums,* from the people, which they use to support themselves and their religious organizations. There are other religious leaders in the Hazarajat, *sheikhs*, who administer to the day-to-day religious needs of the local villages. These needs include teaching the local children to read the Koran, officiate at marriages, and give advice about political or social disputes. *Sheikhs* may or may not also be *sayyids*.

World View

Like those of all peoples, the Hazara way of life, attitudes, and social organizations are shaped by the world in which they live. The salient factors of Hazara life that determine the way they approach and make sense of their world include their low social and political status in the larger Afghan society, their marginal economic condition in Afghanistan, and the remoteness of the Hazarajat. Because of these circumstances, Hazara have a rather inward-looking worldview. By necessity they devote most of their daily attention to surviving, raising their children, and living in a marginal environment. Most Hazara do not have the time or energy to look beyond their immediate needs and as a result they have not played a major role in the larger Afghan society. Also because of this inward-looking attitude, and because of inherent prejudices in Afghan society, the Hazara experience ethnic and racial discrimination, and live at the lowest rung of Afghan society.

To some extent, this inward view has changed in the past three decades of turmoil in Afghanistan. The Hazara not only played an important role in the war of resistance against the Soviet Union in the 1980s, they were also an integral part of the Northern Alliance that took Kabul from the Taliban in 2002. The Hazara suffered greatly under the Taliban, whose religious intolerance led them to attack the Shi'a Hazara in particular. On several occasions, the Taliban government killed large numbers of Hazara civilians, in particular in the fighting in Mazar-i Sharif in 1998. The Hazara have been profoundly politicized by these events of the last three decades, and a newfound ethnic nationalism has developed. As a result the Hazara have formed political organizations, and Hazara leaders are now demanding active participation in the events of Afghanistan and a redress of past wrongs.

The Hazara worldview is also affected by their religion. For one, being Shi'a in a Sunni dominated country opens the Hazara to religious persecution. But also, Shi'ism itself has a particular worldview. Shi'a Islam puts particular focus on the role of the descendants of the prophet Mohammed. The Shi'a believe that the direct descendants of the Prophet, which they call *imams*, are the rightful leaders of Islam and that Mohammed's spiritual essence is passed on through them. There are various branches of Shi'ism, but the branch followed by the Hazara, and also in Iran, believes that the twelfth *imam*, or direct descendant of the Prophet, whose name was Muhammed al-Mahdi, left the physical world and went into the spirit world. This twelfth *imam*, the Shi'a believe, will eventually return to the physical world as a kind of savior. This messianic belief of a returning savior leads to a worldview in which the hardships and suffering of the present antecede a better life in the future.

Threats to Survival

There are several threats to the survival of the Hazara as a people. Among them are challenges to the fragile ecosystem of the Hazarajat and changes in the economic viability of subsistence farming. However, the major threat to the survival of the Hazara is their long and continuing treatment in Afghanistan as a pariah group, for they have been despised, persecuted, murdered, and displaced. The Hazara have been the victims of mass killings by various Afghan governments, of encroachments of their territory by other groups, and of the deliberate undercounting of their populations in national censuses and the drawing of provincial borders so as to split the Hazara population. As a result of such treatment thousands of Hazara have left the Hazarajat to become workers in the major cities or refugees in neighboring countries.

A History of Oppression

The Hazara have a long history of political persecution within Afghanistan. Their location in the remote mountains allowed them to live as relatively autonomous peoples in Afghanistan until late 19th century. The Afghan king Abdur Rahman (reigned 1880–1901) sought to unify Afghanistan into a modern nation-state by ruthlessly bringing the various tribal and ethnic groups of Afghanistan under his rule. In the 1880s he sent military troops into the Hazarajat to subdue the Hazara and to bring them under the control of Kabul. The Hazara resisted, and an armed revolt took place in the years 1891 to 1893. The revolt failed, and the Hazara were brutally punished for their uprising. Among other things, Abdur Rahman partitioned the Hazarajat, making it part of three provinces, Kabul, Bamiyan, and Kandahar, in an attempt to disrupt Hazara unity and independence. He sent Sunni clerics into the Hazarajat to convert the Shi'a Hazara to Sunni Islam (unsuccessfully), and imposed a special tax on the Hazara. Abdur Rahman further imprisoned or executed many of the Hazara khans, or leaders, and as a consequence many Hazara leaders fled the Hazarajat, resettling either in the Pakistan city of Quetta or in Mazar-i Sharif, the Uzbek city in the north of Afghanistan. Hazara were also taken as slaves. In 1904, during the reign of Abdur Rahman's successor, Habibullah Khan (reigned 1901–1919) an amnesty was declared, allowing those who had fled to return. Some did, but many did not and there are still sizeable Hazara communities in these two cities, descendants of those who fled in the 1880s.

Pariah Status

The Hazara's lowly situation in Afghanistan means they can be characterized as a pariah group. Pariah groups are those who are seen by the rest of society as outcast, despised, and to be avoided. The Hazara occupy the lowest status in Afghan society and suffer considerable discrimination and prejudice. They are publicly humiliated with taunts of *Hazara-e mushkhur* (mice-eating Hazara), *bini puchuq* (flat-nose), and *khar-e barkash* (load-carrying donkeys), referring to their racial features or to their role as menial laborers.

Their low status is also seen in the marriage exchanges. In Afghan society marriages are arranged by extended families and marriage is viewed as the exchange of daughters for economic or social gain. Since the family's status is determined by the male's position in society, men often marry women of a lower class or caste, since they can get docile wives cheaply. On the other hand, the reverse—an upper-class woman marrying a lower-class man—would never take place. While most Hazara marriage exchanges are endogamous, that is Hazara marrying Hazara, there is some out-marriage—always Hazara women marrying men of ethnic groups with more status. Being women from a lower-status ethnic group, these Hazara brides are often treated as virtual slaves in their new families.

As discussed above, the situation of the Hazara in Afghanistan has improved, in large part because the Hazara were important members of the Northern Alliance, the movement that drove the Taliban from power. A number of Hazara leaders now hold important positions in the Karzai government. However, while some of the Hazara elite are now doing well, the average Hazara continues to play a subservient role in Afghan society.

Pushtunization

If the Hazara are at the bottom of the Afghan social structure, the Pushtun are at the top. The Pushtun are an ethnolinguistic population organized into several large and powerful patrilineal tribal confederations. They live on both sides of the Afghan-Pakistan border and share a common language, Pashto. Although the Pushtun make up only 40 percent of the population of Afghanistan, they have nonetheless been the rulers of Afghanistan since its beginning, except for brief periods of Tajik rule. Current Afghan president Hamid Karzai is a Pushtun, for instance. Although they once lived mostly in their tribal areas in southern and eastern Afghanistan, over the last 100 years they have used their control of the central government in Kabul to bring much of Afghanistan under Pushtun domination. Historians have referred to this process as the Pushtunization of Afghanistan. It has been accomplished by ceding large areas of Afghanistan that originally belonged to other ethnic groups to the Pushtun tribes to be used for pasturelands or farming, and by encouraging Pushtun to move into other ethnic areas. This has affected the Hazara particularly, since the southern edge of the Hazarajat abuts the traditional Pushtun pasturelands. In the 1890s large sections of the Hazarajat were given to Pushtun nomads or taken by force. This process has continued, albeit more slowly, and large areas of the Hazarajat have been lost to the Hazara.

Pushtun domination over the Hazara and other groups in Afghanistan as well is in part due to the difference in the social structure of Pushtun and Hazara society. The Pushtun, many of whom are, or were, nomadic or semi-nomadic, have a social culture that is particularly nationalistic and bellicose with a strong warrior ethos and tribal codes of manhood and male honor. This warrior culture contrasts sharply with the more passive and inwardly directed culture of the Hazara farmers, and the Pushtun have been able to intimidate and bully the Hazara and other ethnic groups.

The Pushtun dominance of the Hazara in Afghanistan has also forced the Hazara to hide their true identity when possible. For instance, when Hazara are required to register with the government to obtain a state identity card or to register their children in school, they often deny their true heritage. Since their appearance and stature is not similar to that of the taller and darker Pushtun, they often claim they are Tajiks, who, while somewhat different in appearance, are more similar in appearance to the Hazara and also speak Persian. The Tajiks, while clearly not Pushtun, have a higher status than the Hazara. In this way, the Hazara are undercounted in census enumerations. Some Hazara also give their children Pushtun names, instead of the traditional Hazara names, in an attempt to appease the dominant Pushtun. Over the decades some place names of towns or valleys in the Hazarajat have been changed to Pushtun sounding names.

Hazara Out-Migration: Refugees and IDPs

Since the 1880s there has been some migration out of the Hazarajat, in part because of population pressure and economic hardships. In the last 25 years an increase in armed conflict has dramatically increased this out-migration. At times this armed conflict was caused by outside forces, and at other times it arose from internal struggles. During the turbulent times of the Soviet occupation in the 1980s, the Hazarajat's remote location kept the region relatively free of fighting. However, during that period a serious and bloody internal battle occurred among the Hazara: Young radical Islamists, many trained in Iran and supported by Iranian political groups, battled the traditional Hazara khans for control. Several thousand Hazara fled the Hazarajat during that period, many fleeing to the cities of Mazar-i Sharif in Northern Afghanistan or Quetta across the border in Pakistan to join the large communities of Hazara descendants of those who settled there in the 1890s.

However, the bulk of the Hazara refugees who fled Afghanistan in the 1980s went to Iran, largely because they, like the Iranians, were Shi'a Moslems, while most of the refugees from the other Afghan groups fled to Pakistan. In Pakistan, the Afghans were registered, placed in special camps, and given relief support. Such facilities, however, were not available to the Afghan refugees who fled to Iran and most dispersed into the major Iranian cities, primarily Tehran, remaining uncounted and unaccountable. As a result, while it is known that many of the Afghan refugees in Iran were Hazara, it is not known exactly how many fled, where they went, or what they did. Rough guesses range from several hundred thousand to over one million Hazara refugees in Iran.

When the Soviets pulled out of Afghanistan in 1989, and the final Soviet-backed regime collapsed in 1992, some of the refugees began to return to the Hazarajat. Soon, however, a new conflict broke out, this time against the Taliban movement that began to assert its control over Afghanistan in the middle 1990s. Although ostensibly an Islamic movement, the Taliban were mostly Pushtuns, whose goal was not only to create a strict Islamic theocracy but also to return Afghanistan to its Pushtun roots. As the Taliban began to gain control in large areas of Afghanistan, the Hazara put up stiff resistance and a number of battles between Hazara fighters and the Taliban army occurred.

The result of this new fighting was a new wave of displaced people. However, unlike the refugees of the 1980s these people found that the borders with Pakistan and Iran were now closed. Forced out of the Hazarajat by the fighting but unable to leave the country to safety, they became displaced within their own country: internally displaced persons (IDPs).

Beginning in 1999, Taliban forces began to move into the Hazarajat and fighting erupted around the major towns of Bamiyan, Yakawland, and Dar-e Souf. The United Nations estimates that over 50,000 Hazara were displaced in this fighting and moved to safer regions in other parts of Afghanistan, particularly to the north along the Oxus River, or fled into nearby mountains.

Many of the displaced left with few, if any, possessions; and since many of their homes and their crops were lost in the fighting, they had neither food nor shelter. Disease and chronic conditions caused by poverty and extreme cold were pervasive among the elderly and the young alike. Cholera epidemics broke out, too, as the displaced were forced to use water from open irrigation canals that also serve as wastewater runoff ditches.

Killing and Terror

Although several thousand Hazara had been killed in the Afghan conflicts since 1975, including those who were murdered or imprisoned in the demonstrations in the Chindawul, the Hazara ghetto in Kabul, in June 1979, the Taliban government pursued a new and more purposeful killing of Hazara civilians. A major incident took place in the northern city of Mazar-i Sharif in August 1998. When the Taliban forces captured that city, more than 2,000 civilians, most of them Hazara, were killed. This killing was in reprisal for the summary execution of over 2,000 Taliban prisoners in May 1997. The newly installed Taliban governor at that time called the Hazara infidels and threatened to kill the rest of them if they did not convert to Sunni Islam.

Several mass killings have also taken place in the Hazarajat itself. In May 2000, a number of Hazara were killed near the Robatak pass on the border between Baghlan and Samangan provinces. Thirty-one bodies were found at one site to the northwest of the pass. Twenty-six were identified as Hazara civilians from Baghlan. It was later found that all were unlawfully detained for four months, and some were tortured before they were killed.

In January of 2001 the Taliban entered the Yakaolang district of the Hazarajat to conduct a search operation following the recapture of the district from Hazara groups. The Taliban forces detained over 300 civilian adults, including staff members of local humanitarian organizations. The men were herded to assembly points in the center of the district and several outlying areas and then shot by a firing squad in public view. These killings were apparent reprisals for local cooperation with the United Front (The North Alliance) and to forewarn others.

Response: Struggle to Survive

Like all ethnic, linguistic, or racial groups that suffer from oppressions and discrimination, the Hazara have adapted to their plight in several ways. As already discussed, on the political side the Hazara have increased their participation in the national government as a result of their important role in the liberation of Afghanistan, first against the Soviet occupation in the 1980s and then against the Taliban in the 1990s. The Soviet Union's occupation of Afghanistan led to armed rebellion in most of Afghanistan, including the Hazarajat. This occupation also led to the emergence of ethnic awareness and nationalism among various ethnic and tribal groups who began to demand a say in the events in Afghanistan.

However, the beginning of the Hazara awakening can be traced to the 1970s, when the relatively stable, post Second World War period in Afghanistan was coming to an end. In the 1970s, a small number of Hazara, mostly young men who had traveled outside of the Hazarajat, began to become politically active. Several political groups were formed among Hazara groups living outside of Afghanistan, mostly in Quetta, Pakistan, that expressed the early seeds of a new ethnic nationalism and ethnic pride, including the *Jawanan-Mongol* (Mongol Youth), and *Tanzim-e Nazl-e Nau Hazara* (Organization for the New Generation of Hazara). A number of Hazara youth also began to organize within Afghanistan, on the campus of Kabul University. Political awareness and the number of organizations grew dramatically with the coming of the Marxist government in Kabul in 1977 and the Soviet invasion of Afghanistan beginning in 1979. There were numerous demonstrations and rebellions against the Soviet-led government in Kabul's traditional Hazara neighborhoods in the 1970s and the early 1980s. One of the first massive demonstrations against the Marxist government, in fact, took place in the Hazara neighborhood of Chindawul in June 1979. There was also an armed uprising in the Hazarajat, in Bamiyan, in May 1979. A large number of Hazara were arrested because of their participation in these demonstrations and many were killed. However, for the first time since before 1880 the Hazara were unified, organized, and fighting back. It should be pointed out, however, that some Hazara intellectuals supported the Marxist government and took positions of power in Kabul during this period.

As the war of resistance against the Soviet Union intensified in the 1980s, several Hazara political parties emerged. These parties represented diverse elements of the Hazara population, and in some cases fought among themselves. The first major attempt to form an organization to unite the Hazarajat was the *Shura-e Itifaq* (Council of the Union), formed in the Hazarajat in 1979 by Sayyid Ali Beheshti, an important religious leader and landlord. This party was representative of the traditional Hazara leadership, including both religious leaders and khans. The *Shura-e Itifaq* was effective early in the war of resistance, but by 1983 began to be challenged by younger, more radical Hazara who were influenced by the Iranian revolution. These radical Islamists formed Iranian-style political parties in the Hazarajat and began to challenge the older, more traditional leadership. These new political parties, included *Sazman-e Nasr* (Victory Organization) and *Sepah-e Pasdaran* (the Revolutionary Guards), both modeled after Iranian parties of the same name. From 1985 to 1990 a number of local khans were killed in this conflict, and many suspect that Iran was behind these deaths.

By the late 1980s the revolutionary passion of Iran began to cool, and new, more nationalistic parties arose among the Hazara population, including the *Harakat-e Islami* (the Islamic Movement) and *Hizb-e Wahdat* (Unity Party), political organizations that are still active today.

As members of the Northern Alliance—a confederation of ethnic groups, particularly the Uzbeks, Hazara, and Tajiks, from the Northern areas of Afghanistan—the Hazara played an important role in driving out the Taliban government in 2001. They were therefore given several important cabinet and administrative positions in the Karzai government, and for once the position of the Hazara appeared to be improving. However, the recent resurgence of the Taliban and the ongoing insurgency among the Pushtun tribes in Southern and Eastern Afghanistan have increasingly destabilized the Karzai government, and the gains made by the Hazara, as well as other ethnic groups, in the last five years may be rapidly eroding.

Food for Thought

The Hazara were an isolated and oppressed minority group in Afghanistan who became caught up in two major world events that profoundly changed their society and ways of life. The first was the long and disastrous series of political and military events that rocked Afghanistan beginning in 1973. These events were in some ways catastrophic to Afghanistan and the Hazara. Thousands of Hazara, both civilians and combatants, were killed in the fighting. Yet these events transformed this once oppressed group, creating a strong sense of ethnic pride and unity. Once passive, they now have a more important role in Afghanistan. They demand to be counted fairly, to control their own affairs, and to participate proportionally in the governing of Afghanistan.

The second world event was the Iranian revolution, in 1979. As Shi'a, the Hazara became caught up in the events of the Iranian revolution, in the same way that it affected Shi'a populations in all parts of the world. The passion and ideology of the Iranian revolution intersected with the events unfolding in Afghanistan and brought a new surge of Islamic ideology that challenged the old ways and the old leaders. Again lives were lost, and the Hazara were changed.

The Hazara are an endangered group, their numbers are dwindling, many have been killed, their local leaders have been murdered, many people have fled the Hazarajat, and their traditional way of life is largely gone. But they have also changed, and maybe the change will help them survive.

To Think About

1. What is known about the origins of the Hazara people and their culture?
2. What are the characteristics of the Hazara people and their culture that cause them to be singled out for discrimination and prejudice?
3. What does "Pushtunization" mean and how has this process affected the Hazara?
4. How have the events in Afghanistan since 1973 changed the position of the Hazara in Afghan society? Has their position improved or worsened?
5. What lessons can be taken from the situation of the Hazara that would apply to other groups in other parts of the world?

Resources

Published Literature

Dupree, Louis. 1980. *Afghanistan*. Princeton, NJ: Princeton University Press.
Ewans, Martin. 2002. *Afghanistan*. New York: RoutledgeCurzon.

Farr, Grant. 1988. The Rise and Fall of an Indigenous Resistance Group: The Shura of the Hazarajat. *The Afghanistan Studies Journal* 1: 48–61.

Mousawi, Sayid. 1997. *The Hazara of Afghanistan: An Historical, Cultural, Economic, and Political Study.* New York: St. Martins Press.

Roy, Olivier. 1995. *Afghanistan: From Holy War to Civil War.* London: Darwin Press.

Rubin, Barnett. 1995. *The Fragmentation of Afghanistan.* New Haven, CT: Yale University Press.

Internet

The Hazara World: http://www.hazara.net/

Hazarah Cultural and Historical Archives: http://members.tripod.com/~ismat/

Hazara OnLine: http://www.hazaraonline.f2s.com

Hazara Corner: http://www.afghana.com

Hazara Society: http://www.csun.edu

9

The Wakhi and Kirghiz of the Pamirian Knot

Hermann Kreutzmann

Most of our knowledge about the people of the Pamirs, Hindukush, and Karakoram is influenced by the narratives and travelogues of early 19th century explorers and travelers. They encountered difficult environmental conditions in the remote valleys and high plateaus of High Asia—the "roof of the world" (*bam-e darya*)—and reported on two ethnic groups they met there: the Wakhi and Kirghiz. These groups, who lived with the harsh conditions of altitudes ranging between 2,400 and 4,500 meters, provided transport by yak (*Bos grunniens*), Bactrian camel (*Camelus bactrianus*), and horses for the rare travelers and traders trying to cross the high passes.

The People

Today, 50,000 Wakhi live in remote parts of Afghanistan, Pakistan, Tajikistan, and Xinjiang (a territory in the People's Republic of China [PRC]). There are about as many Kirghiz in this area, though many more—perhaps as many as three million—live in China and in the Turkic-speaking Central Asian republics, most in Kyrgyzstan. The Wakhi and Kirghiz occupy the same general territory, but speak different languages: Wakhi belongs to the Eastern Iranian branch of the Indo-Iranian group, whereas Kirgiz is a Turkic language of the Altaic group. Kirghiz is a written language, but Wakhi has no written form and is transcribed in phonetic notation. The subjects of this chapter are the Kirghiz and Wakhi who live in the high mountains separating Central and South Asia, where cold, dry winters and short summers define the ecological limits to cultivation of cereals like barley and wheat.

The Wakhi's permanent settlements are in deeply incised valleys, their seasonal pastures at higher elevations. Kirghiz are nomadic, and live year-round in yurts. Both groups are agro-pastoralists; they also continue to provide transport, pack animals, and scouting services to trade caravans and the

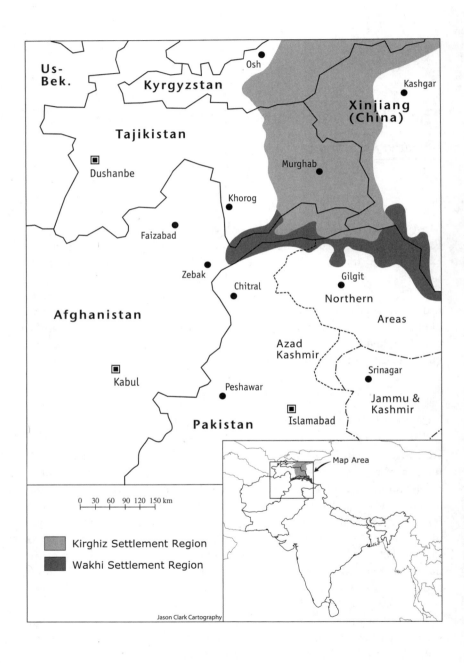

occasional traveler, deriving extra income from these services and from hunting and collecting precious minerals. These nonagrarian activities are the basis of a barter trade, which also involves the exchange of surplus agricultural products and livestock for basic goods like tea, household items, and some clothing. In recent years some of these sources of income have expanded for some people, narrowed for others. Thus economic and sociopolitical conditions further frame the survival of both groups.

The Setting

The Pamirian Knot is a landscape of high mountain valleys and plateaus. Altitude and aridity create natural thermal and hydrological thresholds for farming, though human action and innovation can stretch these limits a bit. Meltwater feeds the manmade irrigation systems. Only Wakhi grow crops, while Kirghiz (in this area) do not practice any form of settled agriculture. Both groups use the high pastures found where groundwater or streams create seasonal meadows: the *pamir* from which the region gets its name. Kirghiz grazing grounds, generally located above 3,500 m, have been praised for their nutritional properties at least since Marco Polo traveled through the area in the 13th century. Livestock from those rich pastures (yaks, fat-tailed sheep, and goats) and game such as Marco Polo sheep (*Ovis ammon*) and ibex (*Capra ibex*) became well known as a source of high-quality meat among consumers in the low-lying Central Asian town oases along the Southern Silk Route. In addition to the seven extended Pamirs (up to 300 km² of pasture area each) there are smaller Pamirs such as the Pamir-e Bugrumal (upper Gunt Valley, Gorno-Badakhshan), Mariang Pamir (Sarikol), Tagarma Pamir (Sarikol) and Shimshal Pamir (Northern Areas of Pakistan). The natural grazing, the major asset of the Pamirs, is augmented by meager cultivation.

Wakhi villages are located in an altitudinal range between 2,150 m and 3,500 m. Arid and semi-arid conditions here require irrigation and allow for a single annual crop (of barley, wheat, potatoes, beans, or peas), which is always supplemented by animal husbandry. With a few exceptions, natural vegetation is scarce and forests almost absent. A few fruit trees such as apple, apricot, walnut, and mulberry are cultivated, and wood for fuel and construction is taken from poplar plantations, a common sight in Central Asia. It is the availability of water stored in glaciers and snow that permits agricultural settlement in this ecological belt.

The overall setting is made up of three areas. The valley bottoms are mainly inhabited by Wakhi and other Pamirian mountain farmers who live in permanent villages and use nearby pastures in the side valleys for seasonal grazing. Above 3,500 m, the Pamir pastures extend through the wider and flatter main valleys, and both Wakhi and Kirghiz use them for grazing and some cultivation. During the cold season, Wakhi retreat from the plateaus to their homesteads in the valleys, while the Kirghiz remain in the mountains. The third area, the high plateaus, is dominated by Kirghiz nomads. The high plateaus favor the nomads whose permanent dwellings are located at high elevations. In modern times, however, the growing demand for natural grazing areas and mutual dependency have resulted in changing land-use patterns, reduced mobility, and political interference.

Traditional Subsistence Strategies

Two major adaptive strategies make use of the pasture potential of Western High Asia: nomadic animal husbandry and combined mountain agriculture, or agro-pastoralism (the combination of mountain agriculture with livestock).

Nomadism's chief advantage is mobility. Traditionally nomadic groups were able to exploit natural resources—pasture—in dispersed locations. Great distances, on the order of several hundreds of kilometers, separated economically valuable mountain pastures from winter campsites, with areas of less economic interest lying in between. In this region, the functional migration cycle alternates longer stays in high-altitude pastures during summer with winter grazing in low-lying basins in the northern foothills or plains of the Inner Asian mountain arc. In both areas the nomads must be permitted to move between pastures, and be able to pay any grazing fees.

Combined mountain agriculture allows the farmer to grow fodder in the permanent homesteads while herds are grazing in the high-lying pastures during the summers. The limiting factor here is the need to provide livestock with as much as nine months of feed, for periods when seasonal pastures are inaccessible; this fodder has to be produced on private or common property village lands. Habitations are usually located at the upper levels of permanent settlements in single-crop farming areas. The access to the Pamir pastures involves shorter migrations and some mobility within the summer habitations. Fodder here is comparatively plentiful but only available for a short period; feed storage and transport to the homesteads are of limited importance.

Both strategies, combined mountain agriculture and mountain pastoralism, can result in competition for natural resources in the same location, and this ecological competition has been expanded to a debate about conflicting economic strategies. In much of the discourse of modernization and social change, the assumption is that nomadism will be superseded by agriculture. The extensive use of marginal resources through pastoralism is then replaced by the intensification and increasing external inputs of agriculture. Thus, it is not surprising that mountain farmers and nomads have been a prime target for "development." The aim is to reduce subsistence-level production and integrate people from the periphery into the mainstream of nation states in the name of development. As a consequence, "traditional" lifestyles and locally developed economic strategies have become endangered.

Sociopolitical Organization

"Wakhi" is the label outsiders use for both the people and their language; they refer to themselves as *xik*; *xik zik* is their language. Their neighbors and visitors identified the Wakhi as the people living in Wakhan, the narrow "panhandle" in modern Afghanistan separating Tajikistan from Pakistan-controlled Kashmir. Until 1883, Wakhan was a principality occupying both banks of the upper Amu Darya (Oxus) and the Wakhan and Pamir Darya. Wakhan was ruled by a hereditary ruler (*mir*) who controlled a territory in which sedentary mountain farmers and Kirghiz nomads lived. Both communities paid taxes and tributes in cash and kind to him. The Wakhi society consisted of an upper stratum: the ruling family (*mir*), some religious leaders (*pir, sayid, xuja*), and a few better-off families (*šana, xaybari*). The vast majority of the people (more than 95 percent) belonged to the "ordinary" people (*xik*), who practiced combined mountain agriculture and were obliged to deliver taxes and corvée services—obligatory work as load carriers and soldiers, for example. Wakhan was no exception in Western High Asia, where many valleys or parts of them were principalities with more or less strong links to mighty neighbors: the Amir of Afghanistan, the Emir of Bokhara (later replaced by Tsarist Russia and still later the Soviet Union), the Chinese Emperor, and British India. The competition among these major players in the Great Game affected diplomatic relations, taxation, conscription policies, and local politics and economy, and finally resulted in the delineation of international boundaries and the termination of independence.

The Kirghiz did not live only within Wakhi administration. Their mobility enabled them to shift to grazing grounds with favorable conditions—not only good forage but also low taxation and tolerable political pressure. The family histories of Kirghiz clans abound in stories about leaving some territories and starting a new life under different conditions, masters, or protectors. Always the search for suitable pastures and low outside interference was the guiding principle. Among themselves, the Kirghiz were organized in a tribal structure. Migratory groups were headed by a camp elder (*beg, khan*), who normally represented the most affluent family. Within their communities a highly stratified hierarchy appeared where the poorer yurts were occupied by shepherds on service for the big herd owners of yaks, sheep, goats, Bactrian camels, and horses. The affluent leaders and rich households profited from the system of renting (*amanat*) their livestock to shepherds. Kirghiz communities formed their own microcosms in the Pamirian pastures with more or less strong relationships to their neighbors. Common goals were the defence of grazing grounds and the avoidance of outside interference.

Wakhi and Kirghiz represent communities long competing for the same resources. Competition was ubiquitous and relations between neighboring groups not always amicable. Both groups were involved in a power struggle for survival where threats came from near and distant neighbors as much as from raiders, slave traders, representatives of administration, conscriptors, and tax officials.

Religion and Worldview

The vast majority of inhabitants in Western High Asia adhere to the Islamic faith. This is a result of historical developments played out over centuries, and the conversion from a local belief system to Islam may have happened a millennium ago or in the last century. A peculiar feature of the Hindukush, Pamir, and Karakoram is that the lowlands are dominated by Sunni Muslims while in the remote mountain valleys live followers of different Shia sects and few Sunni. The Kirghiz would identify themselves—almost without exception, along with most of the Turkic-speaking inhabitants of Central Asia—as members of the Sunni branch of Islam. Visible religious institutions are found mainly in sedentary environments, while architectural symbols of Islam are rarely to be found in mobile Kirghiz encampments, though they are conspicuous in areas where Kirghiz reside in permanent winter settlements.

In contrast, the Wakhi belong to the Ismaili faith, a Shia sect of Islam. The Ismaili faith was brought to Badakhshan long ago by an Ismaili saint sent from Egypt in the 11th century A.D. Since then a dispersed community of Ismailis developed where local religious leaders (*pir*) bound groups of followers (*murid*). Day-to-day practices and rites of passage are executed by lay priests (*xalifa*) in the villages. Only during the last century has this Ismaili group reconnected with mainstream Ismailism under the leadership of the Aga Khan. The present Aga Khan, who operates from Europe, opted for a strong community organization and initiated numerous efforts for community development that have been instrumental in social change.

This brief classification does not address the importance of religious affiliation and worship for the everyday life of Kirghiz nomads and Wakhi mountain farmers, which varies significantly among individuals and households. For long periods of time political circumstances have put many restrictions on public displays of religion in the USSR and the PRC. Nevertheless, more liberal attitudes in recent years and less state interference in religious matters have permitted a revival of devoutness. Oral traditions and local day-to-day practices reveal an underlayer of a much older and still prominent belief system.

Threats to Survival

Demographic Trends

The population of the Wakhi has fluctuated in space and time, with an increase of population from the 19th to the 21st century in the Pamirian Knot as in almost all of High Asia. Only major disasters, crises, and/or exodus have slowed population growth across Asia and for the Wakhi people. Population peaked early at about 6,000 in the principality/mirdom of Wakhan around 1880. Shortly afterwards, the geopolitical confrontation between British India and Tsarist Russia during the "Great Game," as well as the Islamization and expansion program of the Afghan Amir, significantly threatened the autonomy of the small principalities in the Hindukush, Pamir, and Karakoram.

Wakhan was one example (Shughnan and Roshan are others), whose rulers were taken hostage and threatened by one or the other party. In 1883, the Mir of Wakhan, Ali Mardan Shah, organized a preventive exodus for his family and about one-quarter of the population, who took refuge in his father-in-law's territory in Chitral. Subsequently what he feared materialized, and Wakhan was divided in two parts in the same manner as other principalities along the Amu Darya. In the aftermath, the Northern part was controlled by Russia and the Southern part became an extension of Afghanistan's territory. The panhandle-shaped, so-called Wakhan strip was created as a buffer zone between the superpowers of the time, Russia and British India. The artificial boundaries were laid down at the end of the 19th century and remain as the international boundaries of today.

The division of Wakhan led to a refugee crisis that cost many lives; the population of Wakhi decreased by one-sixth. The low point was reached by 1900 and demographic trends have pointed upwards since. The 50,000 Wakhi of today live in four countries: Afghanistan, Tajikistan, the PRC (in the Xinjiang Autonomous Region), and Pakistan. Demographic patterns are linked to divided territories and mobility. The 20th century appears to have been the age of migration. Refugees from Afghanistan still seek shelter and work in Chitral. Migrant workers from Tajikistan end up in Gojal (Hunza). They expect support from local Wakhi residents whose forefathers have been taking refuge here for more than 200 years. Gojali Wakhi participate in transborder trade with their Chinese neighbors. Thus, Wakhi communities are to be found in four countries with different political systems, with market and state-controlled economies, and in regions of contrasting infrastructure, welfare, and educational institutions.

Kirghiz nomads have been affected by the same geopolitical developments. Estimates about demographic trends are more complicated for nomads. The seasonal grazing grounds used by the Kirghiz often belonged to different countries after the delineation of international boundaries. Although in earlier times border crossing was possible, it became next to impossible during the Cold War. The term "closed frontier nomadism" was coined for their case. The Amu Darya, once a permeable boundary, became the almost hermetically controlled interface between the Soviet Union and Afghanistan. The border dispute between the USSR and the PRC led to the introduction of the so-called "system" that identifies a 30 km-wide demilitarized zone with metal fences visible everywhere on the Tajikistan side. Communication and grazing across boundaries and within the "system" became impossible. Kirghiz communities were restricted to their respective countries. The Eastern Pamirs of present-day Tajikistan are predominantly Kirghiz territory, as are the Little and Big Pamir of Afghanistan. The PRC introduced a Kirghiz Autonomous District by the name of Kizil Su (Red Water), and some Kirghiz live in the Tajik Autonomous County of Taxkorgan.

Environmental Crisis

Nomadic pastoralists depend on extensive use of wide-ranging pastures. From their perspective, any restriction on migration and limitation of access to pastures is perceived as an environmental crisis. For most mountain-dwelling nomads like the Kirghiz, maximum use of natural pastures requires grazing the flocks at high altitudes (above 3,500 m) during summer, keeping the herds in low-lying pastures (around 1,200 m) during winter. During winter the urban oases of the Southern Silk Route or in the Fergana Basin offered opportunities for keeping the herds on agricultural fields after harvest. The animals scavenged for crop residues and grass while improving irrigated lands in the oasis with their valuable manure. At the same time Kirghiz participated in business and trade before retreating to the high pastures for the summer. These times are now far in the past. Basically everywhere low-lying winter pastures are missing today. The expansion of cultivation in irrigated oases, the introduction of stationary livestock-keeping there, and the increase in urbanization have led to an exclusion of nomadic entrepreneurs and their herds. Furthermore, political changes such as collectivization and central planning affected the long-established patterns of animal husbandry for all previously involved groups. To sum up, the accessible pastures are to be found nowadays where modernized agriculture failed to grow crops or where political circumstances allow it. Those grazing grounds are generally to be found in remote locations above 3,500 m altitude.

For the Wakhi mountain farmers the situation is modified by irrigated crop farming. The expansion of households predominantly engaged in agriculture has resulted in a higher demand for natural resources which are rather limited. Although there is competition with Kirghiz nomads for high pastures during summer, the real constraint occurs in winter. The fodder production in the homesteads competes with food production as village lands are rather limited (on average less than one hectare per household). Crop farming at the upper altitudinal limit not only faces climatic vagaries but gives comparatively small returns and bears little scope for expansion. Consequently, animal husbandry gains overall importance in the regional production system. Any changes are of major consequence for the livelihood conditions of these peoples.

Sociocultural Crisis

The complexity of sociocultural problems and the manifestations of transforming processes among pastoralists varies from region to region. The Wakhi and Kirghiz in the Pamirs are most affected by external intervention in the livestock sector. Five examples show how geopolitical frame conditions have affected the livelihoods of Kirghiz and Wakhi in Western High Asia during the 20th century, with continuing effects today.

Soviet Sedentarization Programs and Recent Developments in Middle Asia. Most of the Pamirs falls within the Gorno-Badakhshan Autonomous Oblast (GBAO) of the Tajikistan Republic, once part of the USSR; the sedentarization of nomads affected people here during Stalinist modernization programs in the 1930s. Autonomous republics and districts were created in order to elevate segments of society considered primitive. The Autonomous Soviet Socialist Republic of Tajikistan was carved out as a new entity, and nomadic production and the nomads' lifestyle were declared backward and intolerable. Consequently the system of pasture utilization under Kirghiz *begs* was replaced by *kolchoz* (*kollektivnoe chozjajstvo* = collective economy) and *sovchoz* (*sovetskoe chozjajstvo* = Soviet economy) resulting in settlement-centered seasonal migration of herds. Collective and/or Soviet state farming meant that winter quarters were established where the collectivized herds were brought to pasture. The herds were controlled by shepherds of the respective units; during summer, yurt encampments remained as filial branches of the unit. Where it seemed feasible, fodder production was increased and attempts were made to improve the breeding and health of the herds. Permanent winter stables with adequate infrastructure, veterinary treatment, and sufficient fodder contributed to a new settlement cell resembling in some aspects the Pamirian pastoralism of present times. Nowadays in the Eastern Pamirs Kirghiz shepherds and a few Wakhi keep yak, sheep, and goat herds around well-established supply stations. From these bases they undertake seasonal migrations to higher summer pastures. Basically, Kirghiz nomadism was converted into a form of mobile animal husbandry under the conditions of collective resource management.

Similarly, the Wakhi strategy of combined mountain agriculture was adjusted to the new socioeconomic vision. Under Soviet rule Tajikistan's economy was completely integrated into the centrally planned union system and subjected to decrees from the center. This had significant effects even on the remote mountain areas, as the case of Gorno-Badakhshan reveals. The Soviet state-run economy had identified the Eastern Pamirs as primarily a sheep and yak-producing region. All previously practiced agricultural activities were subordinated to the dominant livestock sector. Irrigated village lands formerly used for grain production were converted to fodder production zones. The Wakhi members of *sowchos roi kommunizm* in Rajon Ishkashim kept a sizeable yak herd in the upper parts of the Amu Darya valley and in Khargushi Pamir. Even in low-lying Wakhi villages, alfalfa and fodder crops replaced barley, wheat, and beans. Their whole agricultural system was redirected by decree to animal husbandry; all other food supplies were imported from outside. Even high-protein fodder (50 tons) was annually brought in from as far as Kyrgyzstan to sustain a herd of 450 yaks all year long in the Pamirs.

With the independence of Tajikistan, individual ownership of land (1996–1999) and cattle was reintroduced. Yak herding is now organized through the farmers' association; the shepherds keep 70 percent of the production while the rest belongs to the association. The Wakhi of Ishkashim still control a herd of 300 yak, as well as 15,700 sheep and goats. In neighboring Kirghiz-dominated Rajon Murghab, nearly 14,000 yaks and 38,000 sheep and goats are kept today. The majority of herds are controlled by a diminishing number of state-run enterprises or by dominant private farmers' associations which have replaced the *kolchoz* and *gozchoz* (= state farm). But the adverse economic conditions of the present transformation period have impoverished the Kirghiz herdsmen, whose remaining herds are too small to sustain a household. Food supplies are meager and additional food from the market is expensive. Basically the vast majority of agriculturists in GBAO are dependent on humanitarian aid at present.

After the failure of the Soviet model of modernization came a reversal of the "development" path. Two to three generations ago the Kirghiz nomads and Wakhi mountain farmers were expropriated and their property was collectivized. They became state employees. Though now their resources and their property have been returned to them (at least partially), people were not prepared for this sudden change. They are graduates of the most sophisticated education system in Western High Asia, and they lack their grandfathers' experience in breeding and farming; they adopted different professions during the Soviet era. The present socioeconomic transformation process has forced the majority of Kirghiz and Wakhi to practice subsistence agriculture based on crops and livestock—a return to their fathers' survival strategies, but with very different global and regional conditions. Their present income is much less than during the Soviet period, and it remains to be seen if this resource-based strategy will be sustainable. The level of insufficiency and depression is high as many young people leave and seek low-level employment in Russia and in Pakistan. Tajikistan is one of the areas in the world where substantial migration to Russia is the prime means of poverty alleviation for those in the remote corners of the country.

Competition between Nomads and Mountain Agriculturists in the Pamirs. The Taxkorgan or Sarikol (its former name) area, in the PRC, comprises three different ethnic groups: Sariqoli, Wakhi, and Kirghiz (here less than 5 percent of the population). The former two groups—81.75 percent of the inhabitants (the remainder is composed of Uighur and Han Chinese)—practice combined mountain agriculture, joining crop cultivation and animal husbandry with seasonal utilization of Pamir pastures, while the Kirghiz specialize solely in livestock. All three groups traditionally move their flocks within the Taghdumbash Pamir and once paid tribute to the Mir of Hunza, who exercised control on these pastures until 1937. Kirghiz lived in the higher elevations, while Sariqoli approached high pasture from low-lying villages to the north. Wakhi, stranded as refugees from Afghanistan, founded their settlement of Dafdar (3,400 m) in the heart of the Taghdumbash Pamir about a century ago, with the consent of the Chinese authorities. All three groups compete for the fodder resources.

Since the Chinese Revolution in 1949, and the subsequent formation of the Tajik Taxkorgan Autonomous County (Xinjiang) in 1954, collectivization replaced private ownership, and rural communes (*gungshe*) were established in the villages. The model from the neighboring republics was implemented by Chinese revolutionaries and their Soviet advisors. The basic infrastructure, including schools, police, post offices, health posts, barefoot doctors, as well as commune administration and shops, mosques, and so on, have been provided to all communities of the Taghdumbash Pamir.

In postrevolutionary times the number of livestock increased by a factor of 4.75, reaching 128,800 head in 1984. During the following decade the growth rate slowed, and in 1994 the number of livestock increased according to local statistics only to 147,586 head. This figure encompasses Bactrian camels, horses, donkeys, yaks, other cattle, sheep, and goats. Natural grazing provides the most important local resource exploited through animal husbandry: The area in grasslands extends to 6.09 million *mu* including 97.6 percent natural grazing and 0.13 million *mu* of irrigated meadows (1 *mu* equals 0.067 hectares). More than two-thirds of the overall economic activity of Taxkorgan County derives from animal husbandry.

In 1960, for the first time since the Chinese Revolution, self-sufficiency in food and fodder production was achieved in the Taxkorgan County. Since

1982 the majority of the 11 townships and former people's communes (*renmin gungshe*) have been equipped with a veterinary station supplying vaccines and extension services to the farmers. Experiments with fat-tailed sheep (*dumba, dumbash*) have been successful and their share in the regional flocks has increased. In the heart of the Taghdumbash Pamir a veterinary station specializing in yak-breeding was established in Mazar (south of Dafdar along the Pak-China Friendship Highway) that uses the local knowledge of Sariqoli, Wakhi, and Kirghiz herders who found employment there. About 400 people live in the Mazar breeding farm, which accommodates about 5,000 sheep and 500 yak. Much bigger herds of yaks are kept by the Wakhi and Kirghiz of the Kara Chukur Valley, which drains the westernmost part of the Taghdumbash Pamir. This side valley has become the only Kirghiz-dominated pasture region of Taxkorgan County. In recent years livestock production has become more profitable and found a ready regional market at the Taxkorgan bazaar.

Modernization has reached the Wakhi and Kirghiz the Chinese way. Economic liberalization and political authoritarianism remain the conceptual basis behind land use and economy. Consequently neither group can profit from its location in the border region. Though positioned along the Karakoram Highway, severe restrictions on travel for Chinese citizens apply to them as well. Thus, generating additional income from nonagrarian resources in a peripheral region becomes extremely difficult especially here, where Kirghiz and Wakhi participate in educational programs and professional training to a lower degree than others. Yet given the overall substantial economic growth in China in recent years, these Wakhi and Kirghiz communities are less positively affected than others.

Kirghiz Pastoralists in Kara Köl. The Kirghiz of Kizil Su traditionally migrated over long distances between summer grazing grounds in the Pamirs and the irrigated oases of the mountain forelands. They spent the winter herding and participating in other business in the towns of Kashgar and Yarkand. This pattern has been modified over the last 50 years, and today these Kirghiz nomads are confined with their herds to the Pamir regions all year round. Only when it is time to sell their animals do they leave their mountain abodes and travel with their flocks on foot or on the back of trucks down to the Sunday markets of Kashgar or Yarkand. The herds cover the distance of 280 km easily and without great loss of weight.

The pasture system has been adjusted to these changed conditions. The herds of the Kara Köl Kirghiz average 1.5 horses, 1.4 donkeys, and 2.5 Bactrian camels—preferred for transportation and traveling purposes—with 12.2 yaks, 98.2 sheep, and 40.1 goats. In comparison, in 1976 people in the commune of Subashi (Karakul) owned only 0.5 horses, 0.3 camels, 3.5 yaks, and 74.9 sheep and goats per household. The total number of livestock ranged in this period around 10,300 animals. Beside state ownership of flocks, pastoralists were allowed private ownership of a limited number of animals. The carrying capacity of accessible pastures was estimated at 40,000 animals; by 1991 the number of head had crossed the margin of 30,000 and it is now reaching a critical stage. In comparison with the overall livestock development in the Aqto division, where from 1976 to 1991 livestock numbers grew by a factor of 1.3 and cattle numbers by 1.65 respectively, the growth in Kara Köl is out of proportion. In the remote, high-altitude yak- and sheep-breeding area the livestock numbers grew three times faster. In this area, relaxed attitudes of the Chinese authorities toward agricultural and livestock production, especially since the reforms of 1978, have led to an increased market orientation. The quality of pastures was improved by irrigation and fencing of meadows. Grass is cut by scythe and winter fodder is stored to cover the long period of meager natural grazing in the winter settlement (*kishlok*) of Subashi at an altitude of 3,600 m.

Administratively, the Kara Köl grazing zone forms part of the Aqto division, which is one of the four subunits of the Kizil Su Autonomous Oblast where the majority of China's 119,300 Kirghiz reside (data of 1994). Most Kirghiz of Kizil Su have become sedentary agriculturists, while the inhabitants of the higher Pamirs continue to follow exclusively mobile livestock breeding. The *kishlok* of Subashi is equipped like other communes both with the infrastructure mentioned above and with a veterinary post controlling the quality and health status of animals. Despite harsh environmental conditions, the animals raised in these productive pastures compete very well in the profitable markets in the urban oases along the Southern Silk Route (Tarim Basin). The Kirghiz are respected as one of the most affluent livestock-breeding communities in the region, and Kirghiz state that recent developments have permitted them to operate successfully and they have no cause to be envious of Kirghiz in neighboring states.

Kirghiz Exodus from the Afghan Pamirs. The Great and Little Pamir within Wakhan Woluswali of Badakhshan Province (Afghanistan) have been studied extensively up to the repeated and apostrophized "last exodus" of the majority of Kirghiz nomads from there to Pakistan in 1978. Their fate is one of the most dramatic cases of border delineation interrupting traditional migration patterns.

In 1978 nearly all Kirghiz (inhabitants of 280 yurts) fled to Pakistan; they left their wealth behind. Only a small herd of 6,000 animals could be taken across the high passes to exile in Pakistan, and none at all to Turkey. After four years of exile in Pakistan, Rahman Kul migrated with his 1,132 Kirghiz followers in August 1982 to Eastern Anatolia. Rahman Kul alone had to leave 16,000 sheep and goats, more than 700 yaks, 15 horses, and 18 Bactrian camels behind, while the whole community of the Afghan Pamirs possessed more than 40,000 animals. In comparison, the majority of Afghan Wakhi were much poorer. Wakhi farmers utilizing the Pamirs for summer grazing tried to compete with rich Kirghiz nomads who controlled most of the Pamirs. Some impoverished Wakhi took up jobs as shepherds for Kirghiz herd owners. Eventually they turned to nomadic strategies, one of the rare cases when farmers became nomads.

The Kirghiz community was subsequently established in Kurdish territory as a government resettlement scheme. Since 1986 they have lived in the newly built village of Ulupamir Köyü (1,800 m), where each household was provided with ten sheep and goats as well as three cattle. Rahman Kul became the *muchtar* (village head) of the community where he died in 1990. The leadership was transferred to his eldest son. Presently this community has grown to 2,500 members in more than 400 households; these Afghan Kirghiz exiles practice meager sedentary agriculture and rely mainly on animal husbandry with their herds of 7,000 sheep, 1,000 goats, 6,000 cattle, and 70 horses. In the summer of 2005 there was no sign that the exiles would leave this part of Turkey for an uncertain future in High Asia, although there is conflict between generations: People who were born in the Pamirs dream of a return, as they see the limited natural resources available in Ulupamir Köyü. They remember a life in the Pamirs of abundant pasture and profitable livestock keeping. The next generation of Kirghiz children born in Turkey doubts the prospects of a return to Afghanistan and cannot think of a life without the modern amenities provided in Turkey. Nevertheless, Ulupamir Köyü provides no space for further expansion and for additional pastures. A growing number of people seek employment in nonagricultural activities outside the village.

While the Kirghiz community in Turkey received international attention, a different development occurred within the Pamirs. Unnoticed by interested circles, a small group of 200 Kirghiz refused to follow their *khan* to Turkey; instead they returned to the Afghan Little Pamir from Pakistan by October 1979. Under the leadership of Abdurrashid Khan they settled in Soviet-occupied Wakhan and have remained there since. The community had grown to 102 yurts in Pamir-e Kalan (Great Pamir) and 135 yurts in Pamir-e Khurd (Little Pamir) by 1999. They keep about 1,400 yak, nearly 9,000 sheep and goats, 160 horses, and 90 Bactrian camels. Animal husbandry has been limited to subsistence production in recent years because adverse political conditions have interrupted traditional exchange lines. Presently, the Kirghiz are engaged in livestock breeding and in limited barter trade with entrepreneurs from neighboring Hunza in Pakistan. The itinerant traders supply basic necessities in exchange for yaks and sheep, and livestock products such as wool, hides, yak tails, and *qurut*. Nevertheless, humanitarian aid from outside is regularly needed for basic food supplies. Abdurrashid Khan remembers the period of Soviet occupation in the Afghan Pamirs as the most comfortable period of his life. Prospects for the future are bleak and negotiations with the government of Kyrgyzstan have been started. So far, the majority of Kirghiz refuse to leave the fertile Pamir pastures. Among all the Kirghiz groups the least change has occurred here. No school, no dispensary or hospital is located in the Afghan Pamirs; there are neither bazaars nor shops. Bartering of livestock products and animal husbandry organized through a migratory cycle between winter and summer camps (sometimes an intermediate camp site is occupied in between) remain the prime occupations of this community. Once in a while there is some exchange with neighboring Kirghiz from Tajikistan (when the government permits trade fairs at the border) or with itinerant traders from Afghanistan's bazaars or bartering farmers from Pakistan.

Wakhi Mountain Farmers in Gojal (Hunza, Pakistan) and Wakhan (Afghanistan). There could be no bigger contrast than between Wakhi mountain farmers of Pakistan and Afghanistan. High mountain farmers in Wakhan follow a strict subsistence strategy and are barely able to survive from their fields and pastures. The old capital of the Wakhi, Qala-e Panja, is located in Afghan Wakhan. The ruin of the fort symbolizing diminished autonomy is located within the agricultural fields where there is little state authority to be felt. Before the Afghan crisis, bureaucrats from Kabul were sent to Khandut, the administrative center of Wakhan. But even here, there is little turnover of goods. The spiritual authority of Wakhan, Pir Shah Ismail, has replaced outside players and is accountable only to the commanders of the Northern Alliance. The local commanders demand wheat and livestock and have imposed taxation on the poor mountain farmers. This has exacerbated a severe crisis and has made it extremely difficult for local Wakhi farmers to support their families. Local production is insufficient and resources to purchase external supplies are missing. They are traditional subsistence farmers, without exchange partners for barter trade for the 110 households of approximately 10,000 persons. A very important contribution to previous Wakhi livelihood, the nonagrarian part of the household's income, is no longer accessible. Consequently, subsistence is critically endangered. Regularly, people from here cross the border into neighboring Pakistan to offer livestock and their personal services as wage laborers in exchange for desperately needed flour: Mobility again is a coping strategy for crises. Without these opportunities survival could not be guaranteed in the isolated and remote Wakhan—yet Pakistan talks of sealing this border with fences and land mines.

To a lesser degree, poor Wakhi can be found in communities in Pakistan: in Baroghil (Yarkhun Valley, Chitral), Darkot (Yasin), and Ishkoman. But in Gojal (Hunza Valley) there is a different development. The Wakhi living here are profiting substantially from development efforts of the Aga Khan Development Network (AKDN) and from migration. As a long-term strategy, the AKDN tried to improve the infrastructure by setting up a health network, educational institutions, and rural development in addition to the efforts by the government of Pakistan. The Wakhi of Gojal adopted the educational goals enthusiastically. Nearly all boys and girls are attending schools, and many have experienced further education and are established in professional careers far from dependency on agriculture. Many Wakhi are working in urban centers of Pakistan (Gilgit within the region, and more distant Islamabad and Karachi), and some are migrants living in the Gulf States, the United States, and Canada.

In Gojal, outside intervention and subsidies supported different communities in expanding their sources of income and building a more diversified foundation for survival in harsh environments. A comparable kind of external support was found in the Soviet era, when basic infrastructure was funded from the center and provided to the remotest locations. The PRC followed the same strategy in principle, although the success rate was far lower, especially in terms of education.

Animal husbandry as part of combined mountain agriculture has ceased to be the major survival strategy for the Wakhi. Cash crop production of potatoes promises much higher returns and is less time consuming. Access to the Karakoram Highway as the major traffic artery linking Pakistan with China has become an additional asset. Gojali Wakhi are involved in Pakistan-China trade as much as in commercial and professional enterprises in Pakistan.

Response: Struggles to Sustain Cultural Survival

There have been many challenges to the Kirghiz and Wakhi; responses have been quite varied. Challenges from outside occurred mainly in the field of political pressure and the external domination of peripheral regions. Wakhi and Kirghiz communities came under political control from nation-states with more or less vested interests in their resource base. In the economic sphere concepts of modernization—be they capitalist or communist—were implemented in the name of development and improvement of living conditions. Wakhi and Kirghiz try to retain elements of their pastoral traditions. Their struggle for cultural survival appears to be a pursuit of territorial control and the search for security in a familiar habitat.

On a different level, the Gojali Wakhi established the "Wakhi Tajik Cultural Association" in 1990. Several objectives are pursued, among which preservation, documentation, and publication of "local culture" are stressed, as is the introduction of a script and its application to school textbooks and dictionaries, and to plays, literature, and radio programs. The association was very successful in organizing cultural festivals and in inviting culture troupes from neighboring states. Cultural preservation in the Soviet and Chinese context has been manifest in the preservation of folklore, and the idea of what constitutes cultural survival varies quite a bit. Some emphasize material expressions such as documenting house-building techniques, carpentry, and agricultural skills and the preservation of secular buildings and religious shrines. Others pursue a strong, conscious literary path. The daily transmission of a half-hour Wakhi radio program named *bām-e dunyā* (Roof of the World) from Radio Gilgit is heard in all Wakhi-speaking areas and creates new bonds.

The positions and experiences of Wakhi and Kirghiz in Western High Asia have been fragmented, as the boundaries between the scattered community territories indicate,—but then they have never been a single unit. Geopolitical events have frequently forced both communities to adjust to altered circumstances, and they have found coping strategies in consequence. The far-reaching effects of international politics on peripheral valleys and plateaus might be surprising for such a remote high-mountain region.

Food for Thought

The two production systems applied by Wakhi mountain farmers and Kirghiz nomads in the Pamirian Knot cannot be treated as just two different strategies for the optimum utilization of natural resources in High Asia. Furthermore, the discussion of the case studies has shown how important social developments and how influential political interventions are to an understanding of the socioeconomic patterns and community status in their respective societies and nation states. In a harsh environment at the upper limit of cultivation, and in remote, peripheral regions, external forces are leaving their mark as much as they are felt at the center. The Wakhi and Kirghiz are communities forced to adjust to changed circumstances. Their varying experience in four different nation-states demonstrates the different pathways to cultural transformation.

To Think About

1. Are ecological and/or sociopolitical conditions what determine the chances of survival in harsh environments?
2. How would you define Wakhi and Kirghiz culture?
3. What are the peculiarities of Kirghiz and Wakhi lifestyles and why are they transforming?
4. Would you say the utilization strategies of Kirghiz and Wakhi are efficient?
5. What could be the scope of cultural survival in the case of Wakhi and Kirghiz?

Resources

Published Literature

Curzon, G. N. 1896. The Pamirs and the Source of the Oxus, in *The Geographical Journal* 8: 15–54, 97–119, 239–264.

Dor, Remy and Clas M. Naumann. 1978. *Die Kirghisen des afghanischen Pamir.* Graz: Akademische Druck- und Verlagsanstalt.

Dunmore, Earl of [= Murray, C.A.]. 1893. *The Pamirs; being a narrative of a year's expedition on horseback and on foot through Kashmir, Western Tibet, Chinese Tartary, and Russian Central Asia.* 2 Vols. London: John Murray (reprint: Lahore: Vanguard Books 1996).

Ehlers, Eckart and Hermann Kreutzmann. eds. 2000. *High Mountain Pastoralism in Northern Pakistan.* Stuttgart: Franz Steiner Verlag.

Felmy, Sabine. 1997. *The Voice of the Nightingale: A Personal Account of the Wakhi Culture in Hunza.* Oxford, New York, Karachi: Oxford University Press.

Felmy, Sabine and Hermann Kreutzmann. 2004. Wakhan Woluswali in Badakhshan: Observations and Reflections from Afghanistan's Periphery, in *Erdkunde* 58(2): 97–117.

Gordon, Thomas Edward. 1876. *The Roof of the World, Being the Narrative of a Journey over the High Plateau of Tibet to the Russian Frontier and the Oxus Sources on Pamir.* Edinburgh: Edmonston and Douglas.

Kreutzmann, Hermann. 1994. Habitat Conditions and Settlement Processes in the Hindukush-Karakoram, in *Petermanns Geographische Mitteilungen* 138(6): 337–356.

————. 1995. Globalization, Spatial Integration and Sustainable Development in Northern Pakistan, in *Mountain Research and Development* 15(3): 213–227.

————. 1996. *Ethnizität im Entwicklungsprozeß. Die Wakhi in Hochasien.* Berlin: Dietrich Reimer Verlag, 488. (Contains English summary.)

————. 1998. The Chitral Trade Triangle: Rise and Decline of Central Asian Trade, 1895–1935, in *Asien-Afrika-Lateinamerika* 26(3): 289–327.

————. 2003. Ethnic Minorities and Marginality in the Pamirian Knot. Survival of Wakhi and Kirghiz in a Harsh Environment and Global Contexts, in *The Geographical Journal* 169(3): 215–235.

Olufsen, Ole. 1904. *Through the Unknown Pamirs: The Second Danish Pamir Expedition 1898–1899.* London: William Heinemann (reprint: New York: Greenwood Press 1969).

Shahrani, M. Nazif. 1979. *The Kirghiz and Wakhi of Afghanistan: Adaptation to Closed Frontiers.* Seattle and London: University of Washington Press, 265.

————. 1984. Afghanistan's Kirghiz in Turkey, in *Cultural Survival Quarterly* 8: 31–34.

10

The Badakshani of the Eastern Pamir, Tajikistan

Stephen F. Cunha

The Badakshani inhabit the eastern Pamir Mountains of Tajikistan. This independent, landlocked, Wisconsin-sized republic is the geographical heart of Central Asia's vast cordillera. Long isolated from the outside world, Tajikistan gained autonomy following the 1991 breakup of the Soviet Union. Unfortunately, independence quickly degenerated into a civil war that stifled economic development, degraded the environment, and displaced half a million people. The direct and now lingering effects of this conflict imperil the Badakshani because their isolation leaves them dependent on a stable and successful Tajik state. A UN-brokered settlement in June 1997 between the Tajik government and Islamic opposition forces initiated a fragile peace. However, regional insurgencies and political isolation combined with a challenging physical environment still threaten Badakshani stability. Until recently, meeting the demand for food and medical supplies—especially in winter—required outside assistance. In this landscape of extreme environmental challenges, a solid partnership with western Tajikistan and more open international borders are prerequisites for economic, political, and cultural security.

The People

Tajiks descend from the old pre-Turkic Iranian population and are one of the most ancient ethnic groups in Central Asia. Persians first settled the Pamir region in A.D.500, and were eventually absorbed into the Achaemenid Empire. A succession of Arabs, neighboring Uzbeks, and Afghans overwhelmed them between 500 and 1400. During this time they developed a sedentary agricultural lifeway—becoming the only Central Asians who were not primarily animal herders. Initially the name "Tajik" indicated all "settled people," but the term evolved to distinguish the Iranian (Tajik) from Turkic (other Central Asian)

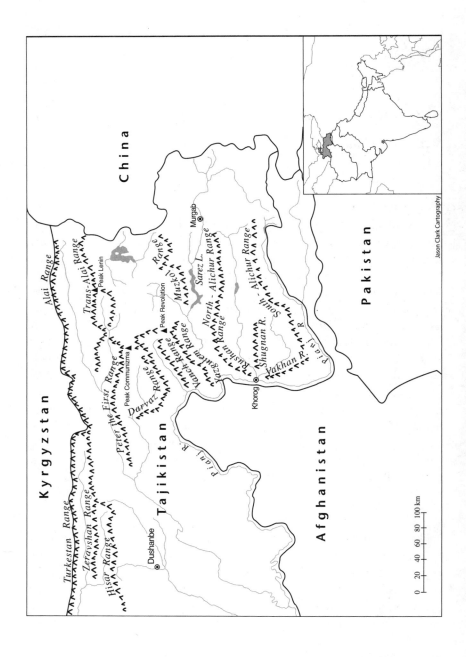

Jason Clark Cartography

subjects of the Arab Empire that stretched from Northern Africa to Central Asia. Western penetration began in the late 1700s, and for the next 200 years, Imperial Britain, Tsarist Russia, and China played the "Great Game" of political and military maneuvering for control of Central Asia. The struggle ended in the 1890s with Russian ascendancy of the Pamir. Through a long period of political change the eastern Pamir became a cultural refuge where early habits and beliefs persevered, some to the present day.

Over half of today's estimated nine million ethnic Tajiks live in Tajikistan as two distinct cultural groups. The majority lowland Tajiks live in western Tajikistan. The minority Badakshani (Mountain Tajiks)—the subject of this chapter—settle the deep canyons of the eastern Pamir and the north bank of the Pianj River (which later becomes the Amu Darya/Oxus). Tajiks also live across the Pianj River in Afghanistan, but seven decades of Soviet rule insured a very different history for those in Tajikistan. Interspersed and included among the Badakshani are six Pamiri clans (Lagnob, Lazgulem, Rushan, Shuganan, Vakhan, and Vanch) of almost pure ancient Iranian heritage. The Badakshani and Pamiri peoples number approximately 200,000, and collectively use *Pamiri*, *Mountain Tajik*, or *Badakshani* (used throughout this chapter) to describe their ethnicity.

Western Tajiks openly discriminate against the Badakshani for their different physical appearance (they are more fair skinned and taller), their Ismaili and Zoroastrian religious beliefs (explained under "Religion and World View" below), and because the Tajiks view Gorno-Badakshan as a backward and secluded place. Badakshani are a low priority for the central Tajik government that is itself besieged with political and economic chaos.

The Tajik language is a Persian variant that belongs to the western division of the Iranian branch of the Indo-European language family. Most other Central Asian languages share Turkic origin, and the difference is important to Tajiks. In addition to speaking Tajik, the Badakshani speak at least one of eight Pamiri languages such as southeastern (Darvaz) and southern (Badakshan, Rog, and Kulyab) sub-dialects. These are not well understood by most lowland Tajiks. As in other Central Asian republics, after the former Soviet Union was dismantled the new Tajik government declared Farsi (Tajik) the national language.

The Setting

The Pamir is a vast rectangular knot of mountains from which the linear Hindu Kush (Afghanistan), Karakoram (Pakistan), and Tien Shan (China/Kyrgyzstan) mountains radiate outward like spokes of a giant wheel. Within Tajikistan, the high Pamir along with numerous valleys and plateaus east of the Pamir crest comprise the Gorno-Badakshan Autonomous Oblast. This poor, sparsely populated, and semi-autonomous administrative unit holds little political influence (and should not to be confused with the even poorer Badakshan Province in adjacent northeast Afghanistan; the wider region and the Wakhi and Kirghiz people who share the Pamirs with the Badakshani are discussed in Chapter 9). Moreover, for much of the year winter snows make this region an enclosed geographical "dead end." Until recently government restraints severely limited travel into adjacent China and Afghanistan. From October to March winter snows block the road to western Tajikistan. There is intermittent winter road access to Osh (Kyrgyzstan), and just-opened access to northern Afghanistan, but for the most part people in Gorno-Badakshan are secluded for the six to seven winter months each year.

There are 300 large glaciers and many peaks exceeding 15,000 ft, including Peak Ismail Saman (24,733 ft), the highest in the former Soviet Union. Numerous deep canyons—some blocked by landslides—drain eastward onto the immense Pamir Plateau. To the south the precipitous Pianj River gorge marks the Tajik frontier with Afghanistan. Riparian stands of birch (*Betula altaica* and *B. tianshanica*) along with hillside juniper (*Juniperus polycarpos seravshanica*) thickets comprise a very thin forest mosaic. The most important wildlife species include the Marco Polo sheep (*Ovis ammon poli*), Siberian ibex (*Capra sibirica*), the snow leopard (*Panthera uncia*), Asiatic bear (*Ursus arctos isabellinus*), and the markhor (*Capra falconeri).*

This multifrontier corner of Central Asia accounts for 44 percent of Tajikistan's land area (64,000 mi²) but only 3.3 percent of the population.[1] The province is divided into seven districts and the capital district of Khorog (population 22,000; also spelled Khorough or Xoroq). The Badakshani share this highland with Kirghiz nomads, a dwindling number of Russians, and a mixture of Uygars, Kazaks, and Mountaineer Tajiks from Afghanistan. Gorno-Badakshan is the poorest part of Tajikistan, which is the poorest former Soviet State, although villagers here enjoy much higher living standards than their ethnic brethren across the Pianj River in Afghanistan, where roads, electricity, schools, and medical clinics are unknown. Cultural pride runs high, and the Badakshani are quick to affirm their distinctiveness from lowland Tajiks.

Located at the same latitude as Washington, D.C., Tajikistan's interior climate is more arid and varies with altitude. A long hot summer (average daily high temperatures exceed 90°F) is followed by a short cold winter lasting from November to March where subfreezing temperatures occur daily. November to May is the rainy period. The average annual temperature at Khorog is 49°F, but temperatures decrease with elevation so even the summer months above 12,000 feet are cool enough to sustain large glaciers. While the western Pamir intercept moisture from distant oceans, very little reaches inside the deep rainshadow canyons on the eastern side. It is here that Badakshani settle and cultivate flat river terraces where melting snow and ice from the high Pamir nourish an otherwise arid land. This contradiction is Tajikistan's wealth and torment: abundant water for irrigation and hydropower development, but terrain that limits farming to narrow valleys under constant threat of flooding, earthquake, and landslides.

Traditional Subsistence Strategies

The Gorno-Badakshan economy revolves around subsistence farming and animal husbandry. In the 1940s Stalin collectivized most farms, which even then only partially supported a growing population. After independence many farms disbanded as vital subsidies from Moscow ended. With little financial capital to upgrade, Badakshani are returning to subsistence agriculture—one of the few locations where traditional farming is increasing.

Badakshani cultivate wheat, barley, maize, apples, pears, walnuts, and apricots. Grains are the most important crops. Drying apricots carpet every roof by late August when both the fleshy fruit and the almond-sized seed become dietary staples. Both collective and private farms cultivate sunflowers as a cash crop, especially along the Pianj River. The Gorno-Badakshan government continues to purchase surplus crops wherever roads allow. Since independence, weapons and opium smuggling is soaring.

Tajiks herd goats and sheep from the valleys up to mountain pasturage in the summer and return to the warmer and often snow-free valleys in fall. Herds move freely across the landscape except where hazardous river crossings or steep terrain prevent safe passage for people and stock. Horses are used for both transport and breeding stock.

Industry is limited to handicrafts such as woolen products (socks and scarves) and mining of piezo-optic quartz for jewelry. A single hydroelectric power station in Khorog produces sufficient energy for those connected to the central power grid. In late 2002, the Aga Khan Fund for Economic Development and the private sector development arm of the World Bank announced plans to develop a new electricity generation and distribution project near Khorog.

Sociopolitical Organization

Seventy-five percent of Badakshani live in small rural *kishlaks* (villages) strung along deep river valleys wherever the alluvial terraces or river bottoms offer flood-safe settlement. *Kishlak* size ranges from 15 to 300 people. Khorog (22,000 people), Murgab (4,000 people) and Iskashim (5,000 people) are the only large settlements. Nearly every *kishlak* connects to the central roads. However, chronic fuel and auto part shortages (Tajikistan produces neither), winter snow and avalanches, flooding, rockslides, and earthflows frequently cut off areas for several months each year. Thus foot and stock trails remain an integral transportation link.

Most *kishlaks* have a ruling council where older men are the primary decision makers. The central political power emanates from Khorog, which has limited semi-autonomy from western Tajikistan, but with little money, population, and no military they still depend upon the federal Tajik capital in Dushanbe. A 1992 Declaration of Independence authored by Gorno-Badakshan nationalists alienated this government, as did supporting the losing side in the Tajik Civil War. The desire for complete autonomy remains high as Gorno-Badakshan struggles to support its population with paltry federal assistance.

Religion and Worldview

Badakshani are Ismaili Muslims. Worldwide, the Islamic faith divides into two main groups, Sunni and Shi'a; the Ismailis are usually considered a small and conservative Shiite branch. In some isolated mountain areas Pamirians also follow Zoroastrian customs (after Zoroaster, the 6th century prophet and religious reformer from northeast Iran). Islam has emerged in the post-Soviet era as vibrant and popular social force despite decades of state sanctioned oppression. The men wear *tubytaka* or skullcaps in allegiance to Allah. Most women wear headscarves of no religious significance, and the *bourka* or complete head to toe veiling is rare here. Compared to other Islamic regions, the society is more open and women have far more contact with nonfamily males and outside visitors. The local mullahs (learned teachers or interpreters of religious laws) and Sufi adepts (those who study and bear the inner message of Islam, and eschew most material goods) are held in high esteem for their spiritual knowledge. Badakshani believe in the *uma*, or worldwide Islamic community. Though proud of their heritage they are friendly and generous to outsiders, and have a keen interest in life beyond the Pamir.

Threats to Survival

Demographic Trends

Demographic (population) trends are a reliable indicator of social health, and in Gorno-Badakshan declining longevity, high infant and child mortality, and the spread of infectious disease is slowing the once rampant pre-independence rate of population growth. Countries with similar profiles such as Mali, Bangladesh, and Haiti are among the poorest.

Surging immigration and high fertility rates more than tripled the population of Central Asia between 1951 and 1989. During this time Tajikistan led all nations with a 3 percent annual growth rate that was among the highest on Earth. Out-migration of Russians (*ostravechnio*) and other non-Tajik minorities, especially younger people, has since reduced annual population growth to just over 1 percent. Children comprise nearly half the population, and their impending reproductive "momentum" will sustain high growth well into this century.

In 1992 the Tajikistan State Republic Committee for Statistics predicted a 20 percent population increase in Badakshani villages by 2005. This optimistic growth was partly based on a predicted drop in infant mortality. This did not materialize as the sudden financial crisis stalled plans to modernize the *kishlaks*. The average extended family size is ten persons with a total fertility rate (the number of children born to each woman) averaging 4.0. The number of children per couple varies between two and 15 offspring. Growth rates are lower in urban areas such as Khorog and Iskashim where housing density, nonagricultural employment, and literacy rates are greater.

The average life expectancy in Gorno-Badakshan recently dropped slightly to 65 years, with a gender differential that favors women by six years. The civil war increased this gap. Infant mortality grew from 41.8 per 1,000 live births in 1990 to a staggering 106 per 1,000 in 2005. In 2005, 117 of every 1,000 children younger than five years of age died from disease, malnutrition, or accidents. Up to 90 percent of births are home deliveries, of which almost half take place without a health care worker present. Between 1950 and independence in 1991, a baby boom created a rural profile where just 38 percent of the population were 20- to 59-year-old "working age" adults. Today 70 percent of the population are either 0–18 year-old dependents or older than 60 years. This "dependency ratio" is the highest in Central Asia and in the upper 10 percent of the world. Moreover, only a fraction of the young end of this ratio will enter the *nonfarm* labor market. Unless alternatives are developed, this distorted age structure will soon require more irrigated agricultural land, increased productivity from existing fields, and increasing emigration from Gorno-Badakshan.

Over 35 percent of Badakshani marry by 20 years of age, but the women marry younger than men do. The woman's median age of first birth is 21 years. The contraceptive prevalence rate is 31 percent for Tajikistan, but if worldwide analogs hold true, it falls below 10 percent for rural Badakshani because most homes lack running water and money for birth control. Family planning here as in the rest of Central Asia raises wider issues about economic and social development. Families are large because education levels, employment, percent of urban dwellers, and the status of women are lower relative to more urban and industrial areas.

The total expenditure on health care is less than 4 percent of the gross domestic product. The World Health Organization estimates that there has been a 100-fold decrease in health care spending since independence. The 2002 per capita state expenditure on health care for Tajikistan averaged less than $6 (U.S.)—but it is less than that in Badakshan where medical personnel and facilities are fewer. The economic crisis has resulted in a major upsurge in communicable diseases including dysentery, typhoid, tuberculosis, and malaria, especially in Gorno-Badakshan. There is an acute shortage of qualified doctors, who are abandoning the profession or emigrating in droves because the salary averages just $4 per month. Although water is one of the country's most plentiful natural assets, it is now a source of disease. The country cannot afford to maintain its treatment plants or to purchase sufficient chlorine, thus contributing to the spread of the above-mentioned diseases.

While the Badakshani were among the most educated Central Asians during the Soviet era, today the education sector is in a precipitous post-Independence downward spiral. In September of 1992, when the University of Central Asia campus opened in Khorog with a class of 200 students and limited resources, the first higher education became available in Gorno-Badakshan. However, in 1997, after reeling from six years of civil war, the government allocated just 12 percent of total public spending to education. By 2000 many of the 305 schools had closed, and two of every five Badakshani children were not enrolled. Fewer girls than boys were enrolled, and the secondary dropout rate for both increased as children entered farm sector employment. While grade school enrolments have been slowly rising since 2000, today there is an acute shortage of teachers, textbooks, and teaching aids, and school maintenance and public transport of students are virtually nonexistent.

Women comprise just over half the population and lag behind men in almost every indicator of social health. The new constitution of the Republic of Tajikistan guarantees equal rights and freedom to everyone, regardless of ethnicity, gender, and national origin, in all aspects of ". . . life and activity." Thus women have the legal rights to seek redress for discrimination in labor problems, marriage and family issues, and have equal protection in the civil and criminal codes. They account for less than 3 percent of elected Federal and Oblast representatives and less than 15 percent of top government ministerial and management posts. In all other key indicators of equal gender status—unemployment, land ownership, violent crime victimization, domestic violence, access to health care—Tajik women lag far behind their male counterparts. Gaining equality is an uphill struggle in a culture that traditionally assigns more status to males. In Gorno-Badakshan women are not well represented in government positions, but relative to elsewhere in Central Asia and the greater Islamic world, they are treated better, are more visible in public, interact more with nonfamily males, and enjoy more status within their families.

Current Events and Conditions

For 70 years the Soviets developed Tajikistan as a colonial state, with goods and services oriented to support Moscow. Within this framework Gorno-Badakshan was merely an outpost to satisfy Russian military objectives. Sudden independence and the end of subsidies in 1991 followed by civil war made Gorno-Badakshan a second-rate province in its own country, precariously short of food, fuel, and medical supplies. Although the extent lessens each year, the Badakshani still suffer from the direct and collateral fallout of these events. The 2004 World Bank *List of Economically Challenged Countries* includes Tajikistan and each neighboring state. The growing presence of clandestine drug smuggling and the many hazards common to mountain habitat—flooding, earthquakes, and landslides—are additional factors that cannot be ignored. Leaving these threats unresolved will almost certainly produce some degree of cultural disintegration, political subversion, and rapid out-migration. The issues are discussed below.

Civil War and Personal Security

Of the emergent former Soviet States, Tajikistan is making the slowest progress toward postcolonial stability and prosperity. Throughout the Pamirs and surrounding lowlands long-standing ethnic rivalries erupted into bloodshed within months following the 1991 Declaration of Independence. The conflict is fundamentally more regional than ideological as clans wrestled both for power in the new Tajik government and for control of smuggling routes used to take opium from Central Asia to Europe. The more developed southern (Kulyab) and northern (Lininabad) regions dominated Tajikistan during the Soviet era. When the controlling grip of Moscow ended, opposition to this dominance grew among people from the poorer and more conservative Muslim regions of Garm and Gorno-Badakshan. The war progressed through two stages: Seven months of full-blown hostility followed by almost five years of temporary peace agreements that repeatedly collapsed into regional guerrilla warfare. Violence impoverished Tajikistan's six million people, deepened ethnic disputes, and thwarted both economic development and natural resource conservation. The conflict claimed 60,000 lives and produced 600,000 refugees, many of whom fled into appalling squatter camps in Afghanistan and neighboring Central Asian republics. The local media operating with post-Soviet freedoms also contributed to feelings of personal insecurity by publishing numerous gory accounts of street crimes, murders, and robberies. In 1999, four United Nations officials were murdered. Since the breakup of the Soviet Union, the Committee to Protect Journalists has ranked Tajikistan as one of the ten most dangerous countries in the world. Although most of the violence occurred in western Tajikistan, several *kishlaks* along the Pianj River within Gorno-Badakshan suffered heavy damage. Downed bridges and land mines repeatedly halted road traffic. After several failed attempts the various rebel factions and the Tajik government signed a United Nations-brokered peace accord in June 1997. Unfortunately, not all militias sat at the table; hence a couple of small ones, especially in the Garm-Nurek area north of Gorno-Badakshan, maintain deep-seated resentment that threatens the larger peace plan.

As has often been the case in the eastern Pamir, the self-interest of distant but powerful nations affects those who live here. The most recent example is the American "War on Terror" which raised the profile of Gorno-Badakshan when American Secretary of Defense Donald Rumsfeld visited Tajikistan in November 2001, one month after the Americans invaded Afghanistan. The Tajik government agreed to let United States and coalition forces use Tajik airspace for aircraft sorties into Afghanistan, and for refueling and emergency landings. The Russians responded in 2003 by increasing their existing military presence by 30,000 troops to help secure Tajikistan's 879-mile border with Afghanistan. In October 2004, the Moscow government also regained control of a former USSR satellite tracking station used to monitor intelligence. In July 2005 the Russians reversed their policy in Tajikistan when they abandoned border garrisons they had occupied for over five decades. In July 2006, Rumsfeld revisited Tajikistan, calling it "a frontline state on the War on Terror," and noted that common American and Tajik interests "involve not only counter-terrorism, but also counter-narcotics, nonproliferation of dangerous weapons, and a common interest in the region's economic growth."

A tangible result of the renewed foreign presence is a $28 million American-funded bridge across the Pianj River between Gorno-Badakshan and Afghanistan, completed in June 2006. During that year the United States contributed another $14 million to strengthen Tajikistan's border security to reduce terrorist and narcotics trafficking. While for the most part Tajikistan now assumes sole responsibility for this contested frontier, the impact of such geopolitical maneuvering on local people is not yet clear.

Food Shortages

Severe food shortages have plagued Tajikistan since independence. They result from falling agricultural production, civil strife, and periodic spring flooding. The end of subsidies from Moscow, which just prior to independence had paid 40 percent of total state expenditures, also contributes to food insecurity. Competing interests in Dushanbe have also been accused of denying Gorno-Badakshan food shipments for political reasons, though food-deficient western Tajikistan may have simply consumed it first.

By the early 1990s irrigated lands in Tajikistan reached a peak of 960,000 hectares and used 81 percent of the total water supply. During the previous two decades the Tajiks exported food and cotton. But the heavy reliance on irrigation, chemicals, and aggressive plantings on marginal lands took its toll. At independence, nearly 80 percent of soils were degraded from various combinations of irrigation erosion, landslides, salinity, and deflation. The war damaged irrigation and road infrastructure nearly everywhere. Within Gorno-Badakshan, communities along the Pianj River on the main road were hit especially hard; the same areas also struggle with soil erosion and contamination.

Food deficiencies are most acute in valleys far removed from the two major roads. The Pianj route connects Khorog with Dushanbe in 18 hours by truck, but winter snows close this from November until March. The Khorog to Osh (Kyrgyzstan) road opens periodically during the winter, but the treacherous journey takes 22 hours by truck and snow strands many vehicles for weeks on end. In May 2004 a new road over Kulma Pass (14,311 ft/ 4,362 m) connected Tajikistan and China for the first time. The artery runs between Tashkurgan in Xinjiang (China) over to Murgab, allowing much faster access to Kashgar, Urumchi, and Pakistan (via the Khunjerab Pass). Winter snowfall and restricted access by Chinese officials kept the first-year traffic very low. The Tajik Ministry of Traffic and Roads counted 17 trucks, 10 buses, 240 tons of cargo, and 171 people over three summer months. There are no railroads in Gorno-Badakshan and air travel is notoriously unreliable because of mountain weather and fuel shortages.

Although meager food supplies are a problem throughout Tajikistan, until recently they reached a crisis stage throughout Gorno-Badakshan each year. Before independence the Red Army supplied this strategic multifrontier with almost 100 percent of its annual grain requirement. The stockpiled food and medical supplies allowed Badakshani and Kyrgyz to survive winter solitude. As mentioned above, these critical shipments suddenly ended when Moscow curtailed the subsidies with Tajik independence and when warfare damaged roads and created fuel shortages. In 1993 road blockades by rebel factions further eliminated almost all summer traffic into Gorno-Badakshan. During that same summer, Badakshani aborted their independence movement from Tajikistan—a move that left them nevertheless politically estranged from the federal Tajik government. During the winter of 1993–1994, reports of famine and death by freezing began surfacing from Badakshani kishlaks, snowbound and saddled with an inefficient Soviet farming system. Outbreaks of dysentery and cholera exacted a further toll. Between 1994 and 1996, acute childhood malnutrition doubled to nearly 6 percent. By 1997 almost half the children of Gorno-Badakshan suffered from chronic childhood malnutrition, and only continuing aid from the outside alleviates winter food shortages in the remote parts of the region.

Opium and Marijuana Farming

Although illegal, the increasing cultivation and smuggling of opium poppy (*Papaver somniferum*) and marijuana (*Cannabis sativa*) is a bright spot in the regional economy. Central Asians first planted opium in the 19th century but the Russians largely eradicated it during the 1940s. With the Soviets gone, planting narcotic plants over food cultigens is attractive because they thrive in the arid climate and sterile glacial soils of the Pamir. Drug crops are also hardier and easier to transport. They store longer than almost any eatable crop. A government eradication program and the furtive nature of drug cultivation makes it difficult, if not impossible, to determine just how much opium and marijuana are produced in Gorno-Badakshan. An independent and chaotic Tajikistan is once again a favored transshipment point for narcotics from Southwest Asia to Western Europe and the Americas. The porous Afghan frontier to Pakistan and the Alai Pass into Kyrgyzstan are the principal bootlegging routes. Opium traffic into Tajikistan surged after the Americans invaded Afghanistan in 2001. Before their fall from power, the Taliban were the lone Central Asian government to successfully crack down on opium cultivation. The admission of Tajikistan into the Russian Customs Union will almost certainly increase the flow of drugs through this "Heroin Corridor." Russian officials attribute declining heroin prices since the mid-1990s to increased production within Tajikistan and Kyrgyzstan and more smuggling of Afghan opium through Tajikistan.

Tajiks use proceeds from the drug trade to purchase much needed food and consumer goods. But this advantage exacts a price. Here as elsewhere, warlords control the drug trade from planting to profits. Thus local security and labor are tightly regimented by these mostly Afghani tribesmen who derive their authority behind the barrel of *Kalashnikovs*. It remains to be seen if Gorno-Badakshan will join Afghanistan and Southeast Asia's Golden Triangle as a major producer of opium.

Lake Sarez

Often called Central Asia's sleeping giant, Lake Sarez formed when a 1911 earthquake shook loose six billion metric tons of debris, damming the

Murgab River. The Usoi dam, named after the *kishlak* buried under rubble, is the highest dam on Earth. The water level rose 787 feet in three years and inundated 37 miles before filtration through a subterranean outlet reestablished the river. Located in the heart of Gorno-Badakshan, Sarez is the largest natural sediment reservoir in Central Asia. The current estimated volume is 10 square miles. The lake level rises up to 8 inches annually, thus increasing the pressure on the natural dam.

Failure of the Usoi dam is a potential cataclysmic disaster that would alter the economy and sociopolitical environment of Tajikistan. In a worst-case scenario that assumes collapse of the dam, a catastrophic outburst flood from Lake Sarez would inundate settlements and infrastructure in the Amu Darya basin between the lake and the Aral Sea, a distance of 3,200 miles. In 1998 and 1999, the United Nations and private donor funding sponsored the sending of two international monitoring and assessment teams to Lake Sarez. They determined that no simple or near-term technical solution exists because development agencies judged the engineering needed to reduce the hazard posed by the lake would be too expensive in relation to the low risk of a worst-case scenario. Close monitoring and an early warning system installed with World Bank funding in 2004 were favored over the high cost of engineering the stability of the dam. Moreover, the seismic recurrence interval is very long, and because the valley narrows at the landslide site, further water pressure would serve to compress and thus strengthen the dam. At stake are many lives, national pride, future economic development, and significant freshwater resources.

Migration Flux in the Southeastern Pamir

The composition and spatial distribution of Tajikistan's ethnic groups are changing as a result of return migration, dissolving collective farms, *ostravechnio*, and refugee movements. Defining ethnic homelands in this mountainous environment was always difficult. The Soviets uprooted and transferred many groups to dilute ethnic nationalism and strengthen adherence to a Soviet identity. The 1980s Soviet-Afghan conflict compounded this by turning the Pianj/Amu Darya River into the "Berlin Wall" of Central Asia. All bridges connecting Afghanistan and Tajikistan were destroyed (except for one at Termez on the road to Kabul). Land mines and guard towers prevented border crossings. Within Gorno-Badakshan the division of Tajiks forced many clan and family units onto different sides of a war they did not start. The lingering animosity fuels current hostilities in both states. Within Gorno-Badakshan Stalin forced farmers into collectives in the 1930s and 1940s. Others were relocated to western Tajikistan to till cotton used in armaments. The rebounding intra-regional relocation is altering settlement and demographic patterns.

Some collective farms dissolved upon independence. The primary post-colonial migration patterns here are from collective farms to either rural or urban areas, and illegal movement between northern Afghanistan and the Tajik Autonomous County in Xinjiang, China. *Ostravechnio* (Russian out-migration) is not significant as Russians constituted only 3 percent of the pre-devolution population. In addition, 15,000 Badakshani from western Tajikistan returned to Gorno-Badakshan to evade fighting during the civil war. During the conflict Gorno-Badakshan received an influx of 100,000 persons into this already impoverished area.

The ebb and flow of refugee migration, collective farm workers, drug cultivators, and returning countrymen complicates traditional land ownership. The fledgling government struggles to adjudicate land claims and assign tax liability. In this subsistence society as in nearly all others, land is the single most important family asset. The radically altered land tenure system initiated by Soviet collectivization still affects ownership between competing family and ethnic groups. The result spells lasting change for the Badakshani.

Response: Struggles to Sustain Cultural Survival

All efforts to promote cultural survival of the Badakshani must consider three current social and environmental constraints:

1. The Tajik government regards Badakshani as a small minority group with much less political clout than the majority lowland Tajiks of the western Pamir;
2. The convoluted mountain terrain, with poor road and communications infrastructure, complicates development and assistance efforts, especially in winter;
3. The sporadic internal civil strife combined with political turmoil in neighboring Afghanistan consumes both Tajik and foreign resources that might otherwise support social services and economic development.

The interrelated sum threatens the Badakshani and other minority groups who live in this solitary region. Enabling them to achieve economic viability and thus some measure of cultural security will almost certainly require outside assistance such as the current initiatives discussed below.

Humanitarian Aid to Restore Peace, Instill Nation-Building, and Avert Famine

Ending armed conflict and insuring public safety is a necessary precondition to developing a new paradigm for inter-ethnic progress. Shared nation building fosters economic development that in turn creates funding for better schools, health care, and housing. Prior to 2000, Tajikistan's competing rebel factions destroyed infrastructure and forestalled foreign aid. The heavy casualties and upsurge in refugees jarred nearly every family.

Within Gorno-Badakshan the impacts were most severe along the Pianj River and in military garrisons on the Pamir Plateau. Prior regional wars in Southeast Asia, Central Africa, and the Balkans demonstrate that prolonged conflict permanently alters the demographic and ethnic distribution between and among states. Tajikistan will be no different, but an accurate assessment is years away.

The United Nations Development Programme (UNDP) coordinates foreign aid to this new state. In early 1998 the UNDP along with the United Tajik Opposition leader Abdullo Nuri and Tajikistan President Emomali Rakhmonov made a joint appeal to the international community for financial and technical assistance to help Tajikistan recover from recent war and years of Soviet neglect. Donor nations contribute to the UNDP-administered trust fund to reestablish the recently damaged infrastructure (roads, communications, health care, etc.). They also direct a vigorous democracy project to build institutions and services in a country with no history of representative government. The competition for development money within Tajikistan is reigniting ethnic enmity. Thus a second agreement guarantees every minority group a place within the new government. This is slowly providing the Badakshani a voice in both the new Tajik Parliament and among other world states. However, any reconciliation derived from these agreements must counter armed ex-rebels, a porous border with unsettled Afghanistan, limited media freedom, and corrupt law enforcement. This destabilizing milieu will challenge the democracy building required for economic development and cultural stability.

Food Security

While civil unrest and political isolation represent the largest threats to long-term cultural survival, food security remains the most immediate problem. The United Nations estimates that food availability in 1991 dropped to 60 percent of its pre-war amount. Various relief agencies such as the World Food Organization (WFO), the Aga Khan Development Network (AKDN), United Nations Children's Fund (UNICEF) and others have averted famine by providing 80–90 percent of the area's food needs and 100 percent of its fuel. The Tajik government, with assistance from the United States Agency for International Development (USAID), is moving to reform land laws, privatize farms, and improve grain and animal stocks. The reforms are working: In 2005 Gorno-Badakshan produced 80 percent of its own food. Thus while dependence is lessening each year, the survival of this population still depends on food imports along routes vulnerable to environmental closures (snowfall, avalanches, earthflow, and high winds).

Environmental Assistance

Long-term cultural survival of agrarian culture requires sustained conservation of soil, water, and forage. The international community recently cooperated with the Tajik government to mitigate the Lake Sarez threat, study the proposed Tajik National Park, and develop a water management plan for the Syr Darya River.

Recognizing special qualities of the Pamir environment, the United Nations University and the Swiss government supported feasibility studies for the Tajik National Park beginning in the early 1990s. The cooperative effort between government and outside consultants determined potential park boundaries, management options, and tourism potential. They also identified unique cultural, physical, and biological features that deserve special protection. The teams sought input from local villagers who would be directly influenced by the proposed reserve. A fledgling tourist industry attracts more foreign mountain climbers, trekkers, and sport hunters each year. Of these, sport hunters (mostly from North America, Europe, and the Middle East) in pursuit of Asiatic bear and sheep at least theoretically contribute substantial hard currency to the local economy—enough to effectively fund park protection. The 2006 permit for one Marco Polo (*Ovis poli*) ram cost $80,000. Agreements between the Dushanbe Ministry of Environment and European tourist agencies entitle the Gorno-Badakshan government to half the permit fee, though in reality only a small portion is remitted.

The potential to earn hard currency, while providing local employment and sustained resource conservation, is just beginning. Foreign assistance to build guesthouses, develop nature reserves, restore historic sites, and finance private sector tourism companies is growing. For military reasons, the Soviets never opened this intriguing Silk Road corridor with its unusual wildlife and unruly "Roof of the World" scenery to tourism. Central Asia is one of the last frontiers of exotic adventure travel. As part of a regional economic development package to promote both trade and tourism, the UN and several NGOs are also advocating more open borders with Pakistan and China.

International advisors promote water for agriculture, hydropower, and export as the best opportunity for Gorno-Badakshan to develop a renewable and profitable natural resource while concurrently meeting the local demand for clean and affordable energy. In this arena, USAID helped Tajik government officials improve the transborder management of shared water systems. The Tajik government developed a water-use optimization model for the Syr Darya River, adopted a uniform system of calculating operations and maintenance costs for shared basin facilities, and fully implemented the 1998 water and energy exchange agreement with the governments of Kazakhstan and Uzbekistan. They also participated in an energy and water-use roundtable group that met regularly to resolve regional issues on management of water and energy resources. As the upstream state, Tajikistan is pursuing payment for water used by downstream states, especially Uzbekistan.

To date these efforts have met with little success, and some Uzbeks accuse the Tajiks of deliberately withholding or poisoning the water supply. Failure to develop a fair water resources compact will destabilize political relations among the downstream Central Asian states. Since most of the upper Syr Darya and Amu Darya watershed is within Gorno-Badakshan, all parties have much to gain from equitable regional water compacts.

Economic Development

In 2005 the World Bank placed Tajikistan among the world's 20 poorest nations, with an annual per capita income of $330 ($260 in Gorno-Badakshan). Even though economic output is increasing, 64 percent of Tajiks (more in Badakshan) live in poverty. Only one out of every thousand people used the Internet. Ongoing inflation devalues the currency by 8–20 percent each year. Even prior to the civil conflict most families had limited access to potable water and electricity. In rural areas wood and animal dung are the primary energy source. Acute poverty will force Badakshani to seek employment and education opportunities outside of Gorno-Badakshan. This presents a familiar dilemma for traditional societies in the Digital Age: Out-migration leaves fewer mouths to feed and employ, yet significant loss, especially among young adults, permanently alters the cultural fabric. The war-induced return of 15,000 Badakshani from western Tajikistan exacerbated food, housing, and employment shortages, causing observers to recommend immediate outside assistance to avert famine and internal unrest.

The current Asian Development Bank (ADB) strategy urges Tajikistan and international society to:

1. Continue implementing the 1997 peace agreement and foster national reconciliation between Tajikistan's various ethnic groups;
2. Maintain and enhance economic stability;
3. Restore basic social and infrastructure services;
4. Promote programs to stimulate employment and reduce poverty.

The ADB is also reviewing the banking sector. Within Gorno-Badakshan, they will study hydropower potential and ways to improve transport.

The AKDN supports Gorno-Badakshan through the Mountain Societies Development Support Programme (MSDSP—originally the Pamir Relief and Development Programme). Their initiatives include transferring farmland from the inefficient collective farms to "long, inheritable leases" or into private ownership. A second objective improved irrigation systems that brought 10 percent more land into production. The MSDSP also provides farmers with seed, fertilizer, and technical advice to boost grain and potato production. Road construction is one of the most important improvements for increasing economic self-sufficiency in Gorno-Badakshan. Before independence all commerce passed through Kyrgyzstan or western Tajikistan, and thence to Russia. The AKDN recently built two bridges across the Pianj River into Afghanistan. The new Kulma Pass route mentioned earlier now connects Gorno-Badakshan with China. The Tajiks now send meat, minerals, and wool in exchange for low-cost Chinese manufactured goods and other foodstuffs. Making deals with the Chinese will challenge the people of Gorno-Badakshan, who have little practice as entrepreneurs. Another road is planned to northern Pakistan across Afghanistan's narrow Wakhan corridor. In addition, a new rail link connecting Turkmenistan to Iran now allows Tajikistan to bypass Russia.

The new roads will render two new income sources: minerals and tourism. Tajikistan has 28 known gold deposits of over 400 tons, and some of the world's largest silver deposits. The Russian government continues to explore iron, lead, ore, and coal reserves that at this time are located too distant from markets. There are also abundant gems (especially rubies and lapis lazuli) and the further potential to export hydropower. Secondly, new roads will pressure China to loosen tight borders with its Central Asian neighbors. Doing so will unleash tourists on a Silk Road circuit through Pakistan, China, the former Soviet Central Asia, and eventually Afghanistan.

Food for Thought

The Badakshani live in a detached multi-frontier corner of Tajikistan. Though they were initially spared much of the post-Independence violence, the war thrust them into a political hinterland. They were also unprepared for the sudden collapse of the Soviet system that provided most of their food, fuel, and medical supplies. Achieving a stable Gorno-Badakshan requires more than developing agricultural and water resources, improving transportation infrastructure, and opening borders to facilitate tourism and commerce—key initiatives that have partly been realized. Much more difficult will be resolving the incendiary ethno-religious political divisions within the country, neutralizing the highly militarized foreign influence, and reversing the mounting influence of drug warlords—while at the same time attempting to recover from years of Soviet economic plundering. The Badakshani survive today with the help of outside assistance, and face challenges as great as the mountains that hem them in. Without the initiatives discussed above, it is unlikely that key economic and social indicators will improve for this isolated mountain society.

To Think About

1. How does geographic isolation both threaten and secure the cultural survival of the Badakshani?
2. What is the relationship between living standards (e.g., per capita income, longevity, dependency ratios) and total fertility rates in Gorno-Badakshan? What situations must occur for these relationships to change?
3. Why is economic development paramount to the long-term cultural survival of traditional agrarian societies such as the Badakshani?
4. How do new roads alter the economy and traditional society of the Badakshani?
5. How did Gorno-Badakshan, though spared much of the violence associated with the Tajik Civil War, still suffer indirectly from the conflict?

Note

1. The Tajik Civil War made it very difficult for the government to compile accurate data. These and other statistics used in this chapter are taken from the Eurasia Foundation, the Population Reference Bureau, the Soros Foundation, the Aga Khan Development Network (AKDN), and the *CIA World Factbook*. Although these are not Tajik government sources, they represent the most accurate data available in this newly independent and developing country.

Resources

Published Literature

Akiner, S. 2001. *Tajikistan: Disintegration or Reconciliation?* London: Chatham House.

Alford, D., S. F. Cunha and J. D. Ives. 2000. Mountain Hazards and Development Assistance. Lake Sarez, Pamir Mountains, Tajikistan. *Journal of Mountain Research & Development* 20(1).

Bekhrandnia, S. 1994. The Tajik Case for a Zoroastrian Identity. *Religion, State and Society* 22(1).

Cunha, S. 1994. Summits, Snow Leopards, Farmers, and Fighters: Will Politics Prevent a National Park in the High Pamirs of Tajikistan? *Focus* 44(1).

Curtis, G. 1997. *Kazakstan, Kyrgyzstan, Tajikistan, Turkmenistan, and Uzbekistan: Country Studies.* Washington, D.C.: United States Government Printing Office.

Falkingham, J. 2004. Poverty, Out-of-Pocket Payments and Access to Health Care: Evidence from Tajikistan. *Social Science & Medicine* 58(2): 247–258.

Gilmore, G. 2007. Rumsfeld Calls Tajikistan 'Solid Partner' in Terror War. *U.S. Department of Defense, American Forces Information Service News Articles.*

Haslinger, A. 2003. The Challenge of the Tajik National Park: How Can the Tajik National Park (TNP) Contribute to the Conservation of Natural Resources in the Pamir Mountains? Berne: Centre for Development and Environment (CDE), University of Berne (MSc thesis).

Hopkirk, P. 1992. *The Great Game: The Struggle for Empire in Central Asia.* Tokyo: Kodansha.

Kanji, N. and Gladwin, C. 2000. *Gender and Livelihoods in Gorno-Badakshan.* Dushanbe: The Mountain Societies Development and Support Programme.

Ludi, E. 2003. Sustainable Pasture Management in Kyrgyzstan and Tajikistan: Development Needs and Recommendations. *Mountain Research and Development* 23(2).

McLean, J. and T. Greene. 1998. Turmoil in Tajikistan: Addressing the Crisis of Internal Displacement. Pages 313–358 in R. Cohen and F. M. Deng eds. *The Forsaken People: Case Studies of the Internally Displaced.* Washington: Brookings Institution.

Olufsen, O. 1904. *Through the Unknown Pamirs: The Second Danish Pamir Expedition, 1898–99.* London: William Heinemann.

11

The Lezghi

Julian Birch

The People

It is not easy to give a simple answer to the question, who are the Lezghi? Although they are apparently one of the oldest groups settled in the eastern part of the Caucasus mountain range, the written history of the Lezghi (also sometimes *Lezgi*) can be traced back only to the Middle Ages. In the past their name was applied to local mountain peoples as a whole. The Lezghi's only close relations are a number of even smaller ethnic groups in the same area—neither Slav nor Turkic (the major groups of the area) but rather northeast Caucasian.

The latest official census figures claim 411,500 Lezghi in Russia's Daghestan republic (2002) and 178, 000 in Azerbaijan (1999), though some complain that the Azeri census deliberately underreports Lezghi numbers.

The Setting

The Lezghi are settled in the territory of southeastern Daghestan in southern Russia, and in northwest Azerbaijan; there is a very small community in eastern Georgia as well. The present division between Russia and Azerbaijan dates from 1860 when Tsarist Russia split its recently acquired colonies here between Daghestan province (which remains a part of Russia's post-Soviet territory) and Shemakhanskaya governorship (now in Azerbaijan). Not only were the Lezghi thus spread over two connected and yet distinct topographical zones—the highlands and the lowlands—the ground was also set for their division between two countries when the Russian Empire's successor, the Soviet Union, fragmented in 1991.

In Russian Daghestan, where Lezghi are one of some 34 distinct and indigenous ethnolinguistic groups, they are to be found along the middle and

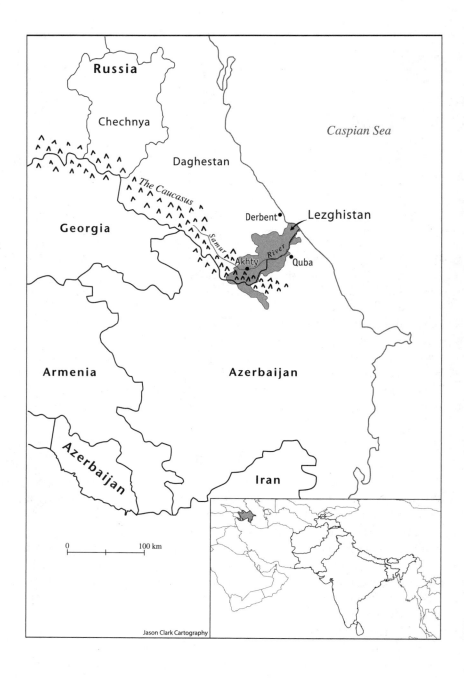

Jason Clark Cartography

lower reaches of the river Samur and along the Kurakhchai and Gyulgerichai valleys in the southeastern districts of Magaramkent, Kurakh, Akhty, Dokuzpara, and Suleimanstal'skiy, with smaller numbers in the Khiv and Rutul districts. The most ancient and largest settlement in Lezghi territory is Akhty, set among perpetually snow-capped mountains including Shalbuz-dag—the so-called mountain of light—a site sacred to the Lezghi, who pray in its caves. A large but detached group of them also live in the city of Derbent in south Daghestan—essentially emigrants from the home range.

Across the Azeri border, formed in part by the river Samur, the Lezghi are to be found in the northen districts of Qusar (which has the highest concentration in this area), Quba, Sheki (formerly Nukha), Shamakha, and Khachimaz. Typically they are to be found living in two-storey houses with verandas and flat roofs common through much of the Caucasus region, with fruit trees growing in the attached courtyards.

In terms of numbers, the census returns gathered throughout the last century reveal a steady increase in population:

Census Date	Total Lezghi Numbers
1926	134, 529
1959	223, 129
1970	323, 829
1979	382, 611
1989	466, 833
2002	Approx. 600, 000

The distribution of the Lezghi within the countries where they find themselves is, however, a matter of dispute and conjecture. Many countries are likely to exaggerate or minimize their minority populations—to exaggerate when seeking financial or medical aid, to minimize in an effort to forge the appearance of unity after gaining independence. The Lezghi see Azerbaijan as the chief culprit in underreporting. Officially the figures are as follows:

Census Date	Lezghi Population of Russian Daghestan	Lezghi Population of Azerbaijan
1926	90, 509	37, 263
1959	108, 615	98, 211
1970	162, 721	137, 250
1979	188, 804	158, 057
1989	204, 370	171, 395
	411,500 (Russia as a whole, 2002)	178,000(1999)

Lezghi leaders, however, allege a Lezghi population in Azerbaijan from two to five times as great as officially claimed, with many Lezghi registered in other categories, especially as Azeris, either by careless and generalizing census officials or by the Lezghi themselves who seek to avoid the possibility of acquiring a second-class status. There has certainly been some loss of identification with their original community and a level of assimilation with the Azeris here.

Traditional Subsistence Strategies

The Lezghi have traditionally lived by animal husbandry (together with associated activities) and settled agriculture, reflecting their two areas of residence: They are mountain-dwelling pastoralists to the north, valley farmers to the south. Among the mountain-dwelling Lezghi, sheep and goat breeding is common and has included transhumance from mountain to lowland pastures in the harsh winters. Quite a number once took their herds across what is now the international frontier, from Daghestan into northern Azerbaijan. These pastoral activities have been accompanied by weaving and assorted handicrafts such as gold and silver smithing, pottery and rug making, and some fruit growing. In the lowlands and plains, Lezghi have worked on cattle-rearing and fruit-growing collective farms which outlived the Soviet regime that created them. The fruit commonly grown in the Akhty and Magaramkent districts includes cherries, apricots, apples, and pears. Some of the lowlanders also farm wheat and maize. Still other Lezghi in the lowlands work in a variety of manufacturing occupations in the larger settlements, including fruit processing. Indeed, the level of urbanization has markedly increased over the last century, though a majority of Lezghi remain rural inhabitants.

Sociopolitical Organization

In the mountain areas, a patriarchal, clan-based village society still exists, with extended families founded on common ancestry. These village clans differ internally and in their marital preferences and practices. Land and property here have traditionally been held in common by the clan. The existence of the clans has certainly slowed down the consolidation of the Lezghi into a more united ethnic entity; that said, the clans have often linked into small-scale federations. While the Lezghi of Daghestan never formed a principality or Khanate of their own (unlike the Avar and other neighbors), they retained the federation model up to the 19th century, and three main federations (the Akhty, Alty, and Dokuz Para) along with some clans among the Rutul people united to form the core of the modern Lezghi people. Those in Azerbaijan formed part of the Quba Khanate, followed briefly in the 18th century by the Kazikumukh Khanate.

From the arrival of the Russians, who established a protectorate in 1812, Lezghi identity and role in the larger scheme of things evolved slowly but steadily: from members of a clan, a village, then clan-federation, to membership of mountain peoples in general and a greater Muslim community, to being full inhabitants of the Russian Empire by 1864. They played no significant role in resisting the Russian incursion into the area, unlike the Avars and the Chechens. After 1917, of course, they became Soviet citizens.

The Soviet system, ideologically committed to internationalism and the creation of a new Soviet identity bestriding all forms of localism, nevertheless had great difficulty in coping with and organizing the multiplicity of distinct peoples and languages of the north Caucasus. The common Moslem identity of many of these peoples (together with a common Arabic literary and educational usage) could have served, as many wished, as a basis for creating a common identity. Even a common usage of Turkish would have served this purpose. Such might have been the case had it not been for the Soviet Bolsheviks' hostility, on gaining power in 1917, to religion and subsequently to Pan-Turkism (a movement for unity among the Turkic peoples of the world). Instead, despite their earlier opposition to federalism, the Soviets settled on a pseudo-federal structure, creating ethnically based units with little real power or autonomy within a federation. Nevertheless, the act of creating such units and defining the distinct peoples more clearly, both in census returns and actual territories in the 1920s and '30s, served to clarify identities around distinct ethnicities and to reinforce the separate nature of the identities. Once categorized, ethnic labels proved almost irreversible in subsequent constitutional readjustments of the constituent parts of the Soviet Union. Moslem, Arabic-aware mountain clans had become Lezghis, Kumyks, Laks, and so on, and even by the 1979 census only 5 percent of Lezghi declared Russian as their first language.

Being partly a lowland people, the southern Lezghis have historically been more open to dominant and more modernizing Azeri influences, even before the 1917 revolution, with a consequent impact on their more traditional social structures. The village community is much weaker and even the clan and sub-clan structures have largely disappeared, along with the extended family. Endogamy, or marrying within the clan, is also less common. Moreover, those Lezghi who have left for cities such as Derbent and Baku make the Lezghi one of the most industrially oriented peoples of the Caucasus.

Religion and Worldview

The early religious history of the Lezghi is one of traditional animistic beliefs based on clan and local deities and on respect for the importance of a variety of holy sites. Zoroastrianism with its fire worship, Judaism, and even Christianity also had some limited early impact, but more important was a series of influences from the Moslem world.

The first wave of Islam arrived in Daghestan with the Arabs in the 8th to 9th centuries. The invasion of Tamurlane and the Mongols in the 14th to 16th centuries expanded Islam's power and reach, which was reinforced by influences from Persian traders in the 15th century. By the 16th century occupation of the Ottoman Turks, Islam was the dominant religion in the region. The work of Moslem Sufi brotherhoods from the end of the 18th century largely completed the process of Islamicization in Daghestan. There was then a steady attempt in the 19th century to eliminate the surviving influence of the old traditional religion, and as a result conservative Islam's annual and life-cycle rites, including circumcision of males, arranged marriages, limitation on intermarriage, bride-price payments and so on, eclipsed the old ways.

With this steady Islamicization of the whole region, the Lezghi overwhelmingly came under the influence of the Sunni branch and its Shafe'i theological school (though a very small community at Miskinji, in Dokuz Para district in the south of Daghestan, have for several centuries followed the Shi'a-Ja'afarite rite form. This distinguishes them from the largely Shi'ite Azeri people to the south.

Opposition to religion in general during the Soviet era (1917–1991) undermined this pattern, such that by 1978 there were no mosques in the majority Lezghi area in Daghestan. Unofficial or underground schools and prayer houses continued to operate, but the secularization process had considerable impact in drawing Lezghis, especially in the urban areas, away from their former convictions.

The breakdown in adherence to secular communism that followed the collapse of the USSR in 1988 has triggered something of a backlash: Many seek either a return to traditional values in the opportunity to practice their Moslem faith openly, or a new focus for belief. The mountain Lezghi are still regarded as a fairly religious ethnic group, though secular values have made big inroads among the lowlanders.

Threats to the Survival of the Lezghi

The Lezghi resisted Azerification tendencies, a more active Russification in the Soviet era, assaults on their religion, changes to their language and culture, attempts to resettle the mountain elements in the more easily controlled lowland collective farms and towns, and their division between two unequal types of administrative units in the Soviet federal system (the so called Azeri republic and the Daghestani autonomous republic). Yet, further formidable obstacles to Lezghi survival have appeared more recently. Together these new problems have prevented their coalescence into a single coherent ethno-political entity and their attainment of a united form of autonomy, let alone independence.

At first sight it might seem obvious that the essential problem facing the Lezghi is being split between two countries. Yet, of course, other peoples have found themselves divided by political borders. Indeed some of their Avar, Rutul, and Tabasaran neighbors are divided by this same border. The Lezghi's divided territory is but part of a broader picture of threats, some the consequence of the divide but others entirely independent of it.

The Border and Problems It Creates

The border was at first a divide in name only. Russia's President Yeltsin's decree making it a full international frontier in June 1992 created a serious impediment, and the closing of the border in December 1993 was a further blow, as until that point there had appeared every prospect of the border remaining open, at least to border peoples. In fact, border and customs posts were constructed in 1994, and a total closure lasted for nearly two years, from December 1994 to the end of the first Chechen-Russian war of the 1990s (13 September 1996). The border's reopening left the uncertainty of an undemarcated frontier line, until further Russian-Azeri agreements in 1996–1997; even those agreements completed only some three-quarters of the job. The consequence of this partially closed, partially open border regime was considerable disruption of social intercourse within families as well as the community as a whole, and the breakdown of new forms of freer market activity that had followed the initial collapse of the controls of the Soviet era. Passport checks and customs inspections led to delays and difficulties in crossing for humans and products alike in what was already, in the case of Daghestan, an area of considerable poverty. The absence of a clearly delineated border created uncertainties over land control and obstacles to transhumance from Daghestan. Illegal crossing could result in death, as happened to two Lezghi shot down by Russian border guards in August 1995—though the situation became much less harsh after the reopening in 1996. Also not to be forgotten was the humiliating impact on the Lezghi of such a border. It was, after all, imposed on their traditional territory by outsiders, and seemed to be open or closed at the whim of these overlords—often manifested in the form of corrupt local officials demanding illicit payments for goods like fruit, which would suffer from any delays in transit. Thus, while the border was a severe imposition in itself, it also has had a wide range of consequences for the Lezghi.

The Problem of Survival as a Single People

The Lezghi are now divided between two states. These states are undergoing processes of re-identifying themselves and forging a new sense of unity; they have been ill-inclined to suffer disruptive and divisive minority separatism, as Russia shows in the case of her treatment of Chechnya. Azerbaijan, too, has been undergoing a period of nationalism, focused on Azeri or Pan-Turkic identity; there is limited concern for minorities. The risk for the Lezghi in the 21st century is that they may be caught between these two stools. Conflicting loyalties and contrasting assimilationist pressures imposed on them could tear their own identity and community apart, or even eliminate it.

Unlike the divided communities of East and West Germany or North and South Korea, which share a language, Lezghi language and culture are threatened by two competing languages with their different alphabets. In the case of the new Azerbaijan, measures ostensibly designed to aid the minorities, such as permission for minority nongovernmental organizations to develop their own newspapers, frequently have not been implemented. Economic circumstances have made such measures unrealistic. Azeri Lezghis have found it next to impossible to subscribe to newspapers and journals from Daghestan. School textbooks in Lezghi have been in a similarly precarious state, while the Lezghi language is no longer even used as the main language of instruction in schools in Azeri Lezghi territory.

Although the pressure on Lezghi culture at present seems to be more from the Azeri side (even though it falls short of outright discrimination against them), growing centrifugal tendencies in Daghestan could see the emergence of more Russifying pressures there as the problems in neighboring Chechnya remain uncontained. All such pressures could undermine the surviving sense of unity among the Lezghi.

The Problem of In-Migration

A problem the Lezghi share with many other minorities throughout the world is what the indigenous group perceives as unwarranted in-migration by outsiders. This is not, in their view, a case of racism or xenophobia. It is the reaction of a fragile minority to what is not simply a natural flow of people to an amenity area (compared to some of the inhospitable lands of the Russian north, for example). Many Lezghi see their traditional lands used as a dumping ground for displaced persons of different ethnic background—part of a deliberate attempt at diluting their claim to traditional territory.

This initially appeared as an issue in 1989 when Meskhi Turks, already once displaced from the western part of Georgia to Central Asia by Stalin, were involved in clashes in Uzbekistan. Some were resettled by the then-Soviet government in Lezghi territory, as were Azeri refugees from the war with Armenia in the early 1990s.

As far back as the 1960s, Lezghi protested about the marked decline in the number of distinct ethnic groups recorded by the census takers in Daghestan, and they are wary that they might join the list of groups absorbed by neighbors or overwhelmed by newcomers. A map produced by an Azeri journal in 1997 indicates a fairly small proportion of refugees in Lezghi lands, though even a small number could potentially upset a delicate balance in minority areas of Azerbaijan.

The Problem of Military Service

Another challenge to their survival from the Lezghi point of view has been the impact on their numbers as their young men were drafted into the Azeri army to fight in the extremely bloody conflict with Armenia in the early 1990s. Much as the Baltic peoples saw the Soviet Union's war in Afghanistan in the 1980s as *Russia's* war, many Lezghi nationalists regard the Azeri-Armenian conflict as none of their business. It is an Azeri problem. Yet to refuse to fight opened them to charges of disloyalty to the state, and consequent imprisonment, if not worse—and the conflict itself could equally kill many.

The Problem of Out-Migration

Also undermining the stability and strength of Lezghi identity is the poverty of the Daghestani part of their territory—one of the poorest areas of Russia. In the long run this will almost certainly result in increased out-migration to cities like Derbent—nearby but not part of the Lezghi heartland. There, despite the presence of many Lezghi already, assimilationist tendencies are likely to take their toll. A parallel economic factor that might have a similar effect has been the reorientation of Azerbaijan's trading patterns and contacts, from overwhelmingly with Russia, to the north, toward Turkey and Iran to the south and west. This has the potential consequence of making Azeri Lezghi territory an even more remote backwater.

A Possible Environmental Problem

An issue that some Lezghi add to these more significant problems is a potential contest over the waters of the river Samur. A 1967 agreement accorded 75 percent of its supply to Azerbaijan. With the designation of the river as an international border, it becomes a potential flashpoint between the two riverine states in times of water shortage or overuse. But as Daghestan has plenty of water sources, this fear is probably exaggerated.

How far these issues are serious threats to the Lezghi as opposed to problems that can be overcome is in part a matter of perception. Nevertheless, the Lezghi, in large numbers, are perturbed at the degree to which their fate is under the control of others. Out-migration of Lezghi, in-migration of others, assimilation, economic disruption, and an overarching political conflict between Azerbaijan and Russia all stand as threats to the future of the Lezghi.

Lezghi Responses to the Threats

Long before the 1991 separation of Russia and Azerbaijan there were protests about the Lezghi situation. Back in December 1921 at the time of the very formation of what was to become the USSR, the Daghestan government assembly called for incorporating the Lezghi of Azerbaijan into its territory, rather than maintaining the artificial divide of the 19th century. Then again, beginning in the late 1950s a small number Lezghi intellectuals protested the unequal treatment meted out to their people in the two constituent parts of the old USSR, and particularly at the hands of the Azeris. An explicit attack on the administrative border between the two territories was even launched by Communist Party member and writer Iskander Qaziev in 1965. He and supporters sought from the Soviet parliament the formation of an autonomous Lezghi entity drawn from lands on both sides of the border. This was not to be granted, however, and some of those who proposed Lezghi autonomy were arrested or exiled.

Subsequently, the Lezghi response to the threats and challenges of the new post-Soviet frontier has taken the form of autonomy- or even independence-minded pressure groups and parties. As they are now locked into two different, sometimes hostile countries, unified action has proved much more difficult. Entirely different bodies representing Lezghi have been formed on either side of the frontier.

On the Daghestan side a national movement called *Sadval* (Unity) was formed in mid-1990 for the purpose of promoting a historic, political, socio-economic, and cultural revival and a union of the two groups of Lezghi, either within their own state or within either Russia or Azerbaijan (more likely Russia). At its All National Congress of December 1991, Sadval called for the formation of a national state: Lezghistan. Its newspaper in the early 1990s even called for an armed struggle against Azerbaijan to that end. As a result of these positions the organization was denied official recognition at first and only gained registration as a legal entity in 1992. This status was revoked again in July 1993, only to be approved once more in 1994 and 1996.

The appearance of Sadval was quickly followed in 1990 by the emergence of the Lezghi National Council, again in Daghestan, which acted as an umbrella organization for a number of similar but separate groups. The Council fused with Sadval in 1993. Some of the movement's more radical goals similarly underwent change and were dropped at its Sixth Congress in April 1996, in part on the grounds that they exacerbated tensions between the Lezghi and the Azeris. Nevertheless, they continued to demand free right of passage across the border, with a customs union and free economic zone between the two states. Further demands were made for an end to the presence of Russian troops and for dual citizenship rights. After a series of internal feuds, however, Sadval split into moderates and radicals at its Seventh Congress in November 1998.

Although popular among some vociferous members of the intelligentsia, Sadval's support among the Lezghi as a whole has been questioned since the heyday of 1991–1993. Most Lezghi have been more concerned with immediate bread-and-butter issues. Nevertheless, residual fear about the Lezghi's fate provides Sadval with a constituency.

A more clearly declared political party, Alpan, was also founded in Daghestan in April 1995. Taking up the same course—unifying the two Lezghi territories— its leader Amiran Babaev openly spoke out about oppression of his people in Azerbaijan.

Although they had some contacts with Sadval in 1992–1993, Azeri officials have been generally hostile to what they view as a terrorist organization. A bombing on the subway in the Azeri capital in March 1994 killed 14 people. Sadval distanced itself from this event, which led to a closed trial and conviction of 11 Lezghi in May 1996. Trials of others involved in the clashes at the frontier in 1991–1993 continued in Azerbaijan into the late 1990s.

A rival body to Sadval, the Lezghi National Center, or Samur, was formed in Azerbaijan in 1990, and was registered officially in January 1992 as a cultural organization of the Lezghi. In 1992 it transformed itself into a social and political body concerned with language and cultural rights. Samur was, however, closely tied in with the Azeri government and stood against any revision of state borders. It was in favor of integration of the Lezghi within Azerbaijan and thus quickly found itself in conflict with Sadval.

In July 1992, a parallel and similarly motivated political party was formed in Azerbaijan: the Lezghi Democratic Party. It too was in all probability sponsored by the government, which has consistently opposed ethnic separatism, and worked in tandem with Samur through the Consultative Council of Small Nations. Having attempted some contact with Sadval in 1992–1993, Samur was proscribed in 1995 and was forced to change its program on the grounds of being a party illegally based on ethnicity and seeking local autonomy. Subsequently, it sought solely to promote the rights of Lezghi in Azerbaijan and has worked in conjunction with the more broadly based Social Democratic Party of Azerbaijan, even working out a joint Lezghi program in 1993.

In addition to establishing these organizations, Lezghi have been activists—particularly after the 1992 decision of the Russians and the Azeris to draw a formal frontier between them. Sadval organized rallies on both sides of the frontier with thousands participating. This seems to have had some impact; the Russians introduced only customs controls, and special measures were taken to ease the situation for those living in the border area. Nevertheless, in 1993, 12 Lezghi were accused in Azerbaijan of involvement in arms trafficking. A major clash in the Gusar region, followed the drafting of Lezghi to fight for Azerbaijan in March 1993, involved about 70,000 Lezghi and resulted in some deaths. Reduction in the level of the Armenian-Azeri conflict softened the impact of this issue by the mid 1990s.

Daghestani leaders met with the Azeris, including President Aliev, in October 1993, and agreed to a transparent border. Despite this, Russia decided in December 1993 to close the border altogether—officially to stop smuggling, but more likely as a reaction to worsening relations between the two countries. In April 1994, even as arrangements to set up full border and customs posts were being signed, violent clashes between Lezghi and police broke out in the out-of-area town of Derbent in Daghestan, resulting in a number of deaths. That same year, a Sadval leader, Mekhraliyev, was charged in Azerbaijan with anti-government activities and sentenced to four years in prison.

In the continued absence of a government commission report on relations with the Lezghi in Azerbaijan, several hundred of them crossed into Daghestan in September 1995 to escape the draft and/or to have their children registered as Russian citizens. The total official closure of the border by Russia in December 1994 as her war in Chechnya developed seemed likely to cause more clashes, but tensions were relieved by subsequent reversal of this decision and a reopening in 1996.

In July 1996, the Daghestani Lezghi activist Nariman Ramazanov was also arrested by Azeri police and accused of calling for armed struggle to change the border regime. Demonstrations in his support were held at the frontier during which the protestors took hostages and blocked the railway across the border. The Azeris eventually released Ramazanov and handed him back to Russia.

In Azerbaijan, the authorities have actually accused the Lezghi nationalists of being in league with the Armenians in their attempt to destabilize Azerbaijan while the conflict between the two countries over Nagorno-Karabagh remains unresolved. There is certainly sympathy from Armenia, but direct support is less easy to demonstrate. Other accusations are that Russia too is using the Lezghi issue to pressure the Azeris in conflicts over such matters as oil pipelines, links with NATO, blocking the transit of Chechen guerrillas, Russia's desire to have a more compliant member of the CIS, and the right to guard the border with Iran. Again, such charges are difficult to prove, though the Russians have openly declared the Lezghi issue a threat to the stability of the area in general.

Some of the earlier militancy has now gone out of the Lezghi situation, but the problems in many respects are ready to reawaken. Following a declaration by an Azeri government advisor in May 1999 that the Lezghi independence movement had no real social base in Azerbaijan and that its power was weakening, a Sadval activist was detained by Azeri police in July 1999, apparently inside Daghestani territory, and, while being transported to Azerbaijan, was rescued by some 200 Lezghi. The Russo-Chechen conflict, which recommenced with a Chechen incursion into Daghestan in August–September 1999, led to tightened security on the Azeri border once again. The Azeri security minister went so far as to declare that Sadval was also stepping up its activities in his country. In November 1999, as its conflict with Chechnya continued, Russia too threatened to tighten the border with Azerbaijan against penetration by pro-Chechen elements. This could clearly have taken the Lezghi back to the situation of the early 1990s.

More recently the situation of the Lezghi and the impact of the new frontier have eased somewhat. The change of leaders in the two countries, the general passage of time, the increase in bilateral trade, and Moscow's less hostile approach to the newly independent states of the area have contributed to this.

If standards of living improve in the area as a result of the prosperity brought by increased oil revenues, and conflict between Azerbaijan and Russia can continue to be avoided, then some potential conflict triggers will be removed. The Lezghi are not actively discriminated against by either regime, but the artificially imposed divisions do still undermine their disposition.

Food for Thought

Their divided situation is far from unique and not even particularly new for the Lezghi themselves. Even in the Soviet era the economies of the two parts were not closely linked: They were governed by different authorities and planning structures. We are thus led to questions about the motives behind the upsurge of apparently nationalist agitation in the 1990s. Does this reflect a genuinely felt set of nationalist aspirations to self-government? Is nationalism a pretext seized upon by criminal elements to gain control in the power vacuum after the collapse of Soviet power? Much the same critique was made of the Chechens in the early part of their revolt in the 1990s. In that case the phrase "criminal elements" tended to become transmuted into "warlords" when it became apparent that there was more Chechen support for the conflict than the anti-nationalists would concede. Ideological support for and against nationalism once again plays a significant part in how this Lezghi conflict is interpreted, and one side is never likely to persuade the other of its claims.

To Think About

1. How can a border-straddling people have its collective rights uniformly and adequately protected?
2. What will be the likely impact of the two dominant cultures of the area on the Lezghi community?
3. Can common Islamic values across the frontier zone serve to lessen the conflict or merely to exacerbate it?
4. Do the Lezghi have a right to autonomous self-government and, if so, should it be in the form of two administrative units within the existing states or in the form of independence?
5. Can improvement in Russo-Azerbaijani relations and in the economic climate remove the threats to the Lezghi without territorial adjustments?

Resources

Published Literature

Akiner S. 1986. *Islamic Peoples of the Soviet Union*, London, 48–50.
Matveeva A. and C. McCartney. 1998. Policy responses to and ethnic community division: Lezgins in Azerbaijan, in *International Journal on Minority and Group Rights* 5: 213–252.
Wixman R. 1994. Lezghins, in D. Levinson ed. *Encyclopedia of World Cultures*, Vol. 6, 1–13.

Internet

Center for International Development and Conflict Management, University of Maryland site: articles by M.L. Haxton: The Lezgins of Azerbaijan, and Lezgins of Daghestan in Russia.

12

The People of Tibet

P. Christiaan Klieger

In 2006, a railroad was opened between Lhasa, capital of Tibet, and Golmud, Qinghai, with direct connections with Beijing. Like the first American transcontinental railroad built in 1869, the China-Tibet railway symbolizes the iron link of a nation finally unified. For the Tibetan people, however, this "last spike" is more like a coffin nail for their embattled culture. Having been annexed by the People's Republic of China in the 1950s, the Tibetan people have struggled to maintain their own identity.

The People

The Qinghai-Tibet plateau, home to approximately six million ethnic Tibetans, was historically divided into three provinces: U-tsang, Kham, and Amdo. Today, U-tsang—the central part of the plateau, in which the Tibetan capital of Lhasa lies—has been designated the Tibetan Autonomous Region (TAR) by the People's Republic of China (PRC), and may also be referred to as Xizang (XAR) in Mandarin. Both Kham and Amdo are considered separate jurisdictional units encompassed within four distinct Chinese provinces: Gansu, Qinghai, Sichuan, and Yunnan. The TAR itself is home to roughly two million—one-third—of the Plateau's ethnic Tibetans. References to "Tibet" in this paper will be limited to the TAR.

Tibet borders the Chinese provinces of Xinjiang, Szechwan, and Yunnan, as well as the countries of India, Nepal, and Bhutan. The TAR is the area of the plateau with the majority of the population, as well as Tibet's capital, Lhasa. While Lhasa is not the geographic center of Tibet, it has long been the key to economic, cultural, and political development on the plateau.

People have lived in Tibet at least 3,000 years, according to archaeologists and Tibetan historians. And according to folklore, 2,000 years ago a blessed

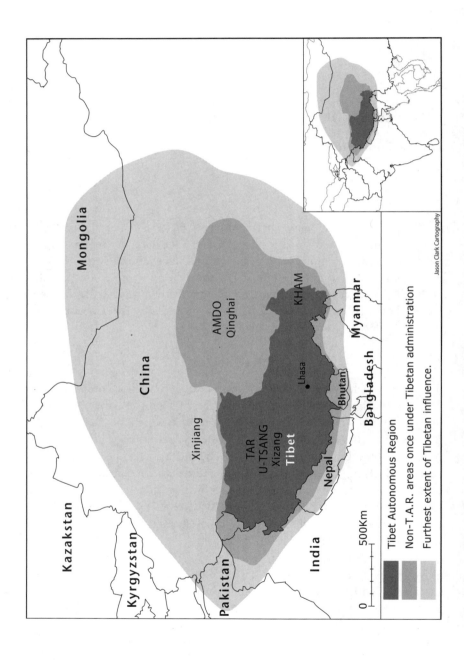

Jason Clark Cartography

monkey mated with a rock demoness who raised their six offspring: the progenitors of the six tribes of Tibet. These tribal groups, known as the Ch'iang, slowly expanded their territory, at one time reaching as far south as central Nepal and as far west as Pakistan. Early settlement centered along the broad Tsangpo River Valley, particularly the Yarlung Valley branch, or "Valley of the Kings," named after the first Tibetan kings (ca. 400–300 B.C.) who built fortress-palaces (*dzong*) atop small peaks along the river flood plain.

Today, in addition to the approximately two million ethnic Tibetans and a small number of Muslims and other ethnic minorities, several hundred thousand Han Chinese live in the TAR. (Access to accurate census data and population statistics is difficult, and the ratio of Tibetan to Han residents varies greatly depending upon the source of the data.) Most people in Tibet reside in the southern valleys of the Tsangpo and Indus rivers, where the higher rainfall and lower elevations concentrate agriculture and urban centers. Lhasa and Shigatse are the two largest cities here. The Changtang plateau, a high arid desert plain that occupies half of Tibet, is home to a half million sparsely distributed semi-nomadic herders. Amdo, in the northeast, is by far the most developed and urbanized portion of the plateau.

Since the instatement of the PRC government in Tibet during the 1950s, Mandarin is the official government language. However, most Tibetans still speak Tibetan as their first language. Street and shop signs are often written in Chinese characters, with smaller Tibetan words scripted underneath. In the primary schools, Tibetan is taught as the primary language, but is replaced by Mandarin in the upper levels. The Tibetan language belongs to the Tibeto-Burman family, its lexography developed from a North Indian Sanskrit script during the 7th century A.D., under the direction of King Songsten Gampo, the most famous of the early Tibetan kings.

The Setting

The Qinghai-Tibet plateau, an area of roughly 1.2 million square kilometers, is bordered by the world's tallest mountains: to the west the Karakoram, to the north the Kunlun Range, and to the south the Himalaya, whose highest peak, Mt. Everest (Chomolungma in Tibetan), straddles the border of Nepal and Tibet and reaches to 29,011 feet (8,848 m.). Tibet is two-thirds the size of the Indian subcontinent, or about twice the size of the state of Texas, and the average altitude of the plateau is 14,000 feet above sea level. Erosional processes have carved out deep valleys and gorges in the rock of the highlands, allowing for human habitation in one of the most extreme environments in the world.

Because of the great height of the Himalaya, most of the moisture-laden, South Asian monsoon rains fall on the southern slopes of the mountains in India and Nepal, leaving Tibet a high, cold desert: Tibet is not a land of great snowfall. Nevertheless, Tibet contains more than 15,000 natural lakes, features leftover from the wetter Pleistocene period (like the Great Salt Lake of Utah). The plateau is also the headwaters of most of the continent's greatest rivers: the Indus, Sutlej, Brahmaputra (Yarlung Tsangpo), Salween, Mekong, Yellow (Huang Ho), and the Yangtse. The waters flowing from Tibet provide for 85 percent of Asia's population: 47 percent of the world's total population. Environmental issues in Tibet are not inconsequential; they affect much of the Earth.

The northern half of the plateau, the Changtang, is a series of valleys and plains averaging 12,000–15,000 feet in elevation, interspersed between mountain ridges with peaks as high as 17,000 feet. The high arid plain receives an average of less than one inch of rain per year; snowfall is low despite low temperatures, and the Changtang is dotted with several brackish and salt lakes. Vegetation, a mix of hardy steppe assemblages of sedges, shrubs, and forbes, must survive the twin stresses of cold and aridity, and gives way to glaciers and bare rock at the highest elevations. Wild fauna includes rare and endangered species such as yak, kiang, snow leopard, and wolf. The Changtang is also home to millions of head of livestock and more than 500,000 pastoralists. The high altitudes and arid-alpine climate preclude much agricultural development. Only 0.12 percent of the land within the TAR is arable, and animal husbandry makes up a large portion (50 percent) of Tibet's total economic output.

The lowland valleys in southern Tibet range from 10,000 to 12,000 feet. Summers are warm but short, temperatures rarely exceeding 80° F. Winters are longer and cold, but not severe, with lowest temperatures at about 3–5°F. Here, monsoonal winds channeled up the river valleys bring summer rains between May and September, resulting in about 18 inches of precipitation per year. The Tsangpo River valley, along with the valleys of its tributaries, the Yarlung and the Kyi Chu, are the most productive agricultural areas in Tibet. Conditions are good for wheat, barley, potatoes, peas, turnips, and apples. Agro-pastoralism defines the economy in Tibet's valleys; land is intensively cultivated at the lowest elevations, while higher elevation areas are used for grazing and for growing animal fodder.

The southeastern part of Tibet is relatively lush and green, receiving far more moisture and warmer temperatures year round, although there are high diurnal fluctuations in temperature. This portion of Tibet is drained primarily by three of the major Asian rivers, the Yangtze, Mekong, and Salween.

Though the subtropical forested zone comprises less than one tenth of Tibet, the majority of its forests (both oak and coniferous forests of spruce and fir interspersed with larch and hemlock) occur here. The highest biological diversity of *Rhododendron* species in the world—more than 400—is also found in the southeastern part of the plateau. Forest grows to about 16,000 ft above this elevation a transition zone leads into alpine scrub, then rock and ice at the highest elevations. Juniper is common on south-facing slopes, and is considered a sacred plant in Tibet, its wood burned ceremonially and in households throughout much of Tibet.

Traditional Subsistence Strategies

Tibet's high elevation and harsh climate make even basic subsistence difficult. Along the Yarlung Tsangpo River Valley, Tibet's farmers raise the primary staple of the Tibetan diet, barley. Barley is toasted like popcorn, then ground into a nutty flour called *tsampa*. This meal is mixed with salted butter tea, and sometimes with grated yak cheese, and rolled into bite-sized balls. Farmers are also able to grow short-season vegetables such as radishes, potatoes, and onions. Outside of the warmer and wetter river valleys, many Tibetans are pastoralists. The majority of these pastoralists are semi-nomadic. Traditionally, purely pastoral nomads, *drogpa,* about one-sixth of the population of Tibet, lived in winter settlements and grazed their animals in adjacent pasture during the winter and on highland pastures in the summer: a mobile animal husbandry system of *transhumance.* Permanent home camps were located near winter grazing grounds, usually near a constant source of water. Temporary camps were set up for a small portion of a family, sometimes a solitary male, to watch summer herds. These summer camps were relatively close to home base, perhaps 30 miles or a two-day walk, primarily because of limited areas where rangeland plants will grow. Wealthier families often stayed put all year and hired poorer herders to manage the summer grazing.

In the warm summer, *drogpa* still use tents made of white cotton with blue appliqué designs; these are replaced in the winter with well-insulated tents made out of tightly spun, felted, and woven black yak wool. A fire in the center of the tent provides for warmth, light, and cooking. Dried yak dung is used for fuel, producing a nearly smokeless and odorless fire.

The yak is the major animal used in herding. The yak is, indeed, an integral component of the livelihood strategies for most Tibetans. The yak provides meat, dairy products, leather, fine wool, and a coarse hair used for making cords and felt tents. The yak is also essential as a pack animal, and is often the main vehicle used for transporting goods to market and for making the long trek between summer and winter encampments. The yak is a hardy, spirited, and agile beast, jumping swiftly over rocks and running about more like a goat kid than a bovine. Yaks are uniquely adapted to life at high altitudes; in addition to their shaggy coat, the yak's red blood cells are engineered to transport oxygen efficiently—critical for an animal that may graze as high as 18,000 feet. Tibetan herdsmen also raise a variety of fat-tailed sheep for meat and wool, plus goats and *dzo*, a more placid and productive cross between the yak and the domestic cow that can thrive at lower altitudes (like the Minhe Mangghuer's *musen,* in Chapter 13).

Nomads churn fresh "yak" milk into butter and dried cheese (yak is the male; females are called *drimo* in Tibetan). This butter is mixed with hot tea and salt to make a soup-like drink, butter tea, which Tibetans enjoy all day long. Nomads traditionally traded with farmers, exchanging meat and dairy products for *tsampa* flour, vegetables, and household goods. Especially important was the annual trek that many drogpa made to exchange salt from high on the plateau for commercial and agricultural products from India and other valleys in the Himalaya (see the discussion of the Humli-Khyampa in Chapter 3, *Peripatetics*). This traditional form of highland-lowland socio-economic linkages allowed pastoralists, who could not produce sufficient calories from their herds alone, to survive. Thus, for pure pastoralists, long-distance trade is essential for subsistence.

Because pastoralists inhabit high mountain regions, their interactions with grain-producing villages are also limited to long-distance treks. Nomads still travel as much as two months' time from home encampments to gather salt each year; they trade this salt for other grains and goods, such as manufactured textiles, from agricultural communities, as well as from Nepalis in bordering towns and villages. The salt/grain exchange was also a large part of the local economy on the Changtang. Of course, this system has also benefited agriculturists and urban dwellers who were able to trade their goods for meat, dairy products, and salt.

Sociopolitical Organization

For most Tibetans, whether they were farmers, traders, or nomads, traditional life was built around this basic unit of the extended family, usually three generations living under one roof. Tibetan society was patrilineal, in that descent from the male line was generally considered superior to the female line and sons inherited property from their fathers. But women had many rights in Tibetan society, and could divorce their husbands easily. Most Tibetan families practiced monogamy, that is, one husband with one wife. Among certain wealthy families, a man had more than one wife. In some families, especially among traders and nomads, a woman could have several husbands—a practice known as *polyandry*. The woman was usually brought into a family of brothers as a common wife: fraternal polyandry. The children of this marriage usually were considered the offspring of the eldest male, regardless of the true relationship. This rare form of marriage reduces overall fertility; it was considered important because it kept the fathers' property from being divided among too many sons.

Traditionally, up to one-third of Tibetan males, and a smaller fraction of females, were sent to monasteries to become monks and nuns. This practice was not only spiritually significant but also meant that the child had a chance for an education, as the monasteries were the primary centers of learning in the country.

Prior to 1959, Tibetan society was organized around estates, or fiefs (*lagyab lhojang*), that were held by monastic leaders (lamas) and their lamaseries, and especially the cohorts of the Dalai Lama and his political rival, the Panchen Lama. These fiefdoms, run by monks and aristocrats, were passed on based on a complex system of inheritance and reincarnation. Fiefdoms contained as many as ten nomad groups holding approximately 2,000 people within a 2,000 square mile area. The lamas and nobles appointed local officials to oversee peasants in the fields and nomads "on the hoof," and to collect taxes.

This system relied heavily upon the intensely religious nature of Tibetans for its stability. While peasants were part of the larger production unit in their specific estate, the household acted as the central production unit. Each household cared for its own privately owned herd and used distinct pastures assigned to it by estate representatives. Some cooperation among families was common during times of high labor requirements, such as during the annual salt trek or during haymaking season. However, as a general rule, each household operated independently and kinship was the primary factor affecting land tenure. The degree to which land and animals were managed cooperatively was limited to the extended family.

Although the survival of this system over hundreds of years points to its long-term stability, it was not without problems. The Marxist Chinese found this feudal relationship between peasant and lama obnoxious. Chinese cadres and officials often invoked the Marxist terminology of feudalism to defend their position as "liberators" of Tibetan "serfs" and "slaves." Chairman Mao Tse-tung's aim of creating an organized peasantry that worked in communes and shared equally in the fruits of labor was viewed by his followers as a substantial improvement over the system of religious "enslavement" in place in Tibet. Many scholars point out a high degree of economic differentiation during this early Maoist era. Yet, while monasteries and nobles high in the religious hierarchy owned a disproportionate share of land, the high degree of loyalty to religious institutions and traditions, and the deep reverence felt by Tibetan citizens toward lamas and other church officials, allowed for a politically stable, albeit unbalanced, system that was able to sustain itself for many generations. The importance of the Buddhist faith, and its role in governing Tibet, was not questioned by Tibetans, as the Chinese government would later be. Moreover, the cultural significance of the Buddhist religion for Tibetans cannot be understated.

Religion and Worldview

Most Tibetans are Buddhists, a religion founded by Prince Siddhartha Shakyamuni in India. Buddhism is said to have arrived in Tibet from India during the 5th century A.D. during a period known as "The Happy Generations." However, Buddhism is not the oldest, or only, religion in Tibet. Before the arrival of Buddhism, the primary religion in Tibet was Bön, the oldest formalized Tibetan religion, and its priests and followers are called "Bönpo." It was founded by Shenrab Miwo in Western Tibet, but diminished with the arrival of Buddhism. The Bön religion is centered on the spirits of the Earth and of trees, rocks, water, and air. Gods are usually contacted through *shamans*, religious specialists who could enter a trance while drumming or dancing and foretell the future or cure illness. While Buddhism is the primary religion in Tibet today, the Bön religion lives on, both within Tibet and among Tibetans living in exile. Indeed, there are many similarities between Bön and Buddhism, and each religion has adopted certain practices and beliefs from the other over the years.

Over the centuries, Buddhism developed to such an extent in Tibet that religious officials eventually became the government. Monasteries, temples, and hermitages were built in every village and town, and every home had its altar for prayer. In 1207, envoys of the Mongol ruler Chinggis (Genghis) Khan demanded the submission of Tibet to his empire. Under this threat, the abbot of Sakya Monastery in Central Tibet was offered the rule of the entire country, under Mongol patronage. He accepted, turning Tibet into a feudal theocracy ruled by a high priest. This system of government has continued up to the present day, represented by the lineage known as the Dalai Lamas. Indeed, Mongol leaders first bestowed the title "Dalai" (meaning "ocean of knowledge") upon this lineage during this time.

From the 13th century to recently, Tibet was ruled by a series of Buddhist priests whose successors were considered reincarnations of their predecessors.

This system was also followed in many of the great monasteries of the land—their abbots were usually considered saintly reincarnations of previous abbots. Although there were secular aspects of Tibetan political life, for most of its recent history Tibet has been governed by a network of Buddhist priests and monasteries, all headed by a supreme lama. The current, 14th, Dalai Lama, Tenzin Gyatso, is perhaps the most well-known icon of the Tibetan people. He fled Tibet in 1959, following an unsuccessful political uprising against Chinese rule. He is now living in exile in Dharamsala, India.

Threats to Survival

Tibet Becomes Chinese Territory

Although the Mongols (Yuan dynasty in China) fell in the 14th century, the rule of Tibet's monasteries continued, often completely independent of Chinese, Mongol, and other foreign intervention. Buddhism continued to flourish. In the 17th century, under the patronage of the Buddhist Qing rulers of China (the Manchus), the lineage of the Dalai Lamas of Drepung Monastery in Central Tibet became rulers of all Tibet. The Dalai Lamas rebuilt Songsten Gampo's ruined fortress palace atop Marpo Ri into a magnificent, 1,000 room palace known as the Potala. The capital itself became known as Lhasa ("gods' land").

For the next 250 years, the emperor in Beijing looked to the Dalai Lama as the high priest of Buddhism, but viewed the country as a protectorate of the Chinese Empire. The Dalai Lama, and the government of Tibet, considered Tibet to be an independent country. This is the core of the Tibetan issue today. The abdication of Emperor Hsuang Tung (Pu Yi) in 1911 brought the end of the relationship between Tibet and the Manchu Empire. The Manchus invaded Tibet in 1910, and maintained it as a protectorate until 1912, when the Qing dynasty was overthrown. At this time, the 13th Dalai Lama declared his country's complete independence, but his declaration was largely ignored by the great powers of the world. Indeed, just before the Manchus fell, during the colonial era, the British signed a treaty (the Simla Accord) with the Manchus declaring China's suzerainty over Tibet.

China itself remained weak until after World War II, when Mao Tse-tung unified China under the communist banner in the late 1940s. Considering it a part of China since the days of the Yuan Mongol dynasty, China invaded Tibet in 1950, forcing the government of the Dalai Lama to sign a 17-point agreement for the "liberation" of the region from "feudal monastic rulers" and foreign "imperialist" influence. To Chairman Mao, Tibet had finally been returned to the Chinese motherland.

The teenaged 14th Dalai Lama lived uneasily under this arrangement in Lhasa until 1959. On March 10, suspecting that the Chinese were planning to kidnap the young Tibetan ruler, the people of Lhasa rose up and encircled the Norbulingka Summer Palace, where the boy was living. On advice from his ministers and the State Oracle, the Dalai Lama escaped under cover of darkness. After several grueling weeks on the road, the Dalai Lama and his party arrived in India and were given asylum by Prime Minister Nehru. Over the next months and years, more than 85,000 Tibetans followed the Dalai Lama into exile. Many died en route. Thousands more back home were killed by the People's Liberation Army of China.

After the 1959 Lhasa uprising, Tibetan culture was actively suppressed. Buddhism was prohibited and the Tibetan language was no longer taught in schools. Further assaults on ethnic Tibetans raged during Chairman Mao's Cultural Revolution (1966–1976), a time throughout China when all old traditions and conservative ways were attacked. During this period, hundreds of thousands of Han Chinese also perished.

The Cultural Revolution is known as one of the most brutal periods in China's history, for Tibetans, other ethnic minorities, and Han Chinese alike. In Tibet, religious persecution was the most brutal aspect of this period. Monasteries were razed and monks and nuns killed, jailed, and tortured. Evidence of these ruined temples dots the hillsides throughout Tibet today. The government banned private practice of religion, and used its military to enforce the ban. A policy known as "destroying the four olds"—culture, ideas, customs, and habits—prevailed.

It is estimated that over 87,000 Tibetans were killed in the first 18 months following the uprising, and up to 1.2 million Tibetans have perished since the occupation—perhaps one-sixth of the total population. Tibetan culture, representing one of the last ancient civilizations still extant, was being destroyed. Most of Tibet's 6,000 temples and monasteries were completely ruined. Golden statues were melted and sacred books were burned. Items associated with Buddhism—but most especially with the Dalai Lama, whom the Chinese labeled a "splittist"—were prohibited. It is not uncommon, today, for private homes to be searched for photos of the Dalai Lama; it is still illegal for anyone in Tibet to possess such photographs.

Sociocultural Crisis

In addition to religious persecution, the Chinese implemented policies that sought to instigate class struggle among the masses. Tibet's farmers and nomadic pastoralists were removed from their ancestral lands, collectivized, and forced to work in factories, large farms, and ranches owned by the state. The family histories and class background of each person were studied in order to determine whether each was poor, middle-class, or rich. Those ranked as rich were labeled class enemies and publicly punished. People who had married into wealthy families were forced to denounce their spouses and in-laws in order to avoid being labeled as such. All class enemies were stripped of their personal assets and forbidden to join communes, often left to fend for themselves without the support of the other commune members.

The full-scale development of communes occurred virtually overnight. All private ownership of livestock was banned and herds became property of the commune. Individual families were at the mercy of appointed commune leaders, and productivity was monitored based upon quotas and requirements handed down from the state. Animals were confiscated and assigned a monetary value, and the commune was given this amount to be divided equally among members. Communes organized tasks according to a "work points" system. Each task was assigned a number of points; a cash value was assigned to the total work points, and taxation was based on this figure. According to the work points earned by each household, food and other necessities were rationed, usually just meeting or below subsistence needs. In addition, long-distance trade fell under heavy regulation from the state; all profits from trade were taxed and then divided among commune members. This system displaced a virtually self-sufficient traditional economy in which each family performed all the tasks necessary for its survival.

These changes resulted in a famine for the first time in Tibetan history. Furthermore, Chinese influence in the schools meant that an entire generation grew up barely able to read the Tibetan language. Education, which had in the past been the responsibility of the local monasteries, was now provided solely by the state. Secular schools developed, but initially the curriculum was entirely in the Chinese language. Today, Tibetan is taught at primary school levels, but Mandarin continues to be the language used in the higher grades.

It is difficult to separate those challenges to traditional Tibetan culture that reflect Chinese occupation from those that may simply be the ramifications of modernization. However, the breakup of the great monasteries of Tibet by the communist regime after 1950 has had the most profound effect on Tibet's culture. Monks and nuns were forced to leave their monasteries, many of which had been highly organized and wealthy feudal estates. Many who were not killed or imprisoned were forced on pain of death to marry. With the destruction of the monasteries, the centuries-old theocracy was swept away. The Dalai Lama and many other high lamas went into exile in India, as did civil leaders, the wealthy, and the educated. The "brain drain," exacerbated by globalization and the ability of more Tibetans to travel abroad and emigrate today, has left Tibet bereft of its traditional ruling class and lacking in skilled Tibetan professionals.

Of the few high lamas who stayed behind, such as the Panchen Lama, most were imprisoned because of their opposition to rule from Beijing. Despite criticism leveled at the Panchen Lama for his cooperation with the Chinese government, he, in fact, spent more than 13 years in prison for speaking out against China.

Han In-Migration

Although the excesses of the past seem to be over, the loss of traditional religious leadership and the in-migration of thousands of Han Chinese into the cities and towns of Tibet gravely threaten traditional Tibetan culture. In particular, the occupation by nearly one million soldiers has had particular demographic ramifications.

The needs of Chinese soldiers and their families have brought many other Han Chinese to settle in the Tibetan cities of Lhasa and Shigatse. Moreover, the Chinese government often provides incentives for Han to move to Tibet in the form of government appointments, land leases, and license to have more than one child. In recent years, great tracts of the old quarter of Lhasa, with its ancient buildings and architecture, have been bulldozed and rebuilt into concrete blocks of high-rise flats. Not only have Tibetans become a minority in their capital, the city itself is beginning to look like so many other strictly functional Chinese towns.

The PRC maintains that many high posts within the government are held by ethnic Tibetans. However, accusations of tokenism abound. A few Tibetans who are known to cooperate with Chinese officials are placed in high-profile positions in order to subdue criticism. Generally, government officials who fail to follow party lines do not last long in their posts.

Environmental Crisis

It was traditionally against Buddhist precepts to kill any animal in Tibet (ironically ignored in the matter of raising large animals for meat—usually a Muslim did the butchering). The natural wildlife of Tibet was largely preserved by this prohibition. Due in part to the Chinese occupation of Tibet and the great increase in nonindigenous population in Lhasa, Shigatse, and other Tibetan cities, the natural wildlife on the plateau has been severely compromised in recent decades. Many species of plants and animals are in imminent danger of becoming extinct. These include animals such as the Himalayan black bear, red panda, musk deer, Tibetan blue sheep, kiang (a wild donkey), gazelle, Tibetan antelope, clouded leopard, the famed snow leopard, and the giant panda. Tibet is also the home of the legendary *migyur* or *yeti*, the ape-man who is said to live high in the mountains. There are 81 endangered species on the Tibetan Plateau; these include 39 mammals and 37 birds. Many medicinal plants, some of which have healing properties that remain unknown, are endangered by contemporary land and resource exploitation.

Changes in the economy because of Chinese occupation and the introduction of Marxist and Maoist socialist economic models have disrupted the ancient balance between the needs of nature and the needs of humanity. It has upset the ability of the land to restore itself. In some former pastureland around the capital of Lhasa, overgrazed during collectivization, the erosion that has followed the loss of vegetation has removed the topsoil all the way down to bedrock. This is largely irreversible. As a result of the loss of fields, crop failures, and poor distribution systems, Tibet experienced episodes of famine for the first time in its history.

In the moist southeastern parts of Tibet, vast old-growth forests have disappeared from overharvesting of forest products. The estimated 25.2 million hectares of coniferous forests here represented a unique global treasure. Unsustainable harvesting has removed much of these virgin forests, an estimated 46 percent of the total by 1985. The ancient old-growth forests of Tibet are largely irreplaceable. In addition, loss of forest causes soil erosion and contributes to flooding. Deposition of silt in the rivers that flow from the Tibetan Plateau is a major problem for the massive populations downstream in China proper, and in Myanmar (Burma), Bangladesh, and India.

Modernization in Tibet has had additional negative impacts on the environment. Dams built to generate hydroelectric power have destroyed the habitats of many plants and animals, and have dried up freshwater sources. A prime example of this process is represented in Yamdrok Tso. Yamdrok Tso is one of four lakes sacred to Tibetans; it was recently dammed to generate hydroelectricity. This is both spiritually and environmentally deleterious. The dam is said to be decreasing water levels, increasing salinity, and contributing to habitat loss for native birds and other species. Plans for larger dams along the Tsangpo River are currently being discussed.

Mining is a further threat to the environment in Tibet. There are thought to be great stores of minerals such as uranium, borax, iron, silver, and copper on the plateau. While the mining efforts in Tibet are currently small-scale because of the difficulty of the terrain, technological developments and the building of infrastructure such as roads and railroads are facilitating the future development of mining industries. There is also substantial evidence that more isolated portions of Tibet are used for Chinese nuclear testing and storage of nuclear waste. The newly completed rail line from Golmud to Lhasa, making Tibet so much more convenient to meet the rapidly accelerating resource demands of China, will exacerbate these problems and bring others.

Response: Struggles to Sustain Cultural Survival

The Tibetan Response: Exile

The 14th Dalai Lama was not the first ruler of Tibet to flee into exile and ask for assistance. In the early 20th century, the 13th Dalai Lama, Thubden Gyatsho, went to India to seek asylum from the excesses of the tottering Manchu dynasty in China. He also sought recognition from the British Empire that Tibet was an independent country. After a time in exile, he was urged to return to his country. Following the fall of the Manchu Dynasty in 1911, the Dalai Lama declared independence in 1914, and the country was left unoccupied by China until 1950.

When Chinese troops arrived in Tibet in 1950, the young Dalai Lama and his government tried to work out a compromise with Mao that would preserve considerable local autonomy for Tibet within the framework of the People's Republic of China. The Dalai and Panchen Lamas even flew to Beijing to hold meetings with Mao, Cho Enlai, and other Communist leaders. Initially, Beijing agreed to keep Buddhism and the monastic ruling order together. Eventually, however, it became clear that the object of the Chinese occupation was to make Tibet a province of China and to dismiss its unique system of governance. The populace was greatly bereaved when the Dalai Lama fled and went into exile in India. Many thousands of Tibetans gave up everything to follow him, and many died on the perilous journey over the high Himalayan passes. Ten to fifteen thousand Tibetans settled in the kingdoms of Nepal, Sikkim, and Bhutan. Several additional thousands were settled in Switzerland and other western countries.

In the first few weeks and months of exile, the Indian government generously provided land for transit camps for the thousands of Tibetan refugees streaming over the border. The most immediate need was for simple housing, food, and medical care. Foreign aid helped provide Tibetans with these necessities. Nevertheless, many immigrants died from diseases not often found on the high Tibetan plateau but common in the tropical environment of India—particularly tuberculosis.

But what the Dalai Lama and his many followers found in India was a chance to reestablish their Tibetan identities and engage in a public discourse about the Tibetan cause with an international audience. Once some of the basic needs were attended to, the Dalai Lama was settled in the old hill station of Dharamsala, about 200 miles north of New Delhi and about 60 miles southwest of the Tibetan border. Here, the Dalai Lama was given the freedom to erect a government in exile, the *Ganden Phodrang*, which is now responsible for establishing schools to teach Tibetan language, music, and the fine arts. Perhaps most important, the Dalai Lama and his subjects were allowed to practice Buddhism freely. Within a few years, Tibetans had reestablished many temples, monasteries, and nunneries in India, the original homeland of Buddhism.

Key to the formation of a Tibetan identity is the acceptance of the Dalai Lama as Tibet's spiritual and political leader. To the Tibetan people he has a special significance. The 14th Dalai Lama is not only considered the reincarnation of his previous 13 predecessors; as Bodhisattva of Compassion he is the guardian of the Tibetan people. He is also considered a reincarnation of King Songsten Gampo, the founder of the Buddhist Kingdom of Tibet. It is not difficult to understand why, despite many attempts by the Chinese to denounce the Dalai Lama and remove him from rule, the Tibetan people both in the homeland and in exile generally refuse to relinquish him. The Dalai Lama forms the link between the secular and the religious. The importance of this dual role is magnified now, as those still living in Tibet are forbidden to learn of their history and are prohibited political freedom to support the Ganden Phodrang; those living in exile cling to the Dalai Lama as the embodiment of the homeland they were forced to leave.

The Chinese invasion that occurred during the 1950s created not only a large wave of Tibetan refugees but also a dichotomy between "us" and "them"—Chinese vs. Tibetan. This forced Tibetans living within Tibet to reidentify their territory as *Tibetan* in order to create legitimate boundaries between themselves and the Chinese. At the same time, Tibetan refugees began to reconstruct Tibet not only as a place inhabited by Tibetans, but as a homeland, a place filled with symbolic and religious geography. It is the refugee community, largely living in India and Nepal, that has constructed Tibet into a homeland and has redefined the sacredness of that landscape for Western audiences, for the Chinese, and for Tibetans still residing within Tibet.

The exile community has been hugely successful in establishing a tie with their unattainable homeland, outside the political boundaries of Tibet. The agricultural settlements in the Himalayan foothills of India are generally more prosperous than those of their Indian neighbors, and Tibetans have succeeded in promoting crafts, industry and education, and hospitals and other institutions. The system of monasteries survives as it had in Tibet. Indeed, the Indian government, while not officially accepting the Dalai Lama as head of a government in exile, has recognized him as the leader of Tibetan communities within India and other refugee areas.

The present government in Dharamsala includes a council of ministers, an elected assembly of legislators, a supreme justice commission, and departments of information and international relations, religion and culture, health, home, finance, education, and security. Notable cultural and educational institutions in Dharamsala include the Tibetan Institute of Performing Arts, Tibetan Children's Village, the Library of Tibetan Works & Archives, and even an accredited college, the Norbulingka Institute. Through the assistance of the Indian government and generous aid from foreign organizations in Europe, America, and elsewhere, refugees have thrived. In Nepal and northern India, Tibetans have been active weaving woolen rugs for the export market, and leading thousands of people on treks throughout the Himalayas. In the southern parts of India, many Tibetans are productive farmers. In New Delhi and other cities, many Tibetans have now earned a college education and are active in business, health care, and engineering.

To represent the Dalai Lama and the exiled Tibetan people, Dharamsala has established several offices around the world, including Tibet House in Delhi and the offices of Tibet in Kathmandu, New York, London, Taipei, Tokyo, Moscow, and other cities. These centers serve as unofficial "embassies" representing the independent government of the Dalai Lama that existed in the homeland prior to the Chinese invasion in 1950.

In the early 1990s, the Tibet–U.S. Resettlement project brought 1,000 Tibetan heads of household to the United States. Tibetans were settled in communities of 20 to more than 100 in a score of cities around the country. They were given permanent visas and jobs. Within a few years, most sent for their spouses and family members. Today, in the San Francisco Bay Area, for example, more than 500 Tibetan refugees have settled. The primary rationale for the exile is to remain strongly Tibetan, in culture, religion, and language, until such time that Tibet is liberated from oppressive rule and exiles may return home to freedom under the Dalai Lama. Most are convinced that this will happen someday.

It has been over 40 years since Tibetans left their homeland with the Dalai Lama. Throughout the exile communities, Tibetan national identity remains strong. All along, the 14th Dalai Lama has maintained that the struggle for Tibetan freedom must be nonviolent. Like Martin Luther King, Jr., the Dalai Lama was strongly influenced by the nonviolent political actions of Mahatma Gandhi, the architect of Indian independence. Nonviolence is also a major religious precept in Buddhism. In 1989, in recognition of his non-violent campaign for the human rights of his people, the Dalai Lama was awarded the Nobel Peace Prize.

Despite the successes of the exile community and the Ganden Phodrang, some interesting conflicts are emerging around the issue of Tibetan independence. The exile community has had access to and the ear of both Western and Indian media and scholars. They have been able to identify and label their historical ties to their homeland and their language, religion, and culture. They have learned to articulate their concerns in order to fit them into an international discourse. For those Tibetans still residing in the TAR, this language is foreign.

Passive Resistance within Tibet

Although Tibetans within the TAR lack access to international media, education and economic development, they engage in resistance to the PRC occupation in more subtle ways. Of course, the more direct means of protest—street demonstrations—do occur, both in large cities and in the hinterlands. The most notable of these protests occurred in 1987.

In the late summer of 1987, with the city of Lhasa full of Western tourists and journalists, a small group of monks and others was arrested by the police for demonstrating for Tibetan independence. The Dalai Lama had just presented a Five-Point Peace Plan to the U.S. Congress, and the world's attention was currently on Tibet. The demonstration in the streets of Lhasa quickly escalated, and the crowd set fire to the police station. Journalists took photographs of horrifying scenes of people being shot and arrested. Many people died, and many more were taken to prison. Tourists were told to leave Tibet immediately. Over the next two years, several other demonstrations were held in Tibet. As a result, many liberalization policies of the Chinese reformist Hu Yao Bang were overturned.

Aside from direct protest, many Tibetans engage in a quieter form of passive resistance to Chinese rule, simply by continuing to engage in Buddhist ritual. The simple act of burning incense or displaying a photo of the Dalai Lama can be seen as an assertion of Tibetanness and as a way of retaining their rights to religious freedoms.

Religious acts, such as pilgrimage, are also a way of maintaining autonomy under the watchful eye of the PRC. Often the pilgrims' journeys are related to the cycle of mountain agriculture and pastoral activities and reflect a plurality of traditions in the most marginal of geographic areas. Pilgrimages are seen as a means to link concrete geographic places with the world of the gods.

Chinese Response to Endangerment (Current Conditions)

Following the death of Mao Tse-tung and the end of the Cultural Revolution, a new economic and social ideology emerged, led by the reformist Deng XiaoPing. Deng's government found communes to be economically untenable and gradually shifted production back to the household level. The centerpiece of this period was the *household responsibility system*. Almost as swiftly as it was implemented, the commune system was abolished; communes officially closed in 1981. Animals were once again allocated for private ownership. Eventually, *complete responsibility* evolved whereby animals and property were allocated directly to individuals, while de facto control remained with the family unit.

The distinction between the household responsibility system and the commune system is an important one. During the Cultural Revolution, the commune represented both the means of production as well as the government structure. Today, the two are separated and the rights and obligations of land management reside within the household. More important, the methods of resource allocation employed by local people are more intimately linked to local environmental conditions and resource availability.

Further, the failures of central planning have been replaced with more liberal practices. In general, most Tibetans keep most of their production for their own use or for sale in the market. All Tibetans, however, have to pay a certain portion to the government as taxes. Medical care has improved over the years, as have telecommunications. Many Tibetans own color televisions. Electricity in Lhasa and many other population centers is quite reliable. New roads are being built, and a railway has been built from Golmud in the north to Lhasa—whether, on balance, for the good or ill of Tibet's people and environment remains to be seen.

The results of reform in Tibet are controversial. Critics of the liberalization policies point out some reversion to old and inefficient practices, such as the use of a yak-pulled plough versus a tractor. The practice of saying Buddhist prayers for a good harvest reemerged during this time as well—stimulating criticism that farmers are likely to abandon modern harvesting techniques in favor of reliance upon mystical forces. In other cases, the resumption of traditional practices meant the reintroduction of rational grazing rotations and barter relationships that have proven helpful in the protection of grassland resources and of the local economies in parts of Tibet.

There have been many positive changes in Tibet's social and political conditions since the worst days of the 1959 uprising and the Cultural Revolution. In the early 1980s, Chinese reformer Hu Yao Bang set out to liberalize the harsh, centralized economy. Mandatory collective farming and ranching were abolished. Tibetan language schools were reestablished, and surprisingly, some monasteries were rebuilt. The state also began to take an interest in promoting tourism in Tibet as a means of generating revenues and foreign exchange, and helping to end the drain on the Chinese economy that the occupation of Tibet had caused. Buddhism was again permitted publicly, although it is still highly regulated; each monastery was allowed only a small fraction of the original numbers of monks and nuns. Most important, each monastery is now controlled by the state, which is officially atheist. Further, any association with the Dalai Lama is strictly prohibited, and mention of him even in his former palace, the Potala, is forbidden.

The important monasteries of Drepung, Sera, and Ganden near Lhasa, and Tashilhumpo in Shigatse have been slowly restored. In the Tibetan capital, the great Potala Palace, although now a museum, was refurbished and opened to the local public for the first time in history. The Norbulingka Summer Palace, the Ramoche and Jokhang temples were also restored. Foreign and internal travel restrictions were liberalized, and tourism to the "Roof of the World" exploded. A new airport was built south of Lhasa, and even a Holiday Inn opened. Whether this form of modernization will be beneficial or deleterious remains to be seen.

In recent years, China has publicly stated that it has made many mistakes in Tibet. Although it steadfastly refuses to acknowledge that Tibet was once independent, it has made many attempts toward bringing Tibet and Tibetans up to an economic level equal to that of the rest of China.

China has made great strides in environmental conservation in Tibet. In cooperation with the United States and other Western countries, China established the Changtang Reserve in eastern Tibet. It is the largest national park in the world, six times larger than Yellowstone in North America. China's efforts to save the giant panda are also well known. In the last few years, China has initiated biodiversity and cultural diversity studies in many isolated regions, such as in Yunnan Province. China has collaborative projects with the California Academy of Sciences in San Francisco and Columbia University in New York on the need to assess and conserve biological and cultural diversity.

Food for Thought

The Tibetan issue is a complex, centuries-old struggle over indigenous peoples' rights to rule themselves. In the almost 50 years since the diaspora, Tibetan exiles have shown themselves to be tenacious in maintaining a Tibetan way of life and a strong faith in Buddhism. And in Tibet itself, Tibetans have been strongly resistant to many attempts by the Chinese to assimilate them into the great motherland. It remains to be seen how long six million Tibetans can hold out against 5,000 years of Chinese civilization, and 1.2 billion people who are rapidly modernizing and becoming relatively affluent at the beginning of the 21st century.

To Think About

1. The Dalai Lama is considered vitally important for the continuation of Tibetan identity. What could happen to the Tibetans in exile and in the homeland once he passes away?
2. Is modernization inevitable in all cultures around the world? If so, does this mean that all traditional societies are doomed to disappear? What are some social factors that may prevent losing one's cultural identity?
3. What are the major reasons that China wants to control Tibet? What possible value is this region to the Chinese?
4. Is it possible for Tibet to somehow obtain a measure of freedom, either within the People's Republic of China or independently?
5. Do you think the nonviolent, Buddhist approach to liberation will achieve its goals in Tibet, or were Tibetans wrong in not fighting the Chinese more diligently?

Resources

Published Literature

Goldstein, Melvyn C. 1989. *A History of Modern Tibet, 1913–1951.* Berkeley: University of California Press.
Grunfeld, A. Tom. 1987. *The Making of Modern Tibet.* Armonk, NY: M.E. Sharpe.
Klieger, P. Christiaan. 1992. *Tibetan Nationalism.* Meerut, India: Archana Press.
Lehman, Steve. 1998. *The Tibetans.* New York: Umbridge Editions.
Lopez, Donald S., Jr. 1998. *Prisoners of Shangri-la.* Chicago: University of Chicago Press.

Films and Videos

"Kundun." 1997. Screenplay by Melissa Mathisson. Directed by Martin Scorsese.
"Seven Years in Tibet." 1997. Iain Smith, producer.
"The Saltmen of Tibet." 1997. Ulrike Koch, producer. Catpics Coproduction.
"A Song for Tibet." 1991. Arcady Films, Anne Henderson, dir. National Film Board of Canada.
"Compassion in Exile." 1992. Lemle Pictures. Direct Cinema Ltd.

Internet

www.tibet.com (Official Website of Tibetan Government-in-Exile)
www.tibet.org (Tibet Online. Resource with films, books, and other information
   on Tibet)
www.chinaembassy.org (Chinese view on Tibet)

Organizations

Office of Tibet
   241 E. 32nd Street
   New York, NY 10016 USA
Department of Information and International Relations
   Gangchen Kyishong
   Dharamsala 176215, H.P.
   India
Central Institute of Higher Tibetan Studies
   Sarnath,
   Varanasi, U.P.
   India 221 007
Library of Tibetan Works and Archives
   Central Tibetan Secretariat
   Gangchen Kyishong
   Dharamsala 176215, H.P.
   India
International Campaign for Tibet
   1825 K Street, NW, Suite 520
   Washington, DC 20006 USA

13

The Minhe Mangghuer

Zhu Yongzhong and Kevin Stuart

Qinghai Province is a vast area situated in the northwest of the People's Republic of China. Occupying the eastern edge of the Tibetan Plateau, the area is the location of Kokonor, China's largest inland saline lake, and home to a varied population of 5.5 million people including Han Chinese, Tibetans, Chinese Muslims (Hui), Monguor (Tu), Salar, and Mongolians.

The People

The Monguor are one of 56 ethnic groups officially recognized by China. With a population of nearly a quarter of a million, the Monguor are a diverse collection of four enclaves of linguistically and culturally different people who share a belief in Tibetan Buddhism, use many Mongolic vocabulary items, and practice a predominantly agricultural way of life.

The largest group of Monguor (more than 50,000) live in Huzhu Monguor (Tu) Autonomous County near Xining, the provincial capital. These Mongour, who represent less than 15 percent of Huzhu County's total population, refer to themselves as "Mongghul," which is the same word they use to classify Mongolians. The second largest group of Monguor (more than 35,000) live 200 kilometers south of the Huzhu Mongghul in Minhe Hui and Mangghuer (Tu) Autonomous County, and call themselves "Mangghuer"—their word for Mongolians. Only a few Monguor living in Datong Hui and Monguor Autonomous County still speak Monguor; most only speak the local Chinese dialect. The people living in several natural villages collectively called "Wutun" in Tongren County, Huangnan Autonomous Prefecture, speak a Creole very different from that spoken by other groups of Monguor, and which is made up of Tibetan, Chinese, Mongolian, and other words of obscure origin. Wutun is famous for its *thankha* painters. Other Monguor speaking still different

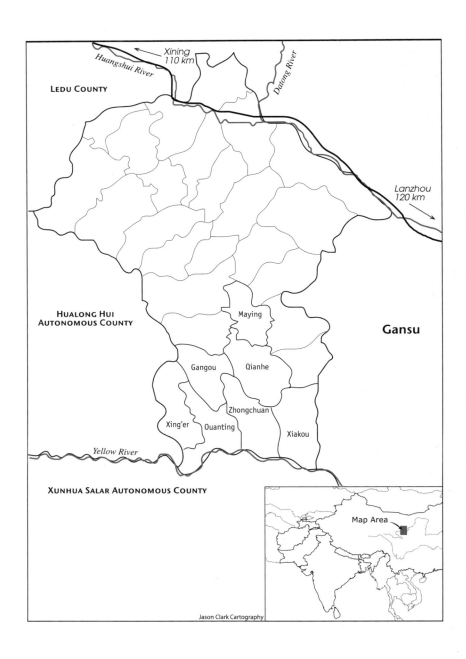

Jason Clark Cartography

dialects live in several villages in Tongren County and in Tianzhu Tibetan Autonomous County, Gansu Province.

The Setting

This chapter will deal mainly with the Minhe Mangghuer. Minhe County is located in eastern Qinghai Province at 35°45' N –36°26' N and 102°26' E –103°04' E and is one of Haidong Region's eight counties. Mangghuer live at elevations ranging from 1,650 to 3,000 meters above sea level along the Yellow River, the boundary between Qinghai and Gansu provinces. The area is characterized by a continental climate: cold winters, warm summers, and little rainfall.

It is densely populated: Though Minhe County's area—1,890 sq km—is only 0.26 percent of all Qinghai's land area, it contains a population of more than 360,000. By contrast, all of Yushu Prefecture (267,000 sq km, more than 33 percent of all Qinghai's land area) has a population of approximately 230,000—a much smaller population than Minhe County's. In short, Yushu's land area is 127 times larger than Minhe's but Minhe has 1.6 times the population of all of Yushu Prefecture.

Minhe Mangghuer are concentrated in areas locally known as Five Big Castles and Three Valleys in the south of the county. Administratively, this area is divided into Zhongchuan, Xiakou, Xing'er, Gangou, and Qianhe townships and Guanting Region. Across the nearby Yellow River lies Jishi Mountain Salar, Dongxiang and Baoan County, Gansu Province. In the Guanting Region and Zhongchuan and Xiakou townships, Mangghuer residents account for 71 to 89 percent of the total population.

Some villages in Zhongchuan, Guanting and Xiakou occupy flat valleys along the Yellow River. Other Mangghuer live on mountains vividly named Zhang Family, Eight Big, Yang Family, Temple, Zhu Family, Village; still others make their homes in such small valleys as Minzhu, Early Shidie Valley, Big Ma Family, Crow, Wushi, and Black Eagle.

Mountains that supported rich forests have long been denuded and the limited amount of grassland is overgrazed by yaks and sheep. Wolves, tigers, monkeys, bears, eagles, wild goats, and foxes appear in local folktales, but no wild animals other than rabbits have been seen in the area for many years.

Traditional Subsistence

In level plain areas, fields are irrigated; in more remote mountain areas, rain-fed agriculture is the norm. Arable land is scarce: On average, there is only about 2 *mu*—about one-third of an acre—of field per person. Before the

Lunar New Year, manure from family toilets and animal pens is put on fields, which are then seeded with wheat and plowed with yaks, yak-cow crosses (*musen*), or mules in mid-February. After the seeds sprout, women and girls weed the fields. Fields that can be irrigated are watered twice. Harvesting begins in early July: Wheat is reaped by hand, put in sheaves on the field, and then carried by donkey or in small hand-pulled carts to threshing grounds where it is threshed by hand or, occasionally, by using a tractor.

Wheat is a family's main food and it is also used to pay a mandatory grain tax to the local government. Grain can also be sold to meet sudden expenses. However, the low price for grain means that most families plant only enough to meet their subsistence needs and pay the tax. Potatoes, prickly ash, English walnuts, edible oil-bearing plants, corn, and beans are raised to supplement the local diet. Apples and pears are grown in plain areas for household consumption and to sell in the local markets.

Nearly every family has a mule, donkey, or *musen* that is used in fieldwork, at least one pig that is slaughtered before the onset of Spring Festival, and several chickens. Some families, particularly in mountain areas, also have a few sheep that are herded in grassland areas.

Mainstays of the Mangghuer diet are noodles, potatoes, salted vegetables, and baked, steamed, and fried breads. Household-based greenhouses were introduced in the area beginning in the 1990s, allowing production of vegetables that may be purchased in the local open-air markets. Mutton, beef, and pork, although also available in local markets, are not eaten regularly by most families because of the expense.

Tea brewed from large bricks of tea is the most common beverage. Locally made liquor was historically popular but now that commercially produced cheap liquor is available, locally made liquor is rarely tasted.

Sociopolitical Organization

Minhe County is divided into 29 townships, each administered by government employees. In practice this means enforcing tax collection and corvée labor, distributing basic food items to impoverished families, and being responsible for the management of local education and health care. Under the township level there are administrative villages that are collections of "natural villages." Theoretically, administrative village leaders contact the township administration when they have problems. It is also the administrative village leaders who are assigned the duty of actually implementing the responsibilities of the township enumerated above.

The names of local mountains, valleys, and villages often beginning with a surname suggest that a family of that name lived there in the past. In villages where many of the residents share a common ancestral root, 30 to 40 related families are part of a *benjia*, or an informal local organization of related families. *Benjia* members help each other when there are weddings and funerals. Although most *benjia* members have the same surname, in some villages the local *benjia* may have members with three to eight different surnames.

A smaller social unit is the *jiawu*, or the households of several male paternal cousins. The number of families in a *jiawu* varies between four and fifteen. *Jiawu* members help each other during weddings and funerals, when a *jiawu* member is ill, and doing collective labor during harvest time. If there are conflicts in a household, the family will invite elders from the *jiawu* and *benjia* to mediate.

Religion and Worldview

Mangghuer religion is a complex blend of Tibetan Buddhism, Sky Worship, animism, shamanism, and the cult of Erlang (a Daoist warrior deity). Before 1949, it was not uncommon for a family with four sons to send two or three sons to the monastery to be monks. Nowadays, however, it is very unusual for a family to have a son who is a monk. Funeral rituals require inviting monks to read Tibetan scriptures to help the deceased's soul reach Heaven.

During Spring Festival, paper money is burnt for the Sky. The Sky is also beseeched to help a family during a critical time of need. Some people believe that old trees are the homes of mountain deities and cutting such trees will bring misfortune to the home of the person who cut the tree. Nearly every Mangghuer village has a temple maintained by an elderly man. Temples house images of local Chinese Buddhist deities, Guanshiyin Bodhisattva, and various Tibetan Buddhist deities.

The temples are sites where mostly elderly women regularly assemble to chant, and for the performance of Nadun, a ritual held in summer to beseech the deities for a favorable harvest and ensure that people and livestock are free of illness. A trance medium (*fala*) performs during many Nadun. He is possessed by a local deity and dances, and the local deity speaks through him to admonish local people of the importance of respecting the local deities. Some of the trance mediums become possessed by Erlang.

Threats to Survival

Demographic Trends

The Mangghuer population has shown dramatic increase. In fact, the area suffers from chronic overpopulation, and beginning in the 1980s some Mangghuer began moving to other areas in Qinghai and Gansu provinces and to Xinjiang Uygur Region. However, distinctive Mangghuer culture is threatened by a variety of factors: the presence of skilled workers from outside the area who move into the Mangghuer regions, poverty, language and culture change, the absence of school texts in the Mangghuer language, and environmental degradation.

Current Events and Conditions. Carpenters, tailors, and barbers from south China have moved into the area and opened business and, increasingly, Hui (Chinese Muslims) come to the area to run restaurants, shops, and buy and sell wood, grain, and livestock. Chinese has gradually become the "important" contact language in the marketplace and for other public interactions, at the expense of Mangghuer.

Many Mangghuer live in dire poverty. In mountain areas where crop yields are low and unpredictable, about one-third of all families borrow food from relatives for three to eight months in a year. Young people leave the area for cities in spring and summer to work at construction jobs and other poorly paid jobs. These circumstances lead many to conclude that Mangghuer as a people, and the Mangghuer language, culture, and homeland, are inferior to the larger outside world where being Mangghuer has no currency. Success can only be achieved in a non-Mangghuer world. This attitude is probably the biggest threat to the survival of a distinctive Mangghuer identity. Local Mangghuer who graduate from university, if given the choice, would prefer to work in non-Mangghuer areas because they believe promotion and ultimate job success are more easily gained outside the Mangghuer area. There is also little sense on the part of these graduates that they should work to improve their home area and the conditions of their ethnic group.

Fundamental claims for a distinctive Mangghuer identity lie in the use of the Mangghuer language, distinctive Mangghuer wedding rituals, and Nadun. While still spoken by nearly all Mangghuer living in Minhe County, the Mangghuer language is undergoing rapid change through the absorption of many Chinese vocabulary items and loss of Mangghuer words. Only a few old Mangghuer can still count in their language; all young Mangghuer can only count in Chinese.

Traditional Mangghuer weddings may require as long as three years from the beginning of matchmaking to the conclusion of wedding rituals. An important part of the wedding is wedding songs (*daola*) that are sung at the bride's and groom's homes. The rituals surrounding bringing the bride to the groom's home are prolonged and complicated, as are the songs: creation accounts, women scolding men, a review of certain gods and goddesses, and lamentations by the bride. As time passes, a number of these songs are no longer being sung and the wedding process is being shortened.

Young people show less and less interest in performing the summer festival Nadun. Often held jointly by two villages, Nadun features a series of singing and dancing performances, worship of local deities and Erlang, the trance medium's dance and speech, and an opportunity to meet relatives and friends in a relaxed festive atmosphere. Historically, every village had a trance medium who played a key role in Nadun and who pierced himself with several spikes during Nadun. Now, in the entire Mangghuer area there are only a few trance mediums. Audience numbers have also decreased. Clearly, Nadun is losing a competition with a modern world where there are many alternative forms of entertainment such as television, video, compact discs, and radio. Furthermore, improved transportation facilities mean that it is possible to be in the provincial capital Xining in six hours, and in Chuankou, the county capital, in three hours. While it may be true that Nadun provides forms of entertainment not otherwise available, interest on the part of the younger generation is clearly on the decline.

The Mangghuer experience with schooling illustrates a number of consequences for minorities living far from an urban center of formal government-sponsored education. Their educational experience confronts such difficulties as an inadequate education infrastructure, minimal financial support by local government, poor quality of teaching, high levels of historical illiteracy, high mandatory school fees, and classes taught in Chinese, a Sinitic language very different from their own Altaic one, which has never been used in education in written form. It is this last point we wish to examine here.

A Monguor written system based on the Huzhu dialect was created in 1979 using *pinyin*. Afterwards, largely unsuccessful attempts were made to popularize the system in Huzhu. To that end, several elementary teaching texts and reading materials have been made available at no charge to some Mongghul children. By 2001, the teaching of written Mongghul in the countryside had nearly ceased. The limited success in teaching literacy in Mongghul results from a number of interacting factors: limited financial resources; criticism by non-Mongghul of expenditures to promote Mongghul literacy; lack of experienced instructors; an attitude among many Mongghul that time spent in becoming literate in Mongghul could be better invested in increasing one's literacy in Chinese, which is seen as useful; the lack of any material written in Mongghul beyond simple texts, further undermining the practicality of a knowledge of the written language.

A written Mangghuer system in Minhe County has never been given serious consideration. The result is education that uses only Chinese-language textbooks. This has resulted in increasing numbers of children speaking Chinese at home. Parents often encourage this, and stress the importance of fluency in Chinese. Textbooks are prescribed by the national curricula and emphasize the importance of Chinese culture, featuring stories of Chinese heroes and history. Schools are thus another site where Mangghuer culture is often ignored. In some schools, there is a policy for students to speak only Chinese while on the school grounds.

Environmental Crisis

Mangghuer also face an enviornmental crisis characterized by the loss of forests without meaningful afforestation efforts, declining rainfall, drying streams and springs, and severe erosion. Local forests have long since been destroyed, the result of many generations of Mangghuer's building adobe homes that use wood for the roofs and supporting columns, and using wood for fuel. Straw and coal are now the main fuels. Burning straw means that it cannot be used as animal feed and recycled as manure.

Yearly precipitation in Minhe County averaged 18 inches in the period from 1956 to 1979, but averaged just 13 inches from 1980 to 1999. For local people, this decline has increased the incidence of droughts, reduced crop yields, and made malnutrition more common. With fewer crops, people have less money with which to buy coal. Some families go to the mountains to sweep up organic material and dig grass roots for fuel. The loss of forest cover and grass from mountainsides has increased the incidence of floods, their intensity, and their devastation: A flood in 2000 washed away three bridges and 30 *mu* of irrigated field.

Drinking water supplies for people and livestock are inadequate at the best of times, and especially during dry seasons. In mountain areas, holes that fill with water from springs are often very dirty. At times, women queue with shoulder poles at such water sources and wait hours before they get their turn to fill their buckets. This can lead to quarrelling and fighting among women. The problem of getting water is especially acute for elderly people who have no animals to haul water from distant valley water holes.

Sociocultural Crisis

Deteriorating environmental conditions, malnutrition, and population growth are encouraging Mangghuer to move to distant places to farm. Many now live in places where Mangghuer is not the lingua franca of village life and culture. Under such conditions, Mangghuer identity quickly disappears. This voluntary resettlement began in the 1980s and, although some families met with conditions less favorable than expected and returned to the Mangghuer areas, most families have stayed in their new locations. As time passes, more and more households are moving away. During Spring Festival, many of these families return to the Mangghuer area to spend the festivities with their relatives. Children who have lived most of their lives in the non-Mangghuer areas do not speak Mangghuer, or speak it poorly. Their first language is Chinese.

Response: Struggle for Cultural Survival

Culture Study

In the early 1990s a few people became interested in writing about Mangghuer culture and recording relevant cultural information. This has led to a number of international publications on various aspects of Mangghuer life. They have also made numerous video and audio recordings of weddings, folktales, folk-songs, Spring Festival rituals, and Nadun; beginning in 2001 these were digitized to be permanently archived in Western libraries. This effort has been recently expanded.

Local Development

Simultaneously, the same people interested in preservation have raised funds from Western sources for development projects. As of 2007 they have implemented more than 100 small-scale development projects in Mangghuer villages that are meant to improve village conditions for water, fuel, education, and health care. Low-cost, locally produced solar cookers, for example, significantly decrease a family's reliance on coal and limit the amount of organic material residents are compelled to gather from mountainsides. Another example is household-based underground concrete water cisterns that provide a family with many of its water needs.

Overall, however, it must be admitted that Mangghuer culture is changing rapidly, and with each passing year, elements that make Mangghuer culture unique disappear. Articles published in international journals and archived video and audio materials provide a valuable record of Mangghuer culture in the late 20th and early 21st centuries. These materials add to our understanding of a much broader "culture of China" and, indeed, world culture. But they do not halt the disintegration of Mangghuer culture nor have they resulted in much improvement in impoverished Mangghuer's lives. Mangghuer lack the written history and culture that surrounds, for example, Mongolian language and culture and that gives at least some Mongolians a strong sense that they must make efforts to preserve their indigenous culture and heritage.

Food for Thought

The situation for the Mangghuer is not unique. Approximately 600 of the world's languages were lost in the last century and it is expected that 90 percent of the world's surviving 6,000 languages will vanish in this century. This is particularly tragic for cultures without written languages to capture their folklore and their traditional knowledge of nature and environmental management. The loss of this knowledge can only adversely affect the environment as it undercuts cultural identity.

Increasingly, Mangghuer families go into debt in order to send their children to colleges and universities where courses are taught in English. Fewer and fewer young Mangghuer know much about their own ethnic group's rich store of folklore and history. They have learned that the "outside Chinese way" is the goal of a "modern life." Expanding markets, good roads and many buses, education in Chinese, a growing access to media offerings in Chinese, job opportunities outside the Mangghuer area, and little detectable interest among most older Mangghuer in preserving their own traditions all combine to reduce the importance of Mangghuer culture and language and its chances for surviving into the next century.

To Think About

1. What is an ethnicity/nationality? How does the Mangghuer/Monguor/Mongghul reality show that the answer to this question is complex?
2. How hopeful do the authors seem to be that Mangghuer culture will continue a century from now?
3. What environmental problems are the Mangghuer experiencing and what impact are they having on the local people?
4. Do the authors believe that the Monguor experience is unique?
5. (a) Who are the Mangghuer? (b) How many officially recognized ethnic groups does China have? (c) Where do the Mangghuer live? (d) How many Mangghuer are there? (e) What is Nadun?
6. What reasons do the authors give for many young Mangghuer having little sense that the preservation of their culture is important? Do you think it is important? Why or why not?
7. If you were in a position to do something to help the Mangghuer, what would it be and why?
8. What may be the relationship between poverty and environmental degradation?
9. What may be the relationship between poverty and continued cultural survival for the impoverished group?

Resources

Published Literature

Anonymous. 1977. Pater Lodewijk, Jozef, Maria Schram (1883–1971), Een Brugs missionaris en etnoloog. *Haec Olim* 21: 16–24.

Berger Patricia. 2003. Empire of Emptiness: Buddhist Art and Political Authority in Qing China. Honolulu: University of Hawai'i Press.

Buck, David D. 1994. Introduction: Dimensions of Ethnic and Cultural Nationalism in Asia—A Symposium. *The Journal of Asian Studies* 53(1): 5.

Chen Qingying and Ma Lianlong, translators. 1988. *Guoshi Ruobi duoji chuan*. Beijing: Minzu chubanshe.

Crossley, Pamela K. 1999. *A Translucent Mirror: History and Identity in Qing Imperial Ideology*. Berkeley: University of California Press.

Dpal ldan bkra shis, Hu Jun, Hu Ping, Limusishiden (Li Dechun), Keith Slater, Kevin Stuart, Wang Xianzhen, and Zhu Yongzhong. 1996. Language Materials of China's Monguor Minority: Huzhu Mongghul and Minhe Mangghuer. *Sino-Platonic Papers* No 69.

Dwyer, Arienne M. 2005. *Language Contact and Variation: A Discourse-based Grammar of Monguor*. http://neh.gov/grants/guidelines/delsamples/mongour.pdf

Ethnologue. 12 June 2004. http://www.ethnologue.com/show_language.asp?code=WUH

Everding, Karl-Heinz. 1988. *Die Präexistenzen der Lcang skya Qutuqtus: Untersuchungen zur Konstruktion und historischen Entwicklung einer lamaistischen Existenzenlinie*. Wiesbaden: Otto Harrassowitz.

Feng Lide and Kevin Stuart. 1992. Interethnic Cultural Contact on the Inner Asian Frontier: The Gangou People of Minhe County, Qinghai. *Sino-Platonic Papers* No. 33.

Field, Kenneth L. 1997. *A Grammatical Overview of Santa Mongolian*. University of California, Santa Barbara. PhD dissertation.

Georg, Stefan. 2003. Mongghul, in Janhunen. 2003: 286–306.

Ha Mingzong and Kevin Stuart. 2006. Everyday Hawan Mongghul. *Mongolica Pragensia* 45–70.

Hasibate. ed. 1986. *Tuzu yu cidian* [Tu Language Dictionary]. Mongolian Language Family Dialects Research Series Vol. 14. Huhehaote: Nei menggu renmin chubanshe [Inner Mongolia People's Press].

Hecken, J. Van. 1977. Schram, Lodewijk, Jozef, Maria, missionaris en etnoloog. *Nationaal Biografisch Woordenboek* 7: 856–865.

Hu Jun and Kevin Stuart. 1992a. The Guanting Tu (Monguor) Wedding Ceremonies and Songs. *Anthropos* 87: 109–132.

———. 1992b. Illness among the Minhe Tu, Qinghai Province: Prevention and Etiology. *Mongolian Studies* 15: 111–135.

Hunsberger, Merril. 1978. *Ma Pu-fang in Chinghai Province, 1931–1949*. Temple University PhD dissertation.

Illich, Marina. 2006. *Selections from the Life of a Tibetan Buddhist Polymath: Chankya Rolpai Dorje (Lcang skya rol pa'i rdo rje), 1717–1786*. Columbia University PhD dissertation.

Janhunen, Juha. ed. 2003a. *The Mongolic Languages*. London: Routledge.

———. 2003b. Shirongol and Shirongolic. *Studia Etymologica Cracoviensia* 8: 83–89.

———. 2006. On the Shirongolic Names of Amdo. *Studia Etymologica Cracoviensia* 11: 95–103.

Juha Janhunen, Lionel Ha Mingzong, and Joseph Tshe.dpag.rnam.rgyal. 2007. On the Language of the Shaowa Tuzu in the Context of the Ethnic Taxonomy of Amdo Qinghai. *Central Asiatic Journal*.

Kämpfe, Hans-Rainer. 1974. *Die soziale Rolle des 2. Pekinger Lcang skya qutuqtu Rol pa'i rdo rje (1717–1786): Beitrage zu einer Analyse anhand tibetischer und mongolischer Biographien*. Bonn: Rheinische Friedrich-Wilhelms-Universität.

Li Keyu. 1987. *Mongghul Qidar Merlong* [Mongghul-Chinese Dictionary]. Xining: Qinghai renmin chubanshe [Qinghai People's Press].

Li Xuewei and Kevin Stuart. 1990. Population and Culture of the Mongols, Tu, Baoan, Dongxiang, and Yugu in Gansu. *Mongolian Studies* 12: 71–93.

Limusishiden and Kevin Stuart. 1994. 'Caring for All the World': The Huzhu Monguor (Tu) *Pram,* in Edward H. Kaplan and Donald W. Whisenhunt, eds. *Opuscula Altaica: Essays in Honor of Henry Schwarz*. Bellingham: Western Washington University Press, 408–426.

———. 1995. Larinbuda and Jiminsu: A Monguor Tragedy. *Asian Theatre Journal* 12(2): 221–263.

———. 1996. Review of Shilaode [Dominik Schröder] ed., translator, Li Keyu. *Tuzu gesaer* [Monguor Gesar]. *Anthropos* 91: 297.

———. eds. 1998. *Huzhu Mongghul Folklore: Texts and Translations*. München: Lincom Europa.

———. 1999. Huzhu Mongghul Language Materials. *Suomalais-Ugrilaisen Seuran Aikakauskirja—Journal de la Société Finno-Ougrienne* 88: 261–264.

———. eds. 2001. *Huzhu Mongghul Texts: Chileb 1983–1996 Selections*. 2 Vols. München: Lincom Europa.

Lipman, Jonathan N. 1981. *The Border World of Gansu, 1895–1935*. Stanford University PhD dissertation. Ann Arbor: University Microfilms.

Liu, Lydia H. 2004. *The Clash of Empires: The Invention of China in Modern World Making*. Cambridge, MA: Harvard University Press.

Lopez, Donald. 2004. Tibetan Buddhism, in Millward *et al.*, eds. 22–32.

Millward, James. Ruth Dunnell, Mark Elliot and Philippe Forêt. eds. 2004. *New Qing Imperial History: The Manchu Summer Palace at Chengde*. London: Routledge/Curzon.

Missions de Scheut. 1920a. *Geschiedenis van de Christenheid Si-ning*, 77–82, 110–116.

———. 1920b. *Lettres du P. Schram*, 38–41.

———. 1920c. *Notes sur la prefecture chinoise d Si-ning (Koukounor)*, 79–85, 112–119.

———. 1921a. *De gelukkigste mens in Kansoe*, 138.

———. 1921b. *L'Immaculee et les paiens de Chine*, 201–220.

———. 1921c. *De zwarte ellende in Si-ning*, 217–223.

Molè, Gabriella. 1970. *The Tu-yü-hun from the Northern Wei to the Time of the Five Dynasties*. Serie Orientale Roma 41. Rome: Istituto Italiano per il Medio ed Estreme Oriente.

Mostaert, Antoine. 1931. The Mongols of Kansu and their Language. *Bulletin of the Catholic University of Peking*, 8: 75–89.

Mostaert, Antoine. 1963–1964. Over Pater Louis Schram CICM. *Haec Olim* 15: 103–108.

Naquin, Susan. 2000. *Peking: Temples and City Life, 1400–1900*. Berkeley: University of California Press.

Ngag dbang chos ldan (Shes rab dar rgyas) and Klaus Sagaster. 1967. *Subud erike, "ein Rosenkranz aus Perlen": die Biographie des 1. Pekinger lCang skya Khutukhtu, Ngag dbang blo bzang chos ldan*. Wiesbaden: Otto Harrassowitz.

Ngag dbang thub bstan dbang phyug and Hans-Rainer Kämpfe. 1976. *Nyi ma'i 'od zer/ Naran-u gerel: Die Biographie des 2. Pekingger lCang skya Qutugtu Rol pa'i rdo rje (1717–1786)*, *Monumenta Tibetica Historica*, Abteilung II: Vitae, Band 1. St. Augustin: VGH Wissenschaftsverlag.

Nian Zhihai and Bai Zhengdeng. 1993. *Qinghai zangchuan fojiao siyuan ming jian [The Clear Mirror of Tibetan Buddhist Temples of Qinghai]*. Lanzhou: Gansu minzu chubanshe.

Norbu, Kalsang. (Skal bzang nor bu), Zhu Yongzhong, and Kevin Stuart. 1999. A Ritual Winter Exorcism in Gnyan Thog Village, Qinghai. *Asian Folklore Studies* 58: 189–203.

Perdue, Peter C. 1988. Comparing Empires: Manchu Colonialism. *The International History Review* xx(2): 255.

Postiglione, Gerard A. ed. 1999. *China's National Minority Education: Ethnicity, Schooling and Development*. New York: Garland Press.

Potanin, G. N. 1893. *Tangutsko-tibetskaya okraïna Kitaya i Central'naya Mongoliya*, Vols. 1–2. St. Petersburg.

———. 1950. *Tangutsko-tibetskaya okraina Kitaya i tsentral'naya Mongoliya (The Tangut-Tibetan frontier of China and Central Mongolia)*. Moscow: State Publisher. (An abridged edition of the 1893 version.)

Qi Huimin, Limusishiden, and Kevin Stuart. 1997–1998. Huzhu Monguor Wedding Songs: Musical Characteristics. Parts I, II, III, IV. *Chinese Music* 20(1): 6–12, 20(2): 32–37, 20(3): 43–52, 20(4): 68–71, 21(1): 10–13.

Qi Huimin, Zhu Yongzhong, and Kevin Stuart. 1999. Minhe Mangghuer Wedding Songs: Musical Characteristics. *Asian Folklore Studies* 58: 77–120.

Rawski, Evelyn S. 1994. Presidential Address: Reenvisioning the Qing: The Significance of the Qing Period in Chinese History. *The Journal of Asian Studies* 55(4): 841–842.

———. 1998. *The Last Emperors: A Social History of Qing Imperial Institutions*. Berkeley: University of California Press.

Schram, Louis M.J. 1912. Kansou. *Missions en Chine et au Congo* 149.

———. 1918. Catholic Missions. *Ethnographic Notes* 229–231.

———. 1927. Christelijke Kunst in China. *Bulletin Catholique de Peking* 368–376.

———. 1932. Le mariage cez les T'ou-jen du Kan-sou [Marriage among the Monguor of Gansu]. *Variétés Sinologiques* 58.

———. 1954a. The Monguors of the Kansu-Tibetan Frontier: Their Origin, History, and Social Organization. Philadelphia: *Transactions of the American Philosophical Society* 44(1).

———. 1954b. The Monguors of the Kansu-Tibetan Frontier: Part II. Their Religious Life. Philadelphia: *Transactions of the American Philosophical Society* 47(1).

Schram, Louis M.J. 1955. *Two letters to Marguerite Hebert*. Hebert (Raphael & Family) Papers Mss. 4769, Subseries 8. Louisiana and Lower Mississippi Valley

Collections, Special Collections, Hill Memorial Library, Louisiana State University Libraries, Baton Rouge, Louisiana State University. See: http://www.lib.lsu.edu/special/findaid/4769_inv.htm

Schram, Louis M.J. 1961. The Monguors of the Kansu-Tibetan Frontier: Part III. Records of the Monguor Clans. Philadelphia: *Transactions of the American Philosophical Society* 51(3).

Schröder, Dominik. 1952/1953. *Zur Religion der Tujen des Sininggebietes (Kukunor)* [On the Religion of the Monguor of the Xining Region (Koknor)]. *Anthropos* 47: 1–79, 620–658, 822–870; 48: 202–249.

———. 1959. *Aus der Volksdicntung der Monguor* [From the Popular Poetry of the Monguor]; *1. Teil: Das weibe Glücksschaf (Mythen, Märchen, Lieder)* [Part 1. The White Lucky-Sheep (Myths, Fairytales, Songs)]. Asiatische Forschungen 6. Wiesbaden: Otto Harrassowitz.

———. 1964. Der dialekt der Monguor In B. Spuler, ed *Mongolistik. (Handbuch der Orientalistik, 1. Abteilung, 5. Band, 2. Abschnitt)*. Leiden: EJ Brill.

———. 1970. *Aus der Volksdichtung der Monguor* [From the Popular Poetry of the Monguor]; *2. Teil: In den Tagen der Urzeit (Ein Mythus vom Licht und vom Leben)* [Part 2. In the Days of Primeval Times (A Myth of Light and Life)]. Wiesbaden: Otto Harrassowitz.

Sechenchogtu [Siqinchaoketu]. 1999. *Kangjia yu yanjiu. Zhongguo xin faxian yuyan yanjiu congshu.* Shanghai: Yuandong chubanshe.

Sheridan, James E. 1975. *China in Disintegration: The Republican Era in Chinese History.* New York: The Free Press.

Slater, Keith. nd. Evidentiality in Minhe Mangghuer: A Case of Contact-Induced Change. University of California-Santa Barbara, Department of Linguistics. Unpublished manuscript.

———. 2003a. Mangghuer, in Janhunen, 307–324.

———. 2003b. *Minhe Mangghuer: A Mongolic Language of China's Qinghai-Gansu Sprachbund.* Curzon Asian Linguistic Series 2. London: RoutledgeCurzon.

Smedt, Albrecht de and Antoine Mostaert. 1929–1931. Le dialecte monguor parlé par les Mongols du Kansou occidental, Ière partie: Phonétique. *Anthropos* 24: 145–166, 801–815; 25: 657–669, 961–973; 26: 253.

———. 1933. *Le dialecte monguor parlé par les Mongols du Kansou occidental, IIIe partie: Dictionnaire monguor-français.* Pei-p'ing: Imprimerie de l'Université Catholique.

———. 1945. *Le dialecte monguor parlé par les Mongols du Kansou occidental, IIe partie: Grammaire.* Monumenta Serica, Monograph 6. Peking.

Smith, Gene. (Kurtis Schaeffer, ed.). 2001. *Among Tibetan Texts: History and Literature of the Himalayan Plateau.* Boston: Wisdom.

Stuart, Kevin and Hu Jun. 1992. Death and Funerals among the Minhe Tu (Monguor). *Asian Folklore Studies* 51(2): 67–87.

———. 1993. 'That All May Prosper': The Monguor *Nadun* of the Guanting/Sanchuan Region. *Anthropos* 88: 15–27.

Stuart, Kevin and Limusishiden. eds. 1994. China's Monguor Minority: Ethnography and Folktales. *Sino-Platonic Papers* No. 59.

Sun Zhu. ed. 1990. *Menggu yuzu yuyan cidian* [Mongol Language Family Dictionary]. Xining: Qinghai renmin chubanshe [Qinghai People's Press].

Thu'u bkwan (III) Blo bzang chos kyi nyi ma. 1989 [1794]. *Lcang skya Rol pa'i rdo rje'i rnam thar.* Lanzhou: Gansu'u mi rigs dpe skrun khang.

Todaeva, Buljash Khojchievna. 1959. Über die Sprache der Tung-hsiang. *Acta Orientalia Hungarica* 9: 273–310.

———. 1961. *Dunsyanskii yazyk.* Moskva: Institut narodov Aziï AN SSSR.

———. 1963. Einige Besonderheiten der Paoan-Sprache. *Acta Orientalia Hungarica* 16: 175–197.

———. 1966. *Baoan'skii yazyk.* Moskva: Institut narodov Aziï AN SSSR.

———. 1973. *Mongorskii yazyk: Issledovanie, teksty, slovar.* Moskva: Institut vostokovedeniya AN SSSR.

Üjiyediin Chuluu (Wu Chaolu). 1994. Introduction, Grammar, and Sample Sentences for Monguor. *Sino-Platonic Papers* No. 57.

Wang Xiangyun. 1995. *Tibetan Buddhism at the Court of Qing: The Life and Work of lCang-skya Rol-pa'i-rdo-rje, 1717–86.* Harvard University PhD dissertation.

Wang Xianzheng (Zhu Yongzhong and Kevin Stuart, eds.). 2001. *Mangghuerla Bihuang Keli* [Mangghuer Folktale Reader]. Chengdu, China-Chengdu Audio Press.

Wang Xianzheng and Kevin Stuart. 1995. 'Blue Skies and Emoluments': Minhe Monguor Men Sing I and II. *Chinese Music* 18(1): 13–18; 18(2): 28–33.

Wang Xianzheng, Zhu Yongzhong, and Kevin Stuart. 1995. 'The Brightness of the World': Minhe Monguor Women Sing. *Mongolian Studies* 18: 65–83.

White, Richard. 1991. *The Middle Ground: Indians, Empires, and Republics in the Great Lakes Region, 1650–1815.* Cambridge, UK: Cambridge University Press.

Zhaonasitu. ed. *Tuzu yu jianchi* [A Brief Account of the Monguor Language]. Beijing: Minzu chubanshe [Nationalities Press].

Zhu Yongzhong and Kevin Stuart. 1996a. Minhe Monguor *Nadun* Texts. *CHIME* 9(Autumn): 89–105.

———. 1996b. A Minhe Monguor Drinking Song. *Central Asiatic Journal* 40(2): 283–289.

———. 1997. Minhe Monguor Children's Games. *Orientalia Suecana* XLV–XLVI: 179–216.

———. 1999a. Education among the Minhe Monguor IN Postiglione.

———. 1999b. 'Two Bodhisattvas from the East': Minhe Monguor Funeral Orations. *Journal of Contemporary China* 8(20): 179–188.

Zhu Yongzhong, Üjiyediin Chuluu (Chaolu Wu), and Kevin Stuart. 1995. The Frog Boy: An Example of Minhe Monguor. *Orientalia Suecana* XLII–XLIV: 197–207.

Zhu Yongzhong, Üjiyediin Chuluu (Chaolu Wu), Keith Slater, and Kevin Stuart. 1997. Gangou Chinese Dialect: A Comparative Study of a Strongly Altaicized Chinese Dialect and Its Mongolic Neighbor. *Anthropos* 92: 433–450.

Zhu Yongzhong, Üjiyediin Chuluu, and Kevin Stuart. 1999. Minhe Mangghuer and Other Mongol Languages. *Archív Orientální* 67(3): 323–338.

Video

Video footage featuring Mangghuer culture (weddings, Nadun, folksong meetings, etc.) is held by Latse Contemporary Tibetan Cultural Library (http://www.latse.org).

Glossary

adivasi   Term translatable as aboriginal inhabitants, used in India in much the same way that "indigenous people" is understood in North America.

agricultural intensification   An increase in food output per unit of land. Such increases are usually made possible by increasing investments or inputs into production, including fertilizers, pesticides, and mechanized planting and harvesting. Simply reducing the periods of fallowing can also increase production. In South Asia, rapid intensification followed the Green Revolution.

Asian Development Bank (ADB)   An international financial institution that provides loans and expertise to developing countries throughout Asia.

bahariya   A servant who lives and works in his or her master's home on a yearly contract.

Bhagat   A devotee of a particular saint or deity in Tadvi and Vassawa societies. The Bhagat movement, active sporadically from the early 20th century to the present day, was a revitalization movement that involved trance and possession and enjoined its followers to abstain from meat eating and drinking liquor. In the colonial period, it preached noncooperation with the British and merchants.

bhanti   A coarse cereal similar to barley, grown on Bhil subsistence plots.

bhuva   A shaman or religious healer in Bhil society. Bhuvas are experts in medical and religious ritual, and possess knowledge of medicinal plants and herbs in the jungles surrounding Bhil villages.

Brahmin   a member of one of the dominant ethnic groups in Nepal; Hindu priests in Nepal are traditionally drawn from the ranks of this ethnic group.

chana   Chickpeas, a lentil.

churaini   A malevolent female ghost.

dakan A woman who is accused of witchcraft in Bhil society. Witchcraft accusations were fairly common in the 19th century, but today few Bhils, or at least Tadvi and Vassawa, believe in the power of witches.

dang A pastoral migration group of Raika, usually including the combined herds of many independent households. Livestock numbers in these migration groups may number as many as 4,000 head. The dang is headed by its leader/representative, the nambardar.

dependency ratio The percent of the *nonworking* population that is below 19 years and above 60 years of age.

Diwali The Hindu festival of lights, usually falling in late October or November.

Dravidian The language family of southern India. It is very different from the north Indian languages in script, grammar, and vocabulary, which were based on Prakrit, the forerunner of Sanskrit.

faliya The major unit of kinship in Bhil society, defined by patrilineal descent and residence.

fallowing Leaving agricultural land without a standing crop. This is done either in the "off season" between crops (short fallow) or for one or more years (long fallow) to rest the soil and allow it to recoup its productivity.

garbhadan A midsummer festival celebrating unmarried women of a village. It involves a three-night cycle of dancing from dawn to dusk.

gher jamai An in-marrying son-in-law who resides with his wife close to her natal household. Although this practice contradicts the ideal of patrilocal residence, it is quite common due to the inflation of bride-price payments.

Gorno-Badakshan Autonomous Oblast A poor, sparsely populated and semi-autonomous administrative unit in eastern Tajikistan with little political influence, and home to most of the Badakshani.

Great Game The 18th- and 19th-century political and military maneuvering for control of Central Asia, played out by Imperial Britain, Tsarist Russia, and China.

Green Revolution The state-sponsored, internationally funded effort, dating from the mid-1960s, to foster agricultural intensification around the world.

This involved the transfer of agricultural technology from major research stations and universities to traditional producers, especially in Mexico, India, Egypt, and the Philippines. The result has been an unquestioned increase in food production but with many unintended consequences including soil degradation, pesticide saturation, and consolidation of agricultural holdings at the expense of small farmers.

jambh   A type of cultivation intermediate between swidden cultivation and intensive agriculture.

jimidar   A revenue collector in premodern Nepal, responsible for both revenue collection and agricultural development; term used today as an honorific for the descendants of jimidars.

khodra   a coarse grain similar to barley.

Khorog   The capital of the Gorno-Badakshan Autonomous Oblast in eastern Tajikistan.

kishlak   Within Tajikistan, the name for a small village.

kul   A group of related patidar (see entry, below); a common ancestor is presumed but not known. Marriage within the kul is prohibited.

Lake Sarez   The largest natural sediment reservoir in Central Asia, with an estimated volume of 10 cubic miles. The lake formed when a 1911 earthquake triggered a massive landslide that damned the Murgab River in eastern Tajikistan.

mahua   A deciduous tree found in the forests of the Satpuda and Vindhya mountains. Flowering in late July and August, its buds are used to make liquor. Its leaves and roots are used as medicines.

mingni   Goat and sheep manure. A major traditional source of fertilizer for agriculture.

monsoon   The prevailing precipitation system of South Asia. The monsoons are driven by a massive body of low pressure over the Asian land mass in summer, which drives winds inland from the Indian Ocean, bringing with them heavy and sustained rains, beginning in May/June and ending in September. Most agriculture in South Asia continues to depend on the monsoon.

moong   A lentil grown on Bhil plots.

mullah   A learned teacher or interpreter of religious laws, highly respected for his knowledge; a learned man.

nambardar   The leader of a Raika dang migration group. The nambardar is selected for his skills in negotiation and group leadership.

neem   A deciduous tree whose leaves and roots have alkaloid properties. Its leaves are used as a pesticide by the Bhils, while its roots are boiled for medicine and its twigs are used as toothbrushes. It has been recently patented by an Australian firm as an ecologically friendly pesticide.

ostravechnio   The out-migration of Russians from Tajikistan following Tajik independence in 1991.

Pamir Mountains   A vast rectangular knot of mountains in Central Asia, located mostly in Tajikistan.

Pamir Relief and Development Programme (PRDP)   A comprehensive program initiated and supported by the Aga Khan Foundation to provide both short- and long-term food security in eastern Tajikistan.

patidar   A lineage; a group of men and their families, usually living in proximity to one another, who trace their descent from a common male ancestor.

puja   A religious ceremony.

purdah   A system whereby males and females are separated by various cultural practices. It typically involves the seclusion of women and is practiced in north Indian upper-caste households, although not among the Bhils.

raiti   Landholding peasants subject to taxation in premodern Nepal.

renunciants   Religious practitioners who renounce worldly goods and desires and live to achieve spiritual understanding.

roti   An unleavened bread made of wheat or corn flour and roasted on a skillet.

scheduled caste   A caste group designated by Indian law to receive special consideration, access to resources, or quotas for political representation. Scheduled castes are those that were historically the most marginal in caste structure, including tribal groups, outcastes, and other "backward" groups that suffered from general discrimination.

shaman   A religious specialist and healer who uses his powers to intercede with supernatural beings.

sinoti   A deciduous shrub whose leaves are boiled to provide a medicine for coughs and colds. It tastes like Vicks tablets.

sitaphul   A deciduous, fruit-bearing tree native to the Satpuda mountains.

Sufi adepts   Those who study and bear the inner message of Islam, and eschew most material goods. They are held in high esteem for their religious knowledge.

Tajik   Descendants from the old pre-Turkic Iranian population that now compose the majority ethnic group in Tajikistan.

tarbandi   A wire fence enclosure, usually one set aside by an official body, like the Forest Department, for management and control.

total fertility rate   The number of children born to each woman. To reach zero population growth, the rate should average 2.2 per woman.

tubytaka   A small skullcap worn by Moslem men to indicate allegiance to Allah.

Zoroastrianism   An ancient faith related to Islam that follows the teachings of Zoroaster, the 6th century prophet and religious reformer from northeast Iran. Its customs include the use of magic and fire worship.

Index

Contributors

Julian Birch is an emeritus member of the International Relations and Area Studies research group and Professor of Politics at the University of Sheffield, UK. His research has focused on the peoples and cultures of Central Asia, especially the constraints posed by the disintegration of the Soviet Union, the rise of nationalism, and ethnic conflict.

Barbara A. Brower is Professor of Geography and International Studies at Portland State University, has researched and written about the intersection of South and Central Asia—the Himalaya-Hindukush—for more than thirty years. She has edited *Himalaya*, the Journal of the Association for Nepal and Himalayan Studies, since 1993, and designs and produces the ANHS Journey to High Asia calendar series.

Michael J. Casimir is Professor of Cultural Anthropology at the University of Cologne. He has conducted extensive fieldwork on the ecology, economy, environmental management and nutritional and socialization patterns among pastoral nomads in west Afghanistan and Kashmir. Together with Aparna Rao he was chairperson of the *Commission on Nomadic Peoples* of the *International Union of Ethnological and Anthropological Sciences* (1995–1998), and co-editor of *Nomadic Peoples*, the journal of the Commission. His major publications include *Flocks and Food: A Biocultural Approach to the Study of Pastoral Foodways* (1991), *Culture and the Changing Environment* (ed., in press) and together with Aparna Rao: *Mobility and Territoriality* (ed. 1992) as well as *Nomadism in South Asia* (ed. 2003).

Stephen Cunha is a professor of geography at Humboldt State University. He previously spent ten seasons as a park ranger in Yosemite and Alaska, and four years investigating the potential for a national park and biosphere reserve in the Tajik Pamir. A graduate of the University of California Berkeley and University of California Davis, he writes about environmental issues in Central Asia and the need for more geography education in American schools.

Grant Farr is the Associate Dean of the College of Liberal Arts and Studies at Portland State University. He has been studying Afghanistan for over forty years and has also written on Iran. He is now conducting research on the role of Islamic institutions in Afghanistan, especially the Madrassas and their role in the development of militant Islam.

Arjun Guneratne is Associate Professor of Anthropology at Macalester College in Saint Paul, Minnesota. His previous research has focused on the shaping of an ethnic identity among the Tharu of the Nepal Tarai. He is currently editing a volume of papers exploring how environment is conceptualized in different Himalayan societies, and researching the development of environmentalism in Sri Lanka.

Barbara Rose Johnston is an anthropologist and senior research fellow at the Center for Political Ecology, Santa Cruz, California. Her work in political ecology and human rights and the environment has included a focus on vulnerable populations, especially indigenous groups and ethnic minorities. Her recent work includes documenting involuntary resettlement, massacre, and genocide associated with the Chixoy hydroelectric dam in Guatemala, and the consequential damages of nuclear militarism in the Marshall Islands.

P. Christiaan Klieger is a leading authority on the historical development of the Tibetan nation. Currently head of the History Department at Oakland Museum of California, he has held positions in anthropology at the California Academy of Sciences and Bishop Museum in Honolulu. His latest book will compare the nationalisms of seven microstates of Europe.

Hermann Josef Kreutzmann is professor of Human Geography and Director of the Centre for Development Studies at the Institute of Geographic Sciences, Freie Universitaet Berlin. His field work experience covers more than 30 years in Central and South Asia resulting in more than 100 publications (journal articles, book chapters, edited books) on the region. He is the co-editor of "Erdkunde - Archive of scientific geography", member of the editorial advisory boards of "Journal of Mountain Science" and "Mountain Research and Development".

Aparna Rao's work is well known among those who study nomadic ("peripatetic") peoples, pastoralists, or peace and conflict in Kashmir. A prolific writer on her own, with husband Michael Casimir she also co-edited *Nomadic Peoples*, and co-authored many books and articles. She was a lecturer in anthropology at the University of Cologne, acted as Head of Department, Anthropology, South Asia Institute Heidelberg, and was to become Directeur de Recherche at the École des Hautes Études, in Paris, when she died unexpectedly in June 2005.

Paul Robbins is associate Professor of Geography at the University of Arizona. His work focuses on the ecological and political entanglement of humans (herders, homeowners, bureaucrats, hunters, scientists) with non-humans (turfgrass, elk, West Nile Virus, DDT, fire), and the implications of those encounters for sustainability and social justice. His recent projects include work on human/wildlife conflicts along park boundaries in northwest India, and the political economy of corruption that inevitably accompanies bio-diversity conservation.

Anna Schmid is an anthropologist and director of the Museum der Kulturen (Museum of Cultures) in Basel, Switzerland. Her research and publications focus on interethnic relations, minorities, popular culture in South Asia. Recently she started working in the field of museum studies.

Kevin Stuart is a specialist in cultural study specializing in ethnic issues in China's Qinghai Province, a small-scale community development specialist, and an English teacher. Since first coming to China in 1984, he has done research and training, recorded three English teaching programs in minority languages with local colleagues in Inner Mongolia and Qinghai Province, and has raised approximately 2 million dollars for more than 100 grassroots development projects. He was a United Nations Volunteer for 6 years under the auspices of United Nations Development Project in both Mongolia and China.

Zhu Yongzhong established one of the first locally registered non-governmental organizations (Sanchuan Development Association) in Qinghai Province, China. He has written and published extensively about Monguor culture and has recorded hundreds of hours of video and audio materials of various Minhe Mangghuer cultural manifestations.

Judith Whitehead, associate professor at the University of Lethbridge, has interests in gender, development, environment and urban anthropology. She has researched a number of topics relating to South Asia, including the Narmada dams project, and gender, colonialism and nationalism. Her most recent research involves the impact of gentrification on the urban poor in Mumbai.